Spartacus
and Me

Life, love and everything in between

VASHTI WHITFIELD
with Sue Smethurst

**SIMON &
SCHUSTER**

London · New York · Sydney · Toronto · New Delhi

A CBS COMPANY

SPARTACUS AND ME – LIFE, LOVE AND EVERYTHING IN BETWEEN
First published in Australia in 2016 by
Simon & Schuster (Australia) Pty Limited
Suite 19A, Level 1, 450 Miller Street, Cammeray, NSW 2062

10 9 8 7 6 5 4 3 2 1

A CBS Company
Sydney New York London Toronto New Delhi
Visit our website at www.simonandschuster.com.au

A cataloguing-in-publication record for this title is available from the
National Library of Australia
Creator: Whitfield, Vashti, author.
Title: Spartacus and Me/Vashti Whitfield.
ISBN: 9781925310306 (paperback)
                9781925310313 (ebook)
Subjects: Whitfield, Andy, 1971-2011.
                Whitfield, Vashti.
                Actors – Australia – Biography
                Cancer – Patients – Biography.
                Welsh – Australia – Biography.
Dewey Number: 306.85092

Cover design: Christabella Designs
Cover photograph by Philip Klaunzer
Typeset by Midland Typesetters, Australia
Printed and bound in Australia by Griffin Press

FSC
www.fsc.org
MIX
Paper from
responsible sources
FSC® C009448

For Andy and my cubs

What if I fall? Oh, but darling what if you fly?

— Erin Hanson

Contents

Foreword

It is appropriate that this book begins with words that immediately bring you into the world of Andy and Vashti Whitfield. You are about to embark on a dramatic, hilarious, raw, honest, sometimes inappropriate, often heart-wrenching, but always forward-moving journey. Regardless of whether the road was wide open or littered with obstacles, Andy and Vashti had the unique ability to keep their focus on moving forward while allowing themselves to experience the present in all its joyful, astounding and gut-wrenching glory.

I first met Andy and Vashti after the first season of Starz Television's *Spartacus: Blood and Sand* had become an international hit, with Andy in the leading role. This was his big break – and with his natural acting talent and good looks, the press, fans and camera are absolutely taken by him. He is the picture of health and with his equally gorgeous wife, the magnetic and effervescent Vashti, and their two beautiful young children, they are on top of the world.

At this time, Andy is feeling back pain which he chalks up to the gruelling workouts of gladiator boot camp, or from doing his own stunts as a sword-wielding gladiator fighting every ancient Roman bad-ass. But he is soon diagnosed with Stage IV non-Hodgkin lymphoma. With Vashti by his side, Andy quietly and quickly goes into chemotherapy and beats the disease.

While gearing up to film Season 2 of *Spartacus*, a routine insurance scan shows the cancer has returned. Andy and Vashti are devastated, but decide to use Andy's new-found star power to share the next part of their journey in a documentary, in the hopes that it may be helpful and inspirational to others faced with challenges. And that's where I come in.

I'd been working with Sam Maydew's company. Sam is a veteran Hollywood manager and producer and we'd been creating a potential television show around Dennis Hopper, who also had developed cancer. Knowing that I was an Academy Award nominated documentary filmmaker and that I was also directing segments for Stand Up To Cancer's live television fund-raiser, Sam asked me if I would speak with Andy and Vashti.

In the early chit-chat that is typical of first conversations, I asked Andy where he was from in the UK. He responded that I would probably not know it because it is a small village, on a tiny island, off the northern coast of Wales. My ears pricked up. More than coincidentally, it turned out to be Bull Bay, where my father grew up, on the island of Anglesey. And there and then, we knew that it was meant to be and we began the epic journey of making the documentary *Be Here Now*.

Little did I know the profound influence Andy and Vashti would have on me, and the friendship that would grow out of making the film. From the very beginning, I was struck by their larger-than-life personalities, positive determination and passion for embracing rather than hiding from what life throws up.

Equally contagious was how they chose to live their lives by setting goals and making them happen. Andy, with Vashti's support, had done this by becoming a star actor at the age of 38. And now, faced with this unexpected challenge, they were focusing that same powerful determination on beating cancer. Yet at the same time, they had the ability to be in the moment – despite the uncertainty of their dramatic roller-coaster ride of highs and lows, good and bad, and the nuances in between.

My goal was to have the camera as invisible and unobtrusive as possible, to be a fly on the wall so I was able to capture the essence of their story as well as its subtleties. I hoped that if the film could convey all this, then their story may be inspiring to others. Simultaneously, I noticed an emerging love story. In their interactions, in shared moments, there was an irrepressible sense of humour and tenderness in the way they played off each other – even when they clashed, disagreed or broke down.

Their love also came through in how they supported each other – Andy sensing when Vashti was feeling the pressure of being his caregiver, and Vashti knowing how to bring Andy back to positive determination after mixed results from his oncologist. Andy attributed this to Vashti's extraordinary emotional intelligence.

Vashti has this rare ability to eloquently and honestly answer a question, while letting herself roll smoothly between her emotions. In my career, I have found it to be rare to interview someone who is comfortable and confident enough to not ask for a tissue or to take a break to compose themselves.

During one interview I asked Vashti how she was always able to turn devastating news into something positive. Without hesitation, she said, 'What else is there to do?' This is what defines their philosophy. As Vashti says, '. . . it does not mean you are going to get happy ever after. But, that's the point. You get what you get, so make the most of it, because it can be something extraordinary.'

Making this documentary also had a big impact on me personally. Throughout the filmmaking process, I'd tell Vashti that I was learning so much from them, but I could not find the words to describe what. I thought I was someone who lives according to the same philosophy, driving hard in my work and play, while remembering to stop, feel and experience the present on a daily basis, sometimes also trying to capture it on camera. But I've come to realise that the second part of this takes practice.

I now try to live my life in smaller increments – in the moments that will add up to days, months and years. I finally understand what the over-used expression 'The journey is more important than the destination' means. That is how Andy and Vashti truly, not theoretically, live their lives. I will be forever grateful for the privilege of being able to follow Andy and Vashti on a short part of their journey and for our invaluable friendship.

As you begin this book, take with you something Andy once said: 'Everyone needs a Vashti.'

Welcome to the forward-moving journey you are about to embark on, with Vashti as your guide. May it be equally as inspiring for you.

Lilibet Foster
Director and Producer, Academy Award nominee

Preface

Vashti is Buddha. Not really ... kind of. But fitter. And funnier. And slightly more sexy.

She has better stories and the best laugh. She's genuine and warm. But won't take any shit. She loves a cup of tea in a glass, makes sandwiches with love and is partial to a margarita. No salt.

She's often pushed for time but is never in a rush. Or is it the other way round? Her hands will be full but she'll always manage to lend one. She's an exceptional negotiator, a disgraceful speller and speaks fluent Italian.

Vashti is the person I call when I'm freaking out. About anything. She won't claim to have the answer but is never short of one. She's pushy. But only in the search for truth. Which doesn't necessarily mean she always tells it.

She has great taste. Usually. An amazing brain, an eye for detail and an open ear. She can't sing to save herself.

She will challenge the way you think about things. Without even trying. She will ask you to ask questions you didn't know you had and help you to see what's been there the whole time.

Vashti is the widow of my dead mate, the mother of my godchild and one of my very best friends. She is the parent I want to become. And she'll never be someone you forgot you met.

Jai Courtney

Introduction

When I let go of what I am, I become what I might be.
— Lao Tzu

8 April 2016

I stumble around in the darkened cinema, desperately trying to find a spare seat next to one of the pockets of wonderful and diverse friends who've travelled from far and wide to share this surreal experience with me in New York City.

It is freezing outside, one of those Manhattan days when the wind whips straight off the East Hudson River and blows ice through your bones. So I am grateful for the warmth in here, not just from the surrounds of this gloriously retro East Village cinema with its lush, red velvet chairs, ornate gold-domed roof and enormous antique chandelier hanging precariously above our heads, but more so from the kindness of treasured friends and complete strangers whose goodwill is cushioning my fragile heart.

As the lights go down and the huge red velvet curtains peel back, Andy's presence on screen is overwhelming. The piercing blue eyes of my beautiful husband, the unmistakable smile of my children's father and the sound of his rich, deep voice soothe me like a cashmere blanket.

On screen he is so alive, so real, I could almost reach out and touch him.

I laugh out loud watching Andy catch his tiny daughter who has, for the fourth time, tumbled in the sand in an attempt to race her big brother. He is so full of love and so happy, it's nearly impossible to comprehend that he is no longer here.

As the frame cuts away from Andy playing with Indi to a scene from *Spartacus*, the television series he starred in, the audience sees this Adonis of a man in full flight, dressed in a loin cloth with muscles rippling. He is utterly captivating, sweaty, rugged and sexy, leaping in and out of sword fights so full of energy and, of course, blissfully unaware that, as he was being filmed, an actual battle was taking place within his magnificent body.

It's inconceivable that this beautiful man we all see on screen, larger than life in so many ways, so full of love, smiling and laughing, so serene and so wise, had Stage IV non-Hodgkin lymphoma roaring through every inch of his body.

On 11 September 2011, my beautiful husband Andy Whitfield, my best friend, my lover and the amazing father of our two gorgeous little cubs, Jesse Red and Indigo Sky, took his last breath and succumbed to cancer. He died one month before his 40th birthday.

So here I am in New York, almost five years later, giving birth to Andy's death, launching *Be Here Now: The Andy Whitfield*

Story, a documentary film that followed his and our journey through cancer, through love, and to a place of life, love and new beginnings.

Andy was the star of the hit TV series *Spartacus: Blood and Sand*. Spartacus was the role of a lifetime for an aspiring actor wanting to crack the US film industry, and Andy, whose big break came at the late age of 36, was an overnight sensation.

Spartacus was set in the Roman Empire, and it was remarkably true to life with its graphic violence and gore, and its sex, nudity and often orgy-like scenes, set around a tragic and tender story of love, loss and vengeance. It was a challenging and incredibly inspiring role for Andy to play, and he immersed himself in it fully. But just weeks after they'd wrapped filming of the first series in New Zealand, he was diagnosed with Stage IV non-Hodgkin lymphoma. Andy had cancer.

Andy had been suffering from terrible back pain for quite some time. We put it down to his physically demanding role as Spartacus. He'd filmed a series of extreme fight scenes and had been training as hard as an Olympic athlete since the day he landed the role. It was exhausting, but exhilarating.

When we arrived home in Sydney for the hiatus before filming Season 2, Andy finally went to a sports physio to get treatment for his back. He was expecting to be told it was a bulging disc or something else treatable, but he rang me from the clinic and said, 'Hon, I think I'm in trouble.'

The scan he'd had showed countless ominous patches throughout his body, and a huge mass in his abdomen, wrapping around his spinal cord. He was told he'd have just three months to live unless urgent and aggressive treatment began immediately.

We were absolutely gutted and completely overwhelmed, but always optimistic about it because Andy was so young and remarkably fit. Together we believed that not only were we an unbeatable force, but also that there was more to this bizarre and unexpected new chapter in our lives than we could absorb in the shock of the moment.

So we decided to focus on the words of Andy's doctor, who said that if you're unlucky enough to get cancer, this is the one you want because there's a very high recovery rate. We didn't doubt for a second that Andy'd be in the 65% who survive beyond five years and, as far as we were concerned, this was just something that, for one reason or another, was here to teach us, challenge us and ready us for whatever lay ahead.

Andy underwent chemotherapy and coped really well with the first round of treatment. After five months of a chemical cocktail pulsing through him every fortnight, he was given the all clear. We were, of course, ecstatic.

In fact, his recovery was going so well that we began preparing for the filming of Season 2 of *Spartacus*. Andy had to undergo tests for the studio's insurance to clear him for filming. When those tests revealed the cancer was back and more aggressive than before, we were devastated. It was like being at sea in a tiny boat and being told a massive storm was on the horizon.

We were so scared – 'fucking scared' as Andy said in his beautiful, soothing, slightly Northern English voice. But he was always very positive, and very open to learning and discovering. Rather than dwelling on the cancer, he asked, 'Well, what are we going to do with this epic storm?'

One of the many amazing things about my husband was that even in the darkest of moments he found light. And from nowhere other than a place in the deepest part of his soul, came Andy's decision to give purpose to his journey into the unknown with cancer, with life and even possibly with death.

We decided to invite a film crew into our lives, to silently follow him, and us, through these uncharted waters, to capture this epic journey with the intention that our story would remind people to live in the moment and to see all of life as an opportunity that happens for you and not to you.

Andy took a very holistic approach to his illness. He grappled with what had caused the cancer and wanted to peel away the layers of why and how. 'If I can't work out what causes it, how can I cure it?' he asked.

As he searched for answers he spent a lot of time reflecting on his life, but he was also very aware of not fearing what he didn't know. He confronted cancer head on with an attitude of 'What can I learn from this?' and 'How can my experience help others?' He gave purpose to an at times hopeless time, knowing that by making a difference to others he could perhaps make sense of why life had brought him to this point.

So here I am in Manhattan, five years after his departure (as I like to call it), sitting in a darkened cinema, bringing this remarkable part of his legacy to life. It is bizarre and overwhelming watching our lives on screen, but equally I love being able to 'hang out' with Andy again for a few hours.

Spartacus was launched in the US in January 2010 and it was an instant hit. It was one month before Andy was diagnosed. There was a massive buzz around the show and huge hype, with red carpet premieres, A-list parties, and Andy's image on a gigantic billboard in Times Square. It was amazing to see my shy, beautiful, humble man shining more brightly than he had ever done before.

It's quite surreal when I think of that enormous image of him – so very gladiatorial, rippled with muscles and incredibly fit – hovering above the hustle and bustle of Broadway, with cancer seeping through his body.

The billboards are now long gone but there is a lingering presence of Andy here that made New York the most appropriate place to give 'birth' to his death. There's a magic about this city that Andy and I shared. He was on the cusp of amazing things and we'd spent some of the best days of our life here; there was a past and a future for us here, even if he was no longer present to share it.

So on 8 April 2016 we gathered at the East Village cinema to launch *Be Here Now*, his friends, former cast mates, managers, producers and directors, as well as journalists, film critics and all sorts of people braving New York's icy weather to celebrate, cry, commiserate and share in Andy's journey with cancer, our journey with cancer.

Releasing this movie was a massive moment. It's his legacy, the kids' and my legacy. We'd always thought Andy would make a huge impact on people's lives; this was just not how we thought it would be.

Andy never set out to be an actor. He was a façade engineer by trade. You could often see him scaling the sides of the Sydney Opera House or abseiling down huge buildings, checking for cracks.

But one day we were walking along Bronte Beach and a woman stopped us and asked if she could take his photo. She was a talent scout for a modelling agency, she explained. Andy thought it was all a bit of a joke and said no, but I pushed him into it! He was physically beautiful, and had a striking feline face that was captivating for the camera.

I never loved Andy for his looks though. He and I clicked on a much deeper level. From the moment we met in England in 1998, we were inseparable.

So he kind of reluctantly went along and did a photo shoot. He was all a bit bemused, I think, but soon he was signed to an agency and was offered all sorts of work. He was cast in ads and started doing modelling shoots. His career took off. Acting was completely natural to him, and he grew to love the craft and technique behind it.

Andy didn't take up acting because he wanted to be famous. He had no interest in seeing his name up in lights – quite the opposite. He was intrinsically shy, but he was a gifted communicator and wanted to do work that would move people. He loved being able to throw himself into a character and he used acting to shed his shyness.

So it's surreal being in New York and watching this film that is utterly gripping. It's the performance of a lifetime, and there's not a moment of acting in it.

New York was always a special place for Andy and me. It had not only been the part of the world that brought us closer to together, but also the one that almost tore us completely apart. Exactly ten years to the minute before his death in 2011, we'd stood together at the bottom of the World Trade Center buildings, watching a river of human beings flowing into their offices to start their working day.

We'd been out for an early morning jog around Manhattan and had stopped to admire these amazing buildings on our way back to the hotel. People were rushing into the Twin Towers, a briefcase under the arm, a Dunkin' Donut bag in one hand, coffee in the other. It was a beautiful snapshot of the hustle and bustle of busy New York, of the normality that I find difficult to reconcile with the horror that followed in the minutes after.

Andy and I had planned on flying to Las Vegas that night to be married. We'd imagined a cheesy, clandestine, drive-through wedding with Elvis or someone silly declaring us man and wife. It was the first time Andy had been to New York and, after a bit of sightseeing, we were going to spend the rest of the day shopping before we flew out. But of course fate had other ideas.

And here I am in New York again and I'm looking at Andy on screen thinking, *But you're not here beside me.*

My love for New York grows and grows; there is something about the city that represents a sense of opportunity and possibility. The solitude and yet connectedness you can feel simply walking through a sea of strangers is liberating. I find serenity in the craziness of people rushing, the human traffic, the horns tooting and the rattle of the subway. I feel completely at peace here, so if felt like the most important place to release this incredible body of work, sharing Andy's most extraordinary step into becoming the man he always could be, even though he was at his most fragile and vulnerable, letting go of his life.

Releasing the film in New York was like putting the last stitch in a gigantic, colourful, wonderful tapestry that was our life. I was standing in this place where we could have both lost our lives in 2001, and exactly ten years after that day, Andy did.

Introduction

Our hearts and our future hopes had been tied up in this city. It was a poetic moment.

That moment I saw Andy on screen in New York, my whole body went into this nervous space. Here was my husband, our children and my life up on screen. To hear his voice, see him running with our children, hear the audience in fits of giggles as the two of us discuss his first 'woody' after chemo rendered him as weak as a kitten for months, is as charming, uplifting and inspiring, as it is thought provoking, challenging and deeply moving.

Then all of a sudden the film ends. The lights go on and the curtain closes and it's all over. The reality hits me that Andy is still gone. That's the moment when the past ends for me, and my present kicks in. My intuition is to turn my body to the man who has always been beside me, the figure I most want to talk to, but like the freezing cold harshness of coming home after Andy's funeral nearly five years ago, the reality that he is actually gone slaps hard across the face.

But just as the years have gone by, so too has the impact of my grief, and in the time it takes for me to exhale the loss of so many beautiful moments gone by, that are so poignantly shared in the film, my thoughts immediately become focused on my new role and the part I have to play honouring the life of the man I so loved. Watching the film multiple times has allowed me to become strangely, yet remarkably, adept at transferring from past to present and from loss to opportunity. So as the film ends and I watch again as my husband disappears from my life, I pose the question to the audience: 'So what does this little story shared, mean for you . . .?'

I have become adept at bringing that jarring moment back into the now, turning to the person beside me or behind me and asking, 'What did you take from that to learn about yourself?'

And for me, that is what this journey and this story is all about. It's about saying, 'Now, over to you. What will you do with this thing called life?'

It's strange to think about time in the context of Andy's absence and I really can't predict how long it will take for me to re-adjust to life without the person who not only played such a significant role in my life, but who made living and loving such a wild and wonderful collaboration of adventure. Some days it feels like forever; on others, it's as though he was here last week. Life moves on and while the love is still very much there, nestled safely on a ledge in my heart that I now only occasionally climb onto, my focus is now very much in the present and on what it takes to inspire endless possibility.

In the final hours of Andy's life, he called Jesse and Indi into his hospital room. He'd been in and out of consciousness for some time but in that moment he drew on something amazing to be so coherent and present with them. They hopped onto the bed and snuggled into their dad. He wanted to explain to these two precious little children whom he absolutely adored that his body was broken and it was time to say goodbye.

'It's like a butterfly when one of its wings is broken,' he said, with Jesse nestled under one arm and Indi leaning her little body onto his fragile leg. 'It can't fly anymore. But don't worry, because I'm going to go up into the sky and every time you look up you'll see me.'

It was the most perfect way of finding beauty even in the most heartbreaking of moments. His wisdom and clarity were breathtaking, and every time our children see a butterfly now they think of their dad. In that one moment, he totally transformed the saddest moment of their lives into something magical, and that's how they will forever think of him.

A few months after Andy died, as I watered the jasmine plants on the deck, I saw Indi running frantically towards me.

'Look, Mummy, look!' she squealed. She lifted up her little hands towards me and there, cupped between her two palms, was a huge black and white butterfly, the size of a man's hand. 'It's Daddy,' she said. 'He's come to see us and he even has a broken wing.'

Jesse and Indi had opened the front door to grab the mail from the mail box and there the butterfly was, perfectly laid out across the doormat, like a gift that had been specially delivered, waiting to be collected by its rightful owner. Indi laid some tissue paper inside a Tupperware container and made a home for her broken butterfly. She carried it around lovingly and told everyone it was her daddy. And that's what the future is about now: Andy's legacy of transforming the ordinary into the extraordinary.

I battled alongside my best friend as we physically but philosophically fought to transition him from shy Welsh engineer to Hollywood heart throb. I have been privileged to have been shown what true love really means by experiencing births, deaths and marriages – of which I have a certificate for each. And I was extremely fortunate to be with my soul mate the moment he left this earth.

These experiences have taught me how precious life really is, and I want to harness the incredible force of that legacy and grief to help others realise their potential and make the most of their lives.

So it's now over to you, beautiful people! I invite you to whole-heartedly take a good old look at who you've become in your life so far, and make sure that you are shaping a legacy worthy of all that you are.

Vashti Whitfield

Part One

A PROLOGUE

1

I am Spartacus

If you can dream it, you can do it,
— Walt Disney

March 2009

When we landed the lead role in *Spartacus*, our lives changed forever. I say 'we' landed the lead role absolutely deliberately, because everything Andy and I did was such a complete partnership that we moved as one. We were totally entwined and wrapped around one another, two people living one life.

Andy's dream to become a successful actor was our dream as a family – and we each had a role to play in making that happen, so equally that our success was shared too.

The inspiring, gentle, beautiful Andy coupled with me the bossy, passionate alchemist, always knew that in whatever direction we were heading, as long as we had each other, the outcome was irrelevant. All that mattered was giving life a go.

So in March 2009 Andy packed up his bags and flew off to pilot season again. Pilot season is three frenzied months in Los Angeles between February and March when television networks cast shows and lock in their filming schedules for the coming years. It is the time and place to be seen.

LA is absolutely bonkers most of the time, but in pilot season, every actor, director, producer, scriptwriter and casting agent hoping for a show to get up or a dream role to land, converges on Tinseltown and the place is in virtual gridlock for weeks.

It sounds very glamorous being in Hollywood where it's sunny and warm and you're mixing with showbiz people day and night. There's auditions and lots of parties and a huge energetic buzz about the place. But in reality, the days are long and the nights even longer. You live off the smell of an oily rag and there's nothing even remotely glamorous about what you need to do to be seen. It is absolutely cut throat and people will stop at nothing to score a highly paid contract.

Dreams are made and lives do change in Hollywood. There's a tonne of work for the film and television industry, but there's also a tonne of people vying for the roles, and although dozens of pilots are made only a handful will ever actually make it to air on TV. When actors turn up for castings they might be one of a thousand faces that have been submitted for the role. That gets whittled down by a casting agent to maybe a hundred who will go through to the first round of audition. There's a lot of waiting around – waiting for auditions, waiting to see directors, waiting and hoping for that magic phone call that says, 'Congratulations, you've got the part.'

From the moment you touch down at LAX you are bang into it. If you've been lucky enough to land an agent beforehand, that agent will have you in front of every person with any shred of importance they can muster up to get exposure; if you don't have an agent you'll be doing workshops and acting classes, and begging for any audition you can get so you can sign with an agent and get on your way to stardom. A producer once described this extraordinary atmosphere as like throwing a single piece of raw juicy steak into the middle of a herd of wild animals who hadn't eaten all year.

There's a lot of would-be actors sleeping on friends' couches, eating $1 tacos from street cart vendors and slugging their guts out to get that one intro that might catapult them into stardom. Young wide-eyed hopefuls slog through five or six auditions every day, riding a constant roller-coaster of nerves, exhaustion, hope, excitement and disappointment – and that's pretty much how it rolls every day.

Another reality of Hollywood is that you're mixing with industry people day and night and are constantly being told in that wonderful west coast way that 'you are so awesome and you must meet this buddy of theirs who would totally *love* you!'

Most of the time the cattle calls don't happen on a glamorous studio lot. You are not going to bump into Angelina Jolie in pilot season! They happen in offices with grey walls and no windows, or in very dull conference rooms in the backblocks of LA. They can be in little theatres that are so dark you can't see who's watching. Or on a stage under intense spotlights with a row of faces right bang in front of you, taking note of every detail.

The tension for an actor walking into that environment is palpable. At first it might be two or three casting directors, who may not even make eye contact with you, so you have a split second to capture their attention, to make them stop playing with their phone, lift their head up out of the pile of scripts and engage with you. It can be quite soul destroying when you're pouring your heart out on stage and the director is checking Twitter, but you just have to suck it up and get on with it.

Most auditions are met with a silent response, despite the enthusiasm of the curly haired assistant who gave you the thumbs up. Often the decisions are totally out of the actor's hands; your future might come down to something as random as the colour of your hair or someone else's.

LA and the entertainment industry are about making money, full stop. If you and what you have to offer are not what they are looking for, there's nothing to be done about it. And the sooner you understand the way it works, the sooner you are able to experience the whole process in a more empowering way.

It's never a case of audition, then bang – you've got the role. The process can be quite drawn out. You'll do a pre-read to narrow down the list from the hundreds, then a producer's session in front of the people who wrote the script and plan to make the show. Then if you get through to the next round, you'll test in front of the studio that the show is being produced for, which is likely to mean a room full of 'suits' staring coldly at you. The final stage, which is the real meat and bones, is a test in front of the network and a meet and greet with very high powered executives, the kingpins.

It is absolutely exhilarating when you get down to the final two or three because you are so hopeful and excited; you are living and breathing this part. But it's gut wrenching when the call comes to tell you, 'Sorry, you've missed out.'

This was the fourth pilot season Andy had done and we were both very hopeful he'd get a role. He'd been close so many times before; he got down to the final two auditions for the lead in the remake of *Tarzan* the year before, just missing out to Travis Fimmel, who'd had great success as a Calvin Klein underwear model. We knew Andy had talent and we had to persevere until the right thing came along. We totally got that the people who seemed to be scoring the big roles were names and faces with a proven record of mass audience appeal, and not a newcomer no one had ever heard of. So Andy allowed himself a healthy 'five minutes' of disappointment, then reflected once again on what had become a hugely valuable learning experience. This was not the first time we had almost started packing our bags, ready to grab a flight to America.

This time was a bit different because Andy had been invited to audition for *Spartacus* and getting invited to audition was a big deal. He'd done some early auditions and come home before getting the call to fly back to LA for another round. It was really exciting. The audition material he'd put down on tape prior and any readings he'd done in LA when he was out there last already had him on the short list. But we'd been here before and knew that until there was literally a printed contract under our noses, nothing was certain.

For others it might have signalled it was crunch time to prepare for the role, but Andy was doing his best to spend time with Jesse and Indi, fill the kitty up with cash so that we could meet the mortgage payments, and spend any spare moments with his number one fan and emotional rudder, me. We needed to stay grounded but at the same time we were both practically peeing our pants with excitement!

Spartacus was a mammoth production, an incredibly challenging and multi-layered role for Andy to potentially take on. Filming would be in LA or Canada or New Zealand. No offence to my lovely Kiwi friends, but you were the bottom of my 'I wanna go there with my kids!' list.

At that time we were living in a beautiful old art deco apartment in Double Bay. You had to climb up the San Franciscan-style hill just to get to the front door and then puff your way up the three flights of stairs that led into our huge, top floor apartment. But it was heaven. Our sun-filled living room windows looked over glorious Sydney Harbour and there were always dozens of yachts dotting the water in front of us. It was the most beautiful place and space to live in.

Andy and I both very much believed that what you focus on, you attract. So for us, in driving toward what most people saw as impossible, we needed all the help and support we could get. For Andy this meant visualising himself in the role.

Andy would stand in front of the windows, the sun streaming in behind him. In the days before he left, with our little son Jesse giggling behind him, and one hand on his chest, he'd be shouting 'I am Spartacus' in a dozen different voices, rehearsing different pitches, tones and monologues.

'Believe it until it is proven otherwise' was our absolute focus and mantra, both of us trusting that if you put a bucket load of negative energy out in the universe, that's exactly what you would get back, one way or another.

So when Andy got the call to fly back to LA, we put a very strategic plan in place to make this role a reality. We wouldn't allow the slightest doubt into our heads that Andy wouldn't be Spartacus. When we spoke about it, we referred to *when* he was offered Spartacus, not if, and we talked of it as a fait accompli. We refused to even entertain that it wouldn't happen.

We had a map of the world up on the kitchen wall with pins dotted on different countries that we might be going to for filming when he landed the role, and encouraging notes all around it. We'd visualise ourselves being there. It was a tangible, strategic plan.

This was something I'd done multiple times with clients in my profession as a coach and facilitator. I'd guide my clients into a space where they totally believed they could make anything happen, with no self-doubt, often using visual manifestations such as notes or pictures placed around the house, and conversational words, talking about 'when' not 'if'. It really works and there are plenty of studies that have proven how the power of manifestation can create positive endorphins.

So Andy packed up his bags and headed back to LA, carrying our hopes and dreams with him, and we waited anxiously back in Sydney for any news.

Each day Andy and I had been sending one another emails saying, 'Congratulations, this is so exciting. You are going to be moving to Canada, America or New Zealand.' And when we spoke on the phone he'd say to me, 'I am Spartacus.'

The kids had drawn a card which we put on the window facing out to the harbour. It said, 'I am Spartacus' and they'd say to Andy, 'Daddy is Spartacus', which was gorgeous.

We had notes on the fridge and in spontaneous places around the apartment. For days I even walked around at home with little notes tucked into each cup of my padded bra (because I have no boobs!) with 'I am Spartacus' written on them. Bonkers as it sounds, it felt like we were so close that any which way I could focus positive energy, instead of focusing on the sometimes rather challenging aspects of my then life as a sleep-deprived mum, I would.

Everywhere we looked, every moment and every thought was channelled towards Andy becoming Spartacus.

Andy would ring me every day from LA. Clearly the process was rigorous. First he had to audition, then he had to go and read again. Then the TV network wanted to see his show reel and he had to meet with them, followed by a live read in front of the executives from the Starz Network.

This process went on for days. He had to keep his energy up and keep himself really focused on what he was doing.

Then one morning, after Andy had been in LA about a week, I was buzzing around doing something very glamorous like changing a nappy, when he called and said, 'Vashti, I am Spartacus. I got the part.'

I had my head squashed onto my shoulder so the phone tucked in between wouldn't fall, and two little toddler cubs beside me, and I thought we were still role playing. I'm like, 'That's great, really great. Congratulations. So how was your day today?'

And Andy says, 'No, Vashti. I'm not joking. I am Spartacus. *We got it!'*

My head buzzed and my stomach churned with excitement. It wasn't about moving country, it was about the massive change under way and knowing intuitively that we would never again live the life we were leading right now.

I didn't pour a glass of champagne or punch the air because it was 'on with the job'. I knew it would happen; I just knew in my heart that Andy would get this, so it was more a feeling of calm and relief than bells and whistles excitement.

Andy had to be in New Zealand to start work in three weeks' time and we'd be living in New Zealand for the next six months. This was when my role kicked in. As Andy transitioned from engineer to leading man, with an entourage of support around him, my new role as head of family logistics, relocation and chief caregiver took on a whole new meaning. I was in charge of packing up our lives and I had to snap into production mode of shutting down our life in Sydney, packing up our apartment and the kids, and getting us set up in New Zealand. And I had three weeks to do it all. We'd lived our life to make this happen. This wasn't just Andy's new career, it was our new career, our new life.

We were Spartacus.

2

Birth of a Queen

Not all those who wander are lost.
— JRR Tolkien

June 1973

My rather dramatic and unconventional arrival into the world was probably a fair signal that my life was always going to be far from ordinary.

On 5 June 1973 my very brave mum gave birth to me on the floor of a tiny cottage in the Welsh village of Capel Iwan, with just my dad and a midwife, who could only speak Welsh, on hand to welcome me into the world. I was the first child of Susi Fisher and Chris Bland, who were ecstatic, thoroughly relieved and both utterly exhausted after many hours of labour, aided by little more than huffing and puffing and some encouraging words to ease my arrival.

Capel Iwan is in the middle of the lush green Cych Valley, on the west coast of Wales. In summer it is a breathtakingly beautiful and totally picturesque place, surrounded by rolling green fields and hawthorn hedges. In winter it rains – a lot. Winter in Wales is damp, grey and muddy. It's the kind of moody setting you'd see on postcards or English television shows, but it's also very remote. (*Harry Potter and the Deathly Hallows Part 2* was filmed there.)

My mum had no support around her when I was born. Her family were back in Bristol and even though Dad was there, they were both very much alone when they were thrust into the wonderful but challenging world of parenthood.

Capel Iwan was a tiny village. To be honest, I think there were more people in the cemetery than the actual town. There's basically one main road that goes through the middle of the village, with a few houses dotted along the roadside tucked in behind moss-covered stone walls that are hundreds of years old. Our cottage was named Llwyn Inon Isaf. It was a few kilometres out of the village, set back, almost hidden, off a narrow winding road. The track to the house, which sat at the bottom of a steep wooded valley, was potholed and muddy.

The house was, to be fair, in need of some repair; it was basically a slate-roofed ruin. There was a little creek running alongside the property, with woods on one side of the house and open fields on the other. The barn adjoining the house was probably once a luxury home for a horse and cart, but it was now the rather less plush digs of Nelly and Babette, our two milking goats. Another long stone barn formed a border around a grassy play area with a swing, a rope ladder and a friendly owl who used to visit at night.

I don't really recall this, but Mum tells me that most days I'd carry a huge jug to fetch fresh milk from the cowshed at the farm opposite us. I think it was an excuse to go and play with their children. How on earth I managed to carry a huge, heavy jug full of milk down our steep, rocky driveway is beyond me, but I guess it was an early sign of my independence and the strength I could muster when I needed it.

The inside of our cottage was pretty basic, just two main rooms really – a kitchen with a small pantry and a little playroom behind it, and a very primitive bathroom. There was an upstairs space which originally had three or four rooms but Dad demolished the walls to make one huge room with old oak beams exposed across the ceiling. For a long time this room was only accessible by ladder, but eventually proper stairs were built.

Two years after I was born, Mum gave birth to my little sister Lowri in that space upstairs.

I remember the cottage being cold. It was open spaces and high ceilings which were very draughty, and it needed a huge amount of work. Dad pottered around and knocked down a wall here and there to make the spaces bigger and the place more comfortable, but even still it was all pretty rustic. This wasn't a picture of modern living for a young, progressive couple with two little babies.

Today Capel Iwan is mainly a bed and breakfast town. The historic cottages with their low roofs are mostly inhabited by holiday makers passing through or old timers who grew up in the town and never left. While the setting looks absolutely idyllic and very romantic, in reality it wasn't the most ideal place when you're trying to cope with a brand new baby and sleep deprivation. It was remote and quite isolated and my parents were a long way from home. There was no one on hand who could come in and cuddle up their babies to give either of them a few minutes' break.

For the first three months of my life I was rather cutely called Plum before my parents settled on Vashti, which I love. Vashti was a queen in the Book of Esther and supposedly the first woman in the Bible to disobey a man. There was also a folk singer named Vashti Bunyan who my mum loved; she was quite ahead of her time too, so the name stuck. However, I'm not entirely sure that during my rather wild teenage years I did my best to honour the feminist legacy that Mum had bestowed upon me!

My parents were the consummate 1970s hippies. They'd spontaneously tied the knot a year before I was born in Carmarthen, a big town in south-west Wales, while they were out shopping at the local market. It was 12 June 1972 and the groom, my dad, was resplendent in his finest dungarees. With long, red hennaed hair flowing down to his bum and dark kohl eyeliner around his eyes, he was every bit of the handsome seventies hipster he sounds.

Mum was gorgeous. With long, sun-streaked brunette hair and beautiful olive skin, she was a cross between Elle Macpherson and Carly Simon. She wore a fabulous flowing kaftan and in lieu of a veil she wore very cool, large-framed seventies glasses and a cracking smile. She was the epitome of hippie chic – very sexy and oozing femininity.

Both Mum and Dad were very avant garde. It was a warm, sunny day, rather out of character for Wales, and intoxicated by hippie love and probably by the heady burst of balmy weather, they decided to marry at the local registry office right there and then on the spot, with the gardener and cleaner as their witnesses.

They exchanged plastic rings that came out of a nearby coin slot machine and they were blissfully happy. After they married, Dad ever so romantically went off and came back with a cow he presented to Mum as a wedding present.

They were totally immersed in the hippie lifestyle. They were living in this little village, painting, growing vegetables in the back garden, hanging out doing their hippie thing, probably smoking a little hashish every now and then, and definitely making a lot of love. They were very happy.

I recall those early years quite fondly. I have distinct memories of my mum and me spending a lot of time fossicking around the nearby gardens and woods. She taught me about flowers and forests, and I know that by the time I was two years old I could name every flower and bud in the area. There's a black and white picture of me that was taken a little later, a tiny little poppet with my long blonde hair in piggy tails and a very straight chopped fringe with a bouquet of flowers in my arms and a smile as wide as a watermelon. That summed me up.

Andy, by contrast, arrived on this earth in a far more traditional way. And he had a far more traditional upbringing. He was also born in Wales, on 17 October 1971, the much adored second child of Pat and Rob Whitfield, and young brother to Laura.

He was born at the local hospital in Altringham, Cheshire. Like so many men during the early 1970s, his dad wasn't even allowed in the maternity ward. He had to pace up and down the waiting room with a bunch of other nervous men while his wife delivered their baby in a starchy white hospital theatre surrounded by complete strangers.

Pat and Rob were a little older than my parents when they married, and they'd had a longer, more traditional courtship. They met at a party one night in their late teens. Pat, in a silky little leopard print dress with her 1960s Sandy Shaw hair-do was smitten by this handsome young fellow with a sporty motorbike. They went out for about four years before Rob finally proposed. Pat gorgeously says that Rob's long wait before popping the question was because he's 'ponderous'!

They married in a traditional ceremony in a little country church at St Mark's in Dunham Massey, near Cheshire. It was a beautiful little historic chapel where all of their family had been married before, so it was a very special place for them. After weeks of rain, the sun burst through momentarily on the morning of their wedding and, as Pat's bridal limousine made its way along the rural roads to the church, the local farmers took a break from harvesting to wave to the beautiful bride and cheer her on.

Andy and I sometimes reminisced about our shared Welsh childhoods. Even though we had remarkably – and I really mean *remarkably* – different upbringings, we both had the same nostalgic memories of getting lost in carpets of bluebells in the woods, making bows and arrows in fern-lined valleys, and nibbling on blackberries and blueberries picked from the fields nearby. Oh, and rain! We both remembered a lot of grey, rainy, gloomy Welsh days.

Mum was a very creative, patient and loving woman and my dad was much the same. If I couldn't sleep, he would sit beside me and stroke my cheeks until I nodded off. They were both ever so gentle and soft and kind, but they were also both fiercely independent and strong-willed and at times they argued.

Sometimes Dad seemed endlessly frustrated, as if there were always ups and downs in his moods. But the isolation of the Welsh countryside would do that to any extrovert who thrives on human connection. When he was up he was great, loving and really fun to be around, but when he was feeling down he could be difficult to be around. It was such a different time and place;

men didn't feel they could express their feelings back then and there were no support services around for either of my parents, who really felt the isolation, unlike today.

Mum and Dad had moved from the city to the Welsh countryside when Mum was pregnant with me. I suspect they thought that remote little cottage away from the pressures of the city would be a wonderful place to soothe their frazzled souls, but it was the opposite. Instead, the charm of the country-side was more like solitary confinement for my Dad. Mum was trying to cope with his moods and two little babies with no support, no friends and nowhere really to escape to. I can see how they thought the cottage might provide the calm they needed, but two stressed out new parents, who are both vibrant, city-loving, worldly individuals stuck in a lonely village far away from what they knew as civilisation, was a recipe for disaster and began to cause a rift.

After three years of renovating, building, plumbing hassles and catastrophes, Welsh rain, mud, mud and more mud, and the arrival of two babies, Mum and Dad were both burnt out and exhausted, and Dad took off travelling to India for a break. I was three years old and Lowri about fifteen months, so we were largely unaware of what was going on between them. All we knew was that one day our daddy who we loved was there, and the next he was gone. My little sister and I didn't know if he was gone for good, or whether he would be away for a while and was coming back. I just knew that I missed him terribly.

When Dad left, Mum decided that being stuck alone for the winter in a partially renovated cottage in the countryside with two small babies wasn't for her either. So inspired by Dad she took off too – with us in tow. And that was the beginning of the whole big adventure that absolutely shaped who I am today.

Mum had been contemplating going to Spain when she came across a newly divorced woman with three children living just up the road from us. She was planning to go to India with her three children and suggested that she and Mum travel together.

My mum had been an amazing student; she'd studied sociology and anthropology, and she'd travelled extensively. She'd travelled overland by bus to India as a student, and she and Dad had their honeymoon in India, so it was a familiar place with lots of warm and happy memories. With Dad now in India somewhere, she felt she was heading in the right direction.

Mum loved travelling, and was fascinated by other languages and cultures. She'd always intended to go off travelling with us at some point, so when fate intervened and she met another single mum wanting to head off to India, she simply decided it was time for us to go too, right there and then. It all seemed very much aligned. She also knew that, while Dad's departure had been somewhat abrupt, at some point we would all reunite, so why not let it be in India.

We packed our less than worldly possessions into a bashed up, green and white VW camper, aka a Kombi van, and along with the other family, took off on the world's longest road trip, driving from the UK across to India. Two mums, five kids, one campervan.

In theory it sounds exotic. What an amazing adventure! But while I was too young to really understand what was going on, and why they'd chosen time apart, the impact of Dad having temporarily left made me a very sad little person at the start of our journey.

My grandparents were absolutely horrified that my mother was taking off in a beaten-up van with two little babies, but Mum was quite determined – and probably blissfully naïve about what was ahead of us – so off we went.

My parents had travelled a lot before I was born. I have beautiful pictures of Mum on the beach in Goa, India, completely naked, hair flowing and pregnant with me. She was stunning, standing in the sand with her arms resting tenderly on her belly. My parents looked genuinely happy then. They'd taken me back there before Lowri was born and we had a wonderful time, so it was not a huge surprise that Mum would want to head back to some of those familiar places. After the cold, rain and wall-to-wall green isolation of Wales, she was headed for a world of sunshine, amazing sights and smells, explosions of colour and noisy excitement, some 10,000 cramped miles in a shitty van away!

It was January 1977 and our first stopover was on a sub-zero night. We were camping in the forest of Fontainebleau, near Paris. It was so cold ice formed on the inside of the campervan windows, and the best intentions of pitching a tent went out the window when the tent froze and ripped. We all crammed into the van to sleep. The two older children from the other family got to sleep on the bunks, but the rest of us and our mums had to squash up on a makeshift bed that was assembled by pushing the seats down and folding them out over the food storage lockers. Lowri was tiny and slept in a carry cot squeezed into a gap between the gas cooker and the sink.

I struggled to cope with this huge shift in our lives. I missed my dad and our home, and the nine-year-old boy who was travelling with us was pretty horrible to me; he was a bully and we didn't get along.

My mum says that for much of the early part of the journey I went from being an enigmatic little ray of light to a very sad little person. But as we travelled further and further away from Wales, I became absorbed in my new surroundings and the adventures that were unfolding, and the melancholy disappeared.

We went via Paris, then across through Greece, Turkey, Iran, Afghanistan, Pakistan and India, along the hippie trail. The hippie trail was hugely popular in the late 1970s and we certainly weren't alone; there were plenty of Westerners doing the same thing, packing up Kombi vans and hitting the road. The hippie trail had really taken off after the Beatles visited India in the late 1960s. My parents, along with just about every teenager in the UK, watched images on their black and white TVs of John, Paul, George and Ringo in this most exotic and majestic place. It opened up their weather-worn, rebellious little hearts to the idea of exploring this extraordinarily decadent country.

India, with its colour, weather and hedonistic lifestyle, was the polar opposite of gloomy, conservative Britain, and Brits couldn't wait to escape. At that time, British passport holders didn't need visas to get into India, and most of the other countries would issue a visa on the spot as you crossed the border. There was very little political tension and you could move freely between countries without any worry.

Sadly, this is not something you could do today, but back in the 1970s borders were open to Westerners and foreigners were very welcome, so it was relatively safe. It cost next to nothing to live, and there were hotels and restaurants along the way that catered for Western travellers, although we often just stopped the van and camped wherever it suited.

Hippies tended to spend more time with the locals and absorbing local culture than taking in the popular tourist locations. They were seeking adventure and spiritual enlightenment, and probably hashish! Sometimes we found ourselves in off-the-beaten-track places where there were literally no other Westerners around, and my sister and I would be running around having a marvellous time with absolutely no boundaries or discipline. We were these little hippie children freely roaming the world!

I distinctly remember one day we were sitting on a Greek beach in the middle of nowhere. Lowri and I were both half naked and had absolute freedom to do whatever we wanted. It was liberating, and we became quite confident little children who had no qualms about wandering the streets of places like Delhi with no adults accompanying us.

Mum recalls that I came back to myself as we travelled. Once I got to these amazing foreign lands, I too fell in love with the colour and excitement and freedom, just as Mum had done years before. I loved seeing the strange men covered in ashes, the women in beautiful saris, and the Muslim women covered head to toe in heavy black burqas. It was sensory overload for a creatively driven child and I thrived on it.

Lowri and I would often roam around the streets and find some interesting person to talk to, an old story teller perhaps, who'd share local myths and legends with us. I learned a huge amount of history on these travels, and developed a real love and appreciation of other cultures before many kids my age would even have known that there were other cultures outside the UK.

Greece was our first major stop. We had driven south through France and Italy via Pisa, where we got to see the leaning tower, down to Pompeii, then taken a ferry across the Adriatic to Northern Greece and stopped in the Peloponnese.

I loved Greece. The weather was sunny and gorgeous, and we camped out on the beach under the stars. It was so good to be out of the campervan and we could swim and play to our hearts' content. There were anemones and irises blooming in the fields near the beach, and on one of our marvellous exploring adventures, we discovered a cave full of relics and bones.

After a couple of months of us all living under one another's feet, the other family decided to go home to England so the kids could go to school. I can't say I was unhappy to see them go. Not long after they left, Dad came to visit. He'd been working in Crete but after a few days with us he decided to stay. He'd missed us. My parents rekindled their relationship and the journey became a family adventure.

We travelled on around Greece. For a while we rented a house, then stayed at a nudist beach, followed by a stint in a camping park on the beach about an hour north of Athens.

Then we moved through Turkey, where we had to put a protective wire grille on the windscreen because the local kids hurled rocks at us. Then we made our way to Pakistan – even less friendly!

By September, we'd arrived in India. My first taste of India was Amritsar, with the magnificent Sikh Golden Temple. The temple guards were dressed in electric blue and orange satin, my first taste of the colour and splendour and contrasts of India. There were white ashen-faced holy men and skeletal paupers sleeping across pavements, the rich and the poor all melted into one. Travelling through India was not like Greece. In Greece you hardly passed another car on the road; in India each day was a dodgem car rally, avoiding bullock carts, motorbikes, rickshaws, bicycles stacked metres high with sugar cane or an entire family, trucks, pedestrians and elephants.

On our way to Delhi, we came across our first elephant. Lowri was mesmerised and couldn't take her eyes off this majestic creature. The handler stopped the elephant in front of us so she could come a little closer. As the elephant stepped towards her, Lowri's mouth dropped so wide open in awe of this huge creature that a biscuit she was eating fell out of her mouth onto the ground. The elephant quickly scooped it up with her trunk and popped it in her mouth. Lowri burst into a fit of giggles, absolutely delighted.

For four-year-old me, India was an incredible circus-like smorgasbord of people and energy and vitality. We went to festivals like Dussehra and Diwali with little boy acrobats, dancers and effigies; we visited ancient temples and palaces; we dipped our toes in the holy river and stayed at Simla, the mountain retreat of the memsahibs of the British Raj.

Delhi was one of my favourite places. There was a huge campsite for Western hippie travellers, so there were hundreds of families just like ours, and lots of people and kids around. It was a rather motley gathering of beaten-up cars, Kombi vans with rainbows and hearts painted on the side, and makeshift tents belonging to a generation of people hoping to find themselves. The air was pungent with the smell of incense and hashish.

Lowri and I were given complete freedom to go wherever we wanted, whenever we wanted. It was safe. I can't remember ever feeling frightened or even cautious. We'd suck up mango lassis that the local Indian women gave us, and they'd dress us up like little dolls in beautiful saris. I suppose weird little white-haired girls were as much a novelty to them as they were to us. They'd stick bindis on our foreheads and paint our faces up with black kohl-rimmed eyes and cherry red lips. We'd be gone for hours, playing with local Indian families and their children. I loved it.

I even got to have my own wedding. I'd watched a traditional Indian wedding take place. The bride was resplendent in rich fabrics and more gold jewellery than I'd ever seen in my life. The groom wore a very fancy head-dress and rode in on a white horse. I was absolutely mesmerised. I remember every smell, every detail of the dust and the colours, every inch of the fabrics the women wore, and the feast they shared afterwards.

From that point on, according to Mum, I was desperate to have an Indian wedding. So one afternoon the owner of the local hotel staged a mini wedding for me with his son Pushpinder, who was the same age. We'd become good friends, and we must've been very cute. We got all dressed up in the traditional Indian wedding regalia and had a little ceremony in the courtyard of the hotel. It was so much fun and it's a memory I treasure.

We survived on very little on that trip. My mum had a small income from the house she let out in Wales, and I imagine that every now and then she called her disapproving parents asking for help. The conversation would've gone something like, 'Can you wire me some money so I can feed my children?' followed by a decent lecture about the ridiculousness of what she was doing and pleas from her mother to come home.

It was very cheap to travel the way we did, and I became quite independent. When we found ourselves in the middle of nowhere with nowhere to buy food, we learned pretty quickly how to hold our own. Mum had no qualms about sending me down to a Greek fisherman to get fish off the boats, or to a market in India to get vegetables. To the locals, my sister and I were these gorgeous, bizarre-looking creatures. We both had big green eyes, blonde hair and chocolate skin. We'd go and ask the fisherman or market gardener if he could help us with some food, and no one would refuse us. I'd come back with a bucket of beautiful whitebait or fish of some kind or something else to help feed the family. We always came through with the goods.

It was a life without any boundaries at all, and we grew up pretty quickly, which of course had massive implications later on.

In January 1978 we made our way to Nepal. With my obsession for flowers I was taken by the stunning poinsettia and rhododendrons that were the size of trees. I absolutely loved Nepal. We were carried on sherpas' shoulders and we camped in the foothills of the Himalayas. Lowri and I ran around traditional tea houses and had cups of tea and ate dhal bhatt, a traditional rice and lentil dish. Little boy monks would come and play Lego with us, and we used our imaginations to find things to do.

We were exploring remote places of Nepal when no one else was doing it. We went to places well off the hippie trail and often didn't see another Westerner for weeks. It was the most amazing childhood – incredible, adventurous and inspiring. But alongside all of this wonder, there were simmering tensions between my parents. Individually, Mum and Dad were wonderful, creative, intelligent, unique people, but those very traits sometimes didn't go so well together. If they had a row, or if I could feel there was anxiety between them, I would disappear into the amazing landscape and awaiting adventures, rather than being sucked into their world of conflict.

By early 1978 we began to slowly head back to the UK, weaving our way across the cultural patchwork of the sub-continent. I think Mum knew in her heart it was time for her girls to go to school and for life to be a little more settled.

As we made our way through Afghanistan, the decision to get home quickly was rather abruptly made for us. On 28 April 1978, civil war broke out in Afghanistan and we were right there in the middle of it. The situation pretty much brought an immediate end to our travelling adventures.

The Afghan revolution was born with the violent murder of the Afghani leader Daoud Khan and his entire family in a bloody coup in Kabul. We were staying at a campsite right next to the palace where he was killed. Imagine being in the middle of Afghanistan with two babies in a battered old campervan when war breaks out. Not ideal! It was a really dangerous time and the mood in Afghanistan changed virtually overnight. Bombs, gunfire, tanks and fighter planes were all around us. Lowri and I had to lie on the floor of the van, hidden under a sleeping bag, until we made it to the British embassy, where we were locked in with a whole lot of other Westerners seeking sanctuary. It was absolutely terrifying and that feeling of fear stayed with me.

We were given one night of refuge at the embassy then sent on our way. When there was a break in fighting the next morning, we packed up the van and hot-footed it out of town, but as we were making our way towards the Iran border, the starter motor on our beloved Kombi broke down. Dad had to get under the van with a screwdriver every time we needed to start the car. We virtually bunny-hopped our way to the border, where we found a mechanic who could repair the car. But war was following us. The Shah had been overthrown, so we fled to Turkey and over the mountains to the Black Sea, where the van was loaded onto a ferry to Istanbul.

Sadly, the hippie trail and all of its magic came to an abrupt end around this time too. Within a year of the outbreak of civil war in Afghanistan, political tensions erupted across the neighbouring nations and civil war swept through the region. This extraordinary place that I had explored as a child, with its majestic scenery and ancient culture, was suddenly a very dark and dangerous place. The heady days of Westerners freely soaking up the rich atmosphere were over, which is such a shame.

My mum and I have talked about this time often and to be honest we do have some different recollections about it all. Looking back now, she says, 'What on earth was I thinking?' She can't imagine how she made those decisions. There's no way she'd ever do anything like that again. But she doesn't regret it – not for a minute. It fuelled her soul and maybe healed the wounds with my father.

When I think of those years, there are so many inspiring and nostalgic memories that come to mind, but the reality is that often it wasn't the best place to travel with small children. My parents made choices which put us in situations that were either almost like paradise for two little free spirits or more wildly dangerous than you could possibly imagine! But I will always be eternally grateful for the risks they took and the magical faraway places they travelled to with us.

3

School of Hard Knocks

Your mind is a garden, your thoughts are the seeds,
you can grow flowers, or you can grow weeds.
— Author unknown

S ettling back into Welsh life was an enormous challenge after the kaleidoscope of our travels. I don't really remember arriving back in Capel Iwan, but I loved the idea of being settled and having some normality in my life, despite not really understanding what that was. Even though normal in my world was, and still is, being constantly stimulated by change and challenge, I craved structure after so many years of wandering. I needed that security of presence and place in my life to grow and belong.

I do recall a general feeling of excitement about going to school, and I craved that opportunity. Although I lacked the actual experience to support it, I had an awareness of what was potentially on offer in this foreign, strange place of learning.

My mum had been home-schooling us up until then but I desperately wanted to go to school like the other kids in the villages did, and after so long on the road, Mum knew it was time too.

My gorgeous Mum and Dad had always spent hours with my sister and me, teaching us or creating something together with us. Being a natural extrovert in the sense that I drew all of my inspiration from what was going on around me, I was thrilled by the concept of going to school and meeting new people and making friends. I loved learning new things and the thought of having my own desk and pencil case and rules to follow, seemed novel at the time; it was something I'd never experienced before.

On our first morning of school, my mum's hand gripped mine as we walked up the road, coming to a stop beside two large metal milk churns, the dew still fresh on the hedgerow.

We stood there waiting for the school bus to arrive. Catching the bus for the first time was a huge occasion in our lives because while we had grown up 'free range', so to speak, rambling off down the road with a bunch of native Welsh strangers, away from the warmth and nurturing embrace of Mum's way of living and being, was pretty terrifying.

We could hear the noisy rumble of the bus and the kids chattering long before we saw it rounding the corner and, as the squeal of the brakes came to a high-pitched close, the lump in my throat grew to an almost-suffocating size with an overwhelming sense of the unknown. Looking back now, it seems odd that sitting on a sherpa's shoulders, striding ahead and away from my parents in the foothills of the Himalayas, seemed like the most natural thing in the world, and yet clambering up into a small school bus in a tiny Welsh village felt absolutely terrifying to me.

When the doors burst open, we were greeted by a sturdy woman with thick cheekbones and little veins that spread across her face like fine cracks on a well-used china plate – let's call her Miss Llewellyn. She looked Mum up and down over the top of her glasses, and then did the same to Lowri and me. 'I suppose you'd better get on then,' she snarled.

Miss Llewellyn was a harsh, cold woman and we could sense her instant dislike of us. Before even so much as a 'good morning', she had already sized us up as misfits, the town hippie kids, not worthy of anything other than her contempt. It was pretty obvious right from the get-go that Miss Llewellyn was going to be our own Miss Trunchbull; she didn't agree with either us being there, or our lifestyle. She greeted us with the same snarly contempt every single morning, but nothing was going to dampen my excitable little spirit!

The school was set on the narrow main road that ran through the village and comprised a small playground surrounded by a flower-filled hedgerow, and one large long building, a little like a town hall, with a grassy area behind that led to the small toilet block.

I distinctly remember, after having gone for a pee one day, pulling down my tights and to my absolute horror, realising that I had forgotten to put on underwear. I was terrified that someone would find out.

I wanted so much to be able to fit in at school so that I could get on with soaking up all the learning that I sensed was available. Instead of wildly exploring and roaming free on a daily basis, I was learning things that I could instantly do something with. Before, I had learned how to tie a sari from a friendly local, or how to fasten a scarf to carry my eight-year-old Nepalese friend while she fastened her two-year-old brother to her back for most of the day.

The logical, tangible and often very gratifying results instantaneously fed my newfound desire to achieve. We did all sorts of fun things on my first day of school, like cross stitch and art, and you can imagine how different it was for us to be sitting in an actual classroom, complete with desks and chairs and lockers and a chalkboard. It was a momentous change after doing lessons squashed in the back of the campervan or in a makeshift campsite in Delhi. We'd been quite literally worlds away.

Schoolwork was relatively easy for me and I loved the challenge of putting my brain to work and being pushed in a way that wasn't necessarily familiar. English was a second language in Wales, so everything was taught in Welsh. The harshest challenges involved grasping the routines of school life, learning the rules of the playground and adapting to the discipline. For so long, we'd just done whatever we liked without anyone telling us what to do, so it was confusing to suddenly be immersed in schoolyard politics and to have to follow rules that we didn't know or understand.

I had my first real taste of schoolyard life at lunchtime one day when a girl pushed me over in the playground. To this day, I have no idea what caused her to do such a thing. I had no one to play with so was just wandering around on my own, minding my own business, and she walked up behind me and gave me a shove in the back with such force that I was knocked off my feet. A beautiful girl named Hevina, with short home-cut hair and wonky blue National Health-provided glasses, came over and introduced herself. She was very sweet and kind and said, 'I'll play with you!' And so lovely little Hevina became my first school friend.

After we'd been outside for a little while, the headmaster came out into the yard. He was wearing a red and white gingham shirt. He had pinkish skin with circles of red rosacea across his cheeks; his hair was bright red and wiry and looked like a little nest of pubic hair resting on the top of his soon-to-be-balding head. He had a flat piggy nose, and the seams of his shirt were stretched to their limits and nearly popping his buttons, his tubby belly straining under the tight checked fabric.

He began swinging around a large brass bell on a long black handle. The only bell I'd ever heard before was a Tibetan prayer bell in Nepal. You don't actually ring a prayer bell; you run your hand around the rim to make the sound, which is rich, serene and soothing. Obviously, the clanging of that school bell signalled something as all of the children began running in different directions, as though they were in on a secret that I knew nothing about. Kids were pushing past me and it was quite chaotic so I began walking over to the hedge alongside the playground, which had all of these beautiful flowers, and did what I knew how to do to get out of the way.

Since I hadn't been included in the game I thought the bloated, red headmaster with his noisy bell and the other children were playing, I was content to amuse myself away from the hustle and bustle. Walking toward the hedge, I suddenly felt this intense, burning feeling on my back. When I turned around, I realised that the headmaster had slapped me! And then he hit me again, three times in total. He whacked me across my little behind and yelled in my face, 'You're going to have to learn to step in line, you are! You may have done what you liked before, but this is what proper people do!'

I had no idea I'd done anything wrong. It was my first day of school and I been shoved, slapped and punished for being different. It was a pivotal point in my life. Inside my little head, rooted the overwhelming thought that, however hard I tried, I somehow did not belong.

Andy's school life began when his dad was offered a promotion with the Central Electricity Generator Board, as it was known, and the Whitfields moved to Anglesey, an island off the coast of north-west Wales. Anglesey was quite remote but this was a big opportunity for Rob to work on a cutting edge nuclear power plant which had just opened. The family moved into a beautiful new home with views of the beach, and Andy and his big sister Laura filled their days exploring the neighbourhood on their bikes, or crabbing among the rocks on the shoreline.

Andy was only four years old when he began school at Amlwch, and although it wasn't the first time he'd been separated from his mum, they were still very new to the island so arriving at a new school, in a new place without a single familiar face, was as intimidating for Pat as it was for the terrified little boy who had no concept of what was taking place. In the flurry of parents and children, all of a sudden Andy's mum was gone and he found himself among a large crowd of children. But what was strangest for him was that he couldn't understand a word anyone was saying.

It was a Welsh-speaking school and no one had thought to explain to him that was the case. When the teacher asked him to introduce himself to the class, he felt so physically overwhelmed that he couldn't speak and began to cry. Realising that his tears needed an explanation, he pretended that he had an ear ache and motioned that he was in pain. So off he went with the school nurse to the sick bay, where he not only made the conscious decision that he would do everything he possibly could to not stand out, but also that he would do all he could to try to fit in.

When Pat spoke to Andy's teacher, she expressed her concerns that he was 'quite shy' and not responding in class. Pat said, 'Well, that's hardly surprising given he doesn't understand a word you are saying!'

In later years Andy told me that this first day at school was pivotal in who he became later in life. Given the decisions he had come to in the sick bay, it took many years to coax him out of his shell.

While Andy struggled with the lessons to begin with, one thing he was very good at was making friends and he did so easily, both in the playground and the neighbourhood. And some of those school yard buddies remained loyal friends into his adult years and still communicate with his family today.

We hadn't been back in Wales for long before Mum realised that it wasn't the life for us. After all the amazing colour and excitement of our travels, Capel Iwan was too 'beige', too small, too quiet and too judgmental for our little family. When you've spent days trekking in Nepal and been bathing in the Ganges, being in a little white classroom in Wales felt stifling. Mum quickly understood that in the village we would not get the kind of education she wanted for us.

My dad's need to be surrounded by people, creativity and diversity was also fast becoming hugely undernourished. His capacity to cope with the feelings of isolation, along with the endlessly grey, wet Welsh weather, brought his restless side to the surface and subsequently triggered hours of rows with my struggling Mum. Wales was far away from the freedom and space that travelling the world had afforded us. And however much I tried to be the family peacekeeper, the joker and the diplomat, I was failing, in my young mind, at making my parents happy. Once again I was being shown – at least in the mis-interpretation of my young, impressionable mind – that I didn't belong 'here'.

It was time to change the situation and move on, so we rented out our little Welsh cottage, packed our bags and moved to a tiny house in a beautiful, leafy suburb in Cheltenham, England. Even though we only spent a year or two there, I have vivid memories of it being a significant chapter in all of our lives. Moving from the countryside to an urban area, however suburban or small it may have been, exposed both Mum and Dad to the stimuli they both had longed for and that had been lacking in our life in Wales.

Dad, who was an incredibly talented, emerging professional photographer, set up his own darkroom and studio and appeared to be fully immersing himself in the chance to combine his vocation with that of his burgeoning creativity. Mum, buoyed by the emergence of the feminist movement, acquired a whole new set of friends – people who seemed to very much reconnect her with the humanitarian and pacifist activist she had once been, a woman who rallied for the rights of others and stood up against the status quo when justice and equality appeared absent.

We attended the local school, a dull, dung brown in colour, and a short walk away. I was delighted to have my first experience of wearing a school uniform. But, as always and particularly in accordance with where Mum's head was at that time, I literally had to beg and plead for the bog standard version, which was in conflict with her desire to inspire us to hold true to our own uniqueness and originality. I definitely did not want a more contemporary, tampered-with uniform that would, once again, have me standing out as being different!

More than anything, school was incredibly stressful, apart from one term with the tall, handsome and very kind Mr Watson, who read us Tolkien's *The Hobbit* in all manner of brilliant and hilarious voices, and who encouraged us to be as creative as we were academic. Otherwise, it seemed a never-ending flow of teachers who appeared to loathe children and who communicated with us like we were either in the army or in a dog obedience training school. (For those of you familiar with the song or the film, cue Pink Floyd's 'Another Brick in the Wall'.)

Our home in Cheltenham was on a safe little street, teeming with young kids who played in and out of each other's houses. I loved how social and accessible our neighbours were, given how isolating our time in Wales had felt. The street was a wonderful and diverse mix of people, and in a short time we had collectively formed the Dagmar Road street 'gang', its members ranging in age from four to ten years old.

So, there I was, in my flared jeans and with my gap-toothed smile, with my BMX bike and my boyfriend, who lived a few doors down, the first 'Andy' in my life, Andrew Leach. We were both around eight years old at the time and loved to play hair-dressers, which was my idea of heaven. I sat in the chair, outside on our street, and relaxed into hours of having my head and hair played and pampered with until Andrew's parents would shout for his return.

In hindsight, I might have thought Andrew somewhat effeminate were it not for the fact that he and I (as I'd done with Martin, the farmer's son back in Wales) regularly engaged in what we thought was a bit of 'sexy time', playing at being grownups. We fumbled around on my top bunk, experiencing our first sense of excitement within a physical world which even then I clearly knew existed, being a child of the seventies and all that. My first Andy introduced me, rather excitedly, to the idea of what a girl got up to with boys!

During the school holidays that year, my mum, sister and I travelled down to our old home in Capel Iwan to enjoy a vacation. In the middle of the night, someone hammered loudly on the front door of our cottage. It was the local police officer, delivering the news that my father had somehow fallen through the front window of a shop, and a large shard of glass had sliced right through a main artery. He was in intensive care, but was going to be okay. How it happened is a little vague, but after the initial shock my mum was furious.

The months that followed were a mixture of extremes. Lovely cuddles with my dad, trying to massage feeling back into his numb hand. And then the smell of his flesh burning as his cigarette burned down to the skin due to the extreme and irreversible nerve damage to his index finger. I remember plates of dinner being hurled at the wall in misplaced frustration and watching a fried egg slide in slow motion toward the floor. Once again my parents instinctively knew it was time to move on.

The city of Bristol was where my parents originally had met and where my mum attended university. Ahead of the trends, she was one of the first women in the city to open up a macrobiotic store which sold brown rice and whole foods; never one to shy away from a challenge, she'd go for anything she put her mind to with great confidence. Bristol was also where she had managed to gain a grant through her studies to visit India for the first time.

My parents, Chris and Susi, knew Bristol for its vibrancy in the 1970s and for the eclectic group of friends that they had collected there while in their early twenties, the same friends who had introduced them to each other. Both of Dad's sisters also lived in Bristol, and we had often visited them over the years.

My parents were not typical parents, or people for that matter, even for the 1970s. Mum had a stifling childhood. Her parents were Austrian refugees who had escaped the Nazis and fled to England, fuelled by their determination to give my mother and her two brothers the most solid, safe upbringing they could. My grandfather was Jewish and twenty years older than my grandmother; she had been his Catholic housekeeper in Austria and risked her own life to help smuggle him out. They married and went on to set up a successful business in England, manufacturing tacks and tape measures.

Mum was sent to 'ladies' schools' where she was taught how to dress properly and how to be a good wife. Her conservative parents must've been mortified when she completely rebelled and became an adventurer and activist, a woman who constantly questioned the status quo, basically the polar opposite to her parents' way of being and thinking. After everything they had endured and survived in terms of post-Nazi Austria and two horrendous wars, they couldn't understand many of the 'poor' choices their daughter was making – chief among them, aligning with my dad.

To this day, my mother is an incredibly intelligent and forward-thinking woman, despite some of her crazy ideas. She was, and is, an amazing mother, gentle and fun; she has always made us feel completely loved and adored. Although not particularly street-wise, she could talk herself into and out of virtually any situation. She had this dogged philosophical standpoint that you could do anything you set your mind to. I don't think there's ever been a time in my life when I've presented her with the craziest of ideas and she hasn't said, 'Go for it, darling. That's terrific!'

My dad had a very challenging upbringing in Portsmouth, England. His father was in the navy and he didn't actually meet him until he was three years old. Their family had very little money and moved around constantly, depending on where his father was stationed. His mother, trying desperately to cope alone with four small children, suffered from incredible depression and feelings of being overwhelmed.

In Dad's really tough, often loveless, childhood he and his siblings were at one point briefly separated from one another and dropped into government-run children's homes which, as you can imagine, back in the 1950s and 1960s, were rather abusive and destructive places. He once described to me how a teacher regularly took to him with a medicine ball, throwing it at him until he fell over in front of the class. I can only imagine, with horror, the effects that kind of abuse would have on a child's sense of self and their mental health moving forward.

Instead of sticking around and enduring more of a life he could no longer bear, Dad ran far away in search of possibility. At seventeen, he became a waiter on a cruise ship and found himself travelling the world. He went to New York, but eventually ended up back in Bristol, where he met my mother. They were young and very much in love, and they were so happy and carefree.

Now we were all living in Bristol, Dad worked sporadically as a freelance photographer, doing everything from architectural shoots to Walls ice cream. We loved it when he came home with boxes of chocolate flakes, left over from the rather challenging job of snapping ice cream that was melting under the studio lights.

He was a handsome young guy, who also often worked with some fairly glamorous up-and-coming models, and it would be fair to say he sometimes enjoyed their company a little too much. I spent a lot of time in my twenties trying to work through some very deep anger and resentment towards my father on account of how he sometimes behaved – and because I spent a lot of my childhood, especially in Bristol, trying to keep the peace between my parents.

Moving to Bristol, the place where my parents' tumultuous relationship had its beginnings, was like stepping into a whole new world. It was hugely multicultural and urban, especially compared to our very white, suburban existence in Cheltenham and our even whiter stay in the Welsh countryside. There was a vibrant music scene and an abundance of passionate, well-travelled creatives settling in the city. The BBC was also located there, as well as one of England's top universities. It was big, busy and noisy, and we could lose ourselves in the anonymity. It was exactly what Mum wanted and she loved it there.

The eighties scene was coming into its own by now, with its super-sized shoulder pads, eyeglasses the size of tea saucers, big hair and way too many dangly earrings. The music my dad had raised me on – The Eagles, Van Morrison, Patti Smith, Bowie and other legendary staples of the 1970s – had begun to fade into bands with big beats and catchy hooks like The Pet Shop Boys and Culture Club. And there was a huge presence of reggae in the area due to the large Rastafarian, Jamaican and West Indian population.

Bristol is nestled between a harbour and huge sandstone hills, with an enormous suspension bridge over the Avon River Gorge leading into town. It was an incredibly pretty city but also somewhat confusing to me: for the first time in my life, I had to contend with becoming street-smart.

Mum rented a brick semi in Montpelier, where graffiti artist Banksy hails from. His artwork is dotted around the streets.

Our house was small but lovely and had three bedrooms with a beautiful, narrow little garden. All of the streets around us were so narrow that you had to park your car up on the sidewalk otherwise you'd have your car smashed in! If Bristol was the front line of multiculturalism back in those days, then Montpelier was the heart and soul of it. Some might describe it as bohemian, but bohemian doesn't capture the excitement and creativity bubbling away in that multicultural stewpot that was our neighbourhood.

But Montpelier could also be an aggressive place. There was an edginess there, always had been. Bristol is a wonderful, creative city, but you never knew when something was going to flare up in cultural tensions or street rebellion. Mum can't bear that I remember it this way, but as a young kid pottering around, there were a lot of really rough kids out on the street, so I spent a lot of my younger years defending myself. The middle-class streets in Clifton, where my school was situated, presented a very different experience to the sometimes scary scenarios I faced wandering around my neighbourhood which, to me, often felt like a pressure cooker about to explode in a flash into the threat of violence or volatility. When we first moved there, I was worried that I could be set upon by a bunch of girls when I was walking home from school and it was quite an anxious time for me.

Mum enrolled me at a Steiner school where she worked teaching English to foreign students, often refugees. Steiner is both a type of school and a form of education; it was the brainchild of Rudolf Steiner, an anthropologist, who believed in a very different approach to developing young minds. The school suited me perfectly. There was a focus on creative energy, the arts, music and dance, all of the things I loved, and I was actually encouraged to use my imagination. Being different was considered something to be really proud of, so for a unique and free-spirited little soul like me, Steiner schooling cemented my love of learning and helped me feel more confident within myself. It was there that I found space, and the encouragement to come into my own as an individual.

At the start of every day, we studied a main lesson which changed every few weeks – maybe Indian mythology or astronomy, or anything that sparked an interest and switched our brains on. Unlike some of the other Steiner schools around the world with pricey tuition fees, our school had a sliding scale of fees, so there were those who paid more and those who paid less, based on what a family could afford. Other than its lack of sports due to poor funding, it was the perfect learning environment with a diverse student body and its mix of sharp, creative, outgoing and sensitive minds. The school was run on the love and commitment of the teachers and parents.

Settling into urban life in Bristol, I began mixing with kids much older than me, not only at school, but also with the cool street kids in our area. I was learning to be street-smart and resilient. But Mum and Dad would've killed me had they known where I was and what I was up to. They gave me as much freedom and responsibility as they thought I could handle, thinking I was hanging out with my well-educated friends, when I may or may not have been hanging out at nightclubs at the tender age of thirteen.

I wasn't drinking or smoking or doing drugs, I was just trying to fit in. It was also somewhat of a strange experience for me because, on some level, I wasn't interested in fostering my individuality either in school or at home. I wanted to be part of the pack and fit in, which really sums up the contradiction of my life. At school I was this diligent, creative little thing thriving in my individuality. But after school, I just wanted to be like everyone else and not stand out. I wanted to be part of the cool group of kids who hung out in our neighbourhood.

I was becoming very aware of myself. I knew I was different from the other kids; I stood out, and I didn't want to be that. I didn't want to be different from everybody else. All I wanted was to wear a school uniform and fit in, blend in, with the other kids instead of being singled out because of my parents. The extraordinary irony is that now I'm teaching my own children that individuality is key! But when you're eleven and twelve, all you want to do is be like everyone else.

Which brings me to my parents' car. We were still driving around in our beaten-up old campervan that by now looked like it had survived a war, barely, and been blown up and put back together several times over! It had giant rusty gashes in the side panels, and had been so bashed around it looked as if it would fall apart if you touched it.

When you're driving though places like India at night, on roads that don't exist, you have to have these blue sidelights to warn trucks that you are coming; they flash so the oncoming trucks slow down, otherwise they'd never see you and you'd be run off the road. We were oceans away from India in Bristol but we were still driving our appalling camper with its gaudy, flashing blue lights. My mum, however, was very proud of the camper; she loved it because it was a souvenir of our adventures. She even named it Phoebe Hurty. But my dad would've rather worn a paper bag on his head than be seen in it, and my sister and I were equally horrified. That ridiculous car, in my mind, called attention to the fact that we were different. And I was having none of it! I always made Mum drop us off around the corner from wherever we were going.

I spent a lot of time seeking the attention of boys outside of school, which I think subconsciously comes back to wanting the attention of my father who had been absent a lot when I was a small child. It wasn't driven by fun and flirtation or any sort of pubescent hormonal curiosity, but by my all-important desire to be acknowledged and to fit in.

The simmering street tensions of Montpelier were nothing compared to what was happening at home, which was basically all-out domestic warfare. Bristol represented many good things for us, but it was also the absolute pinnacle of volatility in my parents' relationship. My mum and I were always close, but our relationship really deepened during those years.

When tensions rose at home, I took my frustration and anger out on Lowri, and she bore the brunt of me letting off steam. If you ask my sister, she will say it wasn't so bad, but I remember being utterly awful to her. I was very dismissive and overpowering, trying to make her look small in front of other people. As siblings, Jesse and Indi have a wonderful relationship and I'm very proud of how they get along, so reflecting on the way I treated Lowri is not something I'm proud of. Lowri still maintains that I'm hanging on to the bad memories, and my mum insists that when I looked after her I was always very sweet and kind. I hope I was. I love my sister enormously; she's a very smart and talented woman.

During those chaotic times in Bristol, Mum was my best friend, and I defended her and was totally in her corner. We did everything together, we were inseparable.

Despite their difficulties, Mum stayed with Dad because he is brilliant and creative and can be very kind and funny. His challenges are not necessarily his faults, and are a result of a fractured childhood; he needs understanding and compassion. She had immense love for him, she still does, and that's why they've stayed together all these years. In fact, they remain married today, living between the south of France and Bristol, surviving 44 years of a marriage that could be described as part rainbow, part storm cloud.

Today I have gratitude for my upbringing and the things I learnt from my parents, good and bad. There is no point hanging on to what happened in the past. Instead of anger, I now choose to look back with positivity and happiness and remember the wonderful family times we had instead of focusing on the difficulties. I have so much appreciation for my dad's amazing photos from our years of travel.

My childhood also allowed me to foster enormous resilience, and to hone my ability to communicate with anyone, in any situation. Surviving on the streets in places like India and Pakistan required equal parts cunning and curiosity, and I developed a razor-sharp ability to read situations in a split second, along with the skills of diplomacy to get out of those situations as quickly as survival warranted. I developed the ability to make someone feel completely at home, even when they are in an unfamiliar or uncomfortable environment, or they don't speak my language.

So there's good stuff that comes from bad, as there is in any situation life offers us. I don't begrudge the difficult parts of my childhood, because they have helped shape the confident, capable woman I am today.

Oddly, or maybe not, I have been staunchly the opposite in the way I parent my two beloved cubs, Jesse and Indi. We've lived very safe, scheduled lives; the kids have been very settled, and Andy and I built a protective and nurturing fortress around them. They've lived very insular, suburban lives and haven't really been exposed to the wild multiculturalism and carefree life that I experienced. Although, having said that, their lives are far from ordinary, as you'll soon discover.

Now they're eight and eleven years old, having always been embraced by an abiding, deep love and the security of loving parents who also adored each other. Despite the unexpected life lessons thrown at them, they are ready – as I am – for a different type of adventure. It very much feels like the right time, with one cub on either side, to trek further afield on an adventure uniquely our own.

4

No Pain, No Gain

To live in this world, you must be able to do three things:
to love what is mortal; to hold it against your bones
knowing your own life depends on it; and, when the
time comes to let it go, to let it go.
— Mary Oliver

Bristol was a place and time of huge physical and emotional awakening for me. The layers of my complex young life and the years of extensive travels had resulted in a sense of exclusion and isolation which in turn created something of an internal armour. I was already a pretty street-smart kid, and had the confidence to explore people and places, as well as a deep and arguably dangerous desire to fit in.

By the time I was in my mid-teens, I had tasted all that life in colourful Bristol had to offer, including sex and drugs, and had an awareness of life that was well beyond my pubescent years. Drugs and alcohol never really carried an allure though. I'd smoked a bit of pot here and there, usually trying to keep up with the cool cats, and I'd gotten horribly drunk on cider a few times, but I hated the feeling of being out of control, of not being present and sharp.

Sex, however, was something I was always completely intrigued by. Lowri and I had mostly worked it all out for ourselves, just by watching along the way, but we were also taught by our parents that sex, along with drugs, was something we should never be forced into by anyone else. Without disclosing the details of her own experience, my mum encouraged me to ensure that, when the time came, losing my virginity was something I should be certain I wanted to do. And so after one near miss, spread-eagled under a horny fifteen-year-old, while two slightly older friends were doing the deed in a field nearby, I honoured my mum's words. I embraced the world of sex and intimacy surrounded by candles and moody music with a kind, gentle, older boyfriend who believed me to be somewhat older and slightly more 'legal' than I actually was.

There were other men – well, boys really – and I had a few dangerous and often awkward liaisons along the way, but by the time I was seventeen I was in my first serious relationship with a guy named Andy who I met at the gym. This Andy was not the beautiful man I went on to marry, but Andy Bush, a larger than life, volatile and hugely charismatic Bristolian who ran and co-owned a gym in the area.

Around fourteen, like many girls, I'd become conscious of my body, and of what I could do with it, the strength and power I had. I threw myself into my fitness after I started working out with my friend Rosie. Rosie's mum was a runner, and Rosie and I started to go running with her. Soon after we were doing aerobics and a passion within me was awakened. I loved it. I loved the feeling of being fit and challenging myself, and aerobics was super fashionable then, even my parents were doing it. We were in the midst of the whole eighties fitness craze; it was all about matching leotards and leg warmers and white sneakers and grapevine. I thought Jane Fonda, with her pearlescent G-string leotards, was the essence of womanhood; she was so sexy and powerful.

My physique was naturally quite athletic and I had huge amounts of energy, so I loved being anywhere I could jump around with others and found the combination of music, adrenalin and my body's natural force quite addictive. I could quickly lose myself in the movement of an aerobics class and found that even in the middle of a dynamic workout, my mind could retreat to a calm and quiet place. Fitness and anything action related were where I felt most alive and liberated, so I relished this newfound way I could express myself and burn off the incredible energy I had.

As my body shape changed I became more confident and quite enjoyed the attention that I was attracting. But that also prompted the unhealthy behaviour of looking for external acknowledgement, and a period of several years of making really poor choices around men. I forgive myself for those things – but there is no excuse for some of the ridiculous outfits I wore! I will always be grateful for the amazing acceptance my dear hipster friends showed me when I turned up at a class wearing a fluoro green thong leotard (think Borat) with lacy black, Madonna's 'Like a Virgin'-style, see-though cycling shorts.

The gym was a happy place for me and it became a huge part of my life. It transported me far away from the mundaneness of yet another cold, wet evening in the UK, while most of my friends would be happily settling into a pint at the pub, or cozying up on the couch to watch *EastEnders*. It was also where I could dodge the darkness of my father's up and down moods, or my friends who thought smoking pot or getting drunk was cool, despite my hating it passionately. Above all, it gave me an escape from the relentless, ever-present thoughts of not belonging anywhere that pounded inside my head and churned at my stomach.

By the time I was sixteen I was living a strange double life. I was studying for my A-levels at the Steiner school and being with these wonderfully creative, artistic people during the day, then at night throwing myself into crazy aerobics and hanging out with kids who were edgy and doing drugs and clubbing.

After A-levels I did a year of what was called Art Foundation, which is a year of preparing your art folio before you go off to art school. Our classes were held at the magnificent Ashton Court mansion, an extraordinary 850-acre estate that was run by the council. It was a seriously amazing place to go to school. We had deer skipping around the grounds and beautiful woodlands carpeted with flowers as far as your eye could see. I remember rows and rows of rhododendrons and lush green rolling hills. It was incredible.

So by day, I was at this very posh school, then at night I'd go to the gym, and on the weekends I'd be going out to clubs like Thekla which was a famous nightclub on a boat moored in the Bristol harbour. This was very much the era of white ankle boots and puffy ra-ra skirts. We'd dance all night to Soul to Soul, Salt-N-Pepa, Grandmaster Flash and my absolutely favourite song

'All this love I'm giving' by the late Gwen McCrae. My parents had no idea I was doing these things; they thought I was at my very conservative friends' homes studying.

One night we were at a party and this guy I vaguely knew came up to me and said, 'You've got a fabulous body. Why don't you come and train with us?'

Train for what? I didn't know what 'training' was. He asked me to come along to his gym and see what it was all about.

You'd be forgiven for thinking that a gym around this time was all leotards and leg warmers. But it was the opposite at this place. It was a very beefy, sweaty place, one of those grungy places where really serious body builders go, with giant barbells and stuff. This was men and muscles and I instantly loved it. I was really attracted to the power behind pushing yourself. I'd always had extraordinary strength and tonnes of energy; I was a little pocket rocket and I loved seeing what I could achieve with my body.

The thing that struck me about this gym environment was that there was no class structure. No one was better than anyone else. You could be talking to a bloke who could barely string a few words together or a lawyer or a doctor, and they were all the same. They were there because they were into body building; they shared a passion for pushing their bodies to the limit. There was absolutely no sense of where you came from or how much money you had, and it was a very inclusive and encouraging environment. If you saw some of these blokes walking down the street with their gun arms and thick necks, you'd probably run. But they were a pack of gentle giants, and I always felt very secure among these guys; they looked after me.

So I started hanging out at the gym a lot more often and I got to know everyone so well that after a couple of months they offered me a part-time job as the receptionist. The gym was owned by a very well-known Bristol family, who owned a number of colourful businesses and had a lot of power around town. Their daughter and her boyfriend, a guy named Andy Bush, ran the gym together. He was embedded in the family and her father had given them this business.

Andy Bush was a well-known raconteur and a bit of a lad around the streets of Bristol. He was quite a bit older than me; he would've been in his late twenties when we met, and to me, he was sophisticated and worldly and a lot of fun. He had blazing blue eyes and a laugh that could charm pretty much anyone. He was a ladies' man, witty and funny, and he had this confidence around women that was very sexy. Andy came from a working class background and reminded me of one of those lovable English rogues you'd see in a Guy Ritchie movie. He was razor sharp and, although he wasn't academically educated, he was one of the brightest people I'd ever met. He was 100% man without a sniff of boy.

Andy and I used to flirt a lot, which probably wasn't the smartest thing given that his girlfriend's dad owned the business! But he was clearly attracted to me and I was completely taken by him. I thought he was very much off limits because of his role in the business, and also because I was considerably younger than him, but he didn't seem to see any problem with our mutual attraction and wasn't subtle about how he felt for me. This wasn't a sweet little seduction. Sometimes he'd stand at the end of the reception desk and we'd talk; he made me laugh a lot.

Before long Andy started giving me a lift home after work, and one night after a lingering kiss, which became a rather drawn-out passionate snog, we began having a clandestine relationship. He told me he'd been unhappy in his relationship for a long time but he felt trapped because he was involved with the family and really had no way out. He flattered me by being interested in and inspired by so many things that I just saw as ordinary in myself. My childhood had taught me to gravitate towards the unpredictable and this extended to my interest in men; there's a real sexiness in unpredictable men, so I think I found it really attractive that this man, who I thought I couldn't have, took such an interest in me.

Andy was tall and blond and very attractive. He was well built from years of training at the gym, not a pretty boy at all, but his face told a story and I knew he had grown up in the school of hard knocks. He had a big personality and he was quite a life force; everyone knew when Andy was in the room.

So we had this secret affair, but not surprisingly we got found out. His girlfriend was suspicious he had feelings for me and was furious when she caught him leaning over my desk and flirting with me. The whole thing blew up big time. I was banned from going to the gym and he was kicked out of the family, which was a really big deal. I was warned that I shouldn't be seen anywhere near the gym ever again.

The gym was situated in a part of Bristol that I would never otherwise have reason to visit, so it wasn't difficult to stay away. Shortly after, for one reason or another, Andy dramatically left the bosom of the family and fled across town to Clifton, near where I had attended the Steiner school. He leased a beautiful apartment in a huge old sandstone building and created a space that I could come and go from. Our relationship had suddenly become far more serious.

Every night I'd talk to him on the phone for hours, literally until I fell asleep with the phone in my hands. It's fair to say there wasn't a great deal of depth in our conversation, but this was the early days of mobile phones. I vividly remember the afternoon Dad picked up a 1200 pound phone bill from the mail box and the ensuing blood curdling scream. 'VASHTI!!!!!' What is this phone bill? And who is this man we've never met?'

I shouted back, as innocently as I could, that there must've been some mistake! Taking off out the door as quickly as I could, I belted over to Andy's. When I told him what had happened he took me into his bedroom, lifted up the mattress and pulled out 1500 pounds from a huge pile of cash he had stashed away.

Now I could be gullible and say that the money – and the odd firearm that was also stashed away – came from his business working as a doorman at clubs, having taken this on after he was kicked out of the gym. But it could've come from him selling steroids or drugs or any one of a dozen other things. I'm sure the source of the money was dubious, but I was so smitten with him it was easy enough to legitimise it and make allowances for its presence.

There was a honeymoon period of a few months when things were going really well. Then the relationship started to change. Andy began to show a quite controlling, jealous and aggressive side which I hadn't seen before. In my mind I was going out with someone powerful, but really I was going out with someone who was narcissistic. Andy started telling me how to behave, what to wear and who I could see. If I was some innocent girl it might've rolled, but for me – fiercely independent little Vashti who'd travelled the world with a staunchly feminist mother – it was not on. No man was going to tell me what to say or think or do!

He did start to mess with my head though and strangely, for a while, I said that if he wasn't happy I'd change for him. I was still living with Mum and Dad and would only see him occasionally, but he'd sit outside my house sometimes and wait for me to leave to see what I was wearing and if I was dressed appropriately. It went against my entire being but I was very taken by him and I wanted it to work, but it wasn't long before I was saying, 'Hang on a minute, there's no way I'm doing this.'

Andy wasn't the first man I'd slept with; I'd had physical relationships with men ever since I was fourteen. But he was the first man I really fell in love with and there was something special about that, an intimacy that I hadn't previously experienced.

So here I was at seventeen, having a torrid affair with a part drug dealer, part doorman, part body builder, while spending my days going to a very preppy middle class art school. It was bonkers!

I loved art school and I wanted to go on and study fine arts. I applied for a place at Leeds University and I was accepted, which was fantastic. I moved to Leeds at the start of the summer and for a few months I'd drive back to Bristol every weekend to be with Andy. It was a bit over three hours each way and he worked weekends doing security at various nightclubs, so I really didn't get to see him. He made no effort to make me feel welcome or acknowledge that the time and energy I'd spent driving back and forth to see him was of any value, so the relationship started to fizz out.

During one of my trips home I discovered that Andy had begun seeing another woman. He had met Samantha Mason, a very well-known TV newsreader with BBC Bristol, at another gym. She and I actually look quite similar, so he must've had a thing for brunettes. Samantha was striking, and she was sassy and sharp.

Bristol is a small place so I knew what was going on and, although I was upset, deep down the relationship was struggling so it wasn't a huge shock and I was strangely okay with it. When Andy told me that they'd been spending time together, somewhat bizarrely I was relieved. Our relationship came to a natural end and we remained friends; I actually became quite friendly with Samantha too. I felt a sense of accomplishment that Andy had forged a relationship with someone who was clever, ambitious, charming and who would not take any of his shit.

Andy and Samantha married, and when their daughter Ellie was born they asked me to be her godmother. Now that's a tangled web! Eventually Andy and Samantha split up, but they too stayed good friends, bonded by their daughter.

Over time, Andy had started to move out of some of his more questionable businesses and he'd become a bit more legit with his ventures, running pawn shops and eventually jewellery shops. He was very successful.

In 2014, my mum emailed me a newspaper clipping. The headline boldly declared Andy had died. It was a big story in Wales. He'd been shot dead by a former girlfriend, a 26-year-old Slovakian bikini model who was jealous that Andy had a new lover. Mum later sent me a pile of newspaper clippings about it. One of the headlines read: 'Gold Dealer Millionaire Shot Dead Outside Spanish Home, By Russian Model Girlfriend'.

According to Spanish police, she shot him three times, twice in the head and once in the shoulder, when she arrived at his house in Marbella and found the new girlfriend there. To be honest, I wasn't surprised or shocked that he'd died this way. When you play in that world, anything can happen, but I was sad and my heart hurt a little that the incredible force Andy was, was now gone forever.

Mayka Kukucova was sentenced to fifteen years in jail for Andy's murder. What a waste of two lives. The newspapers described him as Bristol's 'King of Bling'; he'd made a lot of money and was very well known. He was driving around town in a chunked-up Hummer, with two bodyguards alongside him everywhere he went. His house on the outskirts of Bristol was a mansion with a seven foot brick fence around the perimeter, reinforced steel shutters on the windows and doors, security cameras on every corner, and a team of Rottweiler guard dogs. That's some pretty serious security happening right there. Perhaps excessive for the local jewellery store owner, but who am I to question?

There was a soft side to Andy, though. He was an entrepreneur, and when I saw him some years after we broke up he'd matured a lot. I think that was the influence of his daughter Ellie. I haven't seen Samantha or Ellie for a long time, but I am sorry for them that Andy has gone, and grateful for my time with him.

I believe that people come into our lives for reasons, seasons or lifetimes, and the sooner we are able to begin to understand their purpose, then the sooner we are able to learn and connect to the opportunities available from those relationships. As I absorbed the brutality of what happened to Andy, I felt grateful for what he had taught me about men and relationships. Andy taught me that the potential I had so passionately seen in him, my greatest strength, was also my greatest vulnerability. My willingness to see good in everyone blinded me to the potential for bad. So I will always be grateful for the legacy of the sparkly-eyed, larger-than-life, naughty human being that was Andy Bush.

Part Two

FINDING THE
MISSING PIECE

5

Welcome to Leeds

I don't have long-standing regrets;
they pass as I see how things are meant to be.
— Dita Von Teese

I couldn't wait to move out of home and go to university, but admittedly, I didn't exactly fall ass-over-teakettle in love with my new home. Leeds was grey, rainy and rather gloomy, looking basically nothing like the upmarket city it is today.

The act of leaving home was a huge deal for me because I felt very sophisticated and in control of my life. It was the first point in my life where I really felt like I was growing up. However, the reality of being away from home was something altogether different.

I lived in a shared house with two grungy Doc Marten-wearing women, who were, at best, a little bit unusual. One was completely obsessed with her 'stuff' to the point of marking lines on her milk bottle or cereal packets to ensure that nobody was eating her food. The day I moved in, she warned me that if I touched her things, she'd kill me. The other was a sturdy Irish girl who confessed to me that she'd recently tried to commit suicide.

So here I was in this freezing cold, crappy house in a part of Leeds that was far away from where most of the other students lived, in rows and rows of two-up two-down brick buildings, with two human beings who were at the other end on the spectrum from the way I chose to be in the world. I really didn't know what I was doing there, which made me question why I had chosen to go to Leeds at all.

I read once that the thing that screws us up the most in life is the picture in our heads of how life's supposed to be. I'd imagined university would be different, more sophisticated somehow, but it wasn't. Also, when I first arrived in Leeds to study, I was lovesick and homesick. I was still seeing Andy Bush, which meant driving home to Bristol almost every weekend, so I didn't really give myself a chance to get to know my new home or make new friends.

When Andy and I broke up, I began staying in Leeds on weekends. Finally, I started to settle in. By second semester everything began to change. I celebrated my 21st birthday with new friends, and I'd found a gym I could train at. I settled in to a more familiar routine and Leeds began to feel like home.

Similar to the gym I went to in Bristol, the gym I was going to in Leeds wasn't a health club kind of facility, featuring girls in neon leotards and group exercise sessions; this was hardcore training. The Body Balance Gym, owned by famous 'British Storm' wrestler and body builder Ian Harrison, a former

Mr Universe, was a sweaty muscle factory on the outskirts of the city. Harrison's gym was serious business for blokes craving carved-up bodies and world's-strongest-man-issue bodies. But the common denominator among us all was a deep desire for a sense of strength and power. It doesn't take a shrink to work out that most of the people there, including myself, were layering on muscles like suits of armour to protect ourselves from the pain that was buried deep inside, and to keep us safe from anything external that might have us feel anything similar ever again.

On my first day, I drove out there all excited and was greeted by a huge guy, ridiculously out of proportion, sitting behind a tiny reception desk. He had rippling arms that reminded me of the film prosthetics for The Hulk, only his were caramel in colour, not green. He was wider than he was tall, a quintessential English body builder. He was bald and rugged looking, with a heavily lined face and swollen veins popping out around his neck. He had cauliflower ears, probably from too many rugby run-ins, and he looked rough and mean. I soon learned though that he had a heart of gold and a really gentle soul, which had been my experience with most of the men I'd come across in the bodybuilding community.

And then there was me. I had turned up, all very excited and bubbly and chirpy with my little southern English voice proclaiming, 'Hello, I'd like to train with you!'

It was likely no different to how I presented myself as a five-year-old on the streets of India, bowling up to any kid with a ball and asking if I could play.

The environment at Body Balance was stark and, on the face of it, I clearly didn't fit in with the brutish physicality around me.

But like at the gym in Bristol, this subculture welcomed me without question. It's said that you should never judge a book by its cover, and as long as your attitude, humour and determination were abundant, you were guaranteed a lifelong membership of camaraderie and loyalty with these guys.

I struck up friendships straightaway and came to really love being around my training mates. We all had the same goal: to push ourselves and have as much fun as possible in the process. I felt a sense of safety being among them, maybe because they could see some confidence and immature fearlessness in me that needed protection. They opened the door to a whole new world for me, and while I may have taken two steps backward in the evolutionary stages of self-awareness and responsibility for one's own actions, the sense of importance I had adopted had me wanting to take on the north of England!

These guys were lovable rogues, and I know there were some dark backgrounds and some pretty difficult pasts among them, but they were also charming and fun. And they felt like family in a way. I felt like I was part of something, and that I belonged somewhere.

Many of my new gym friends worked as security guards at nightclubs all around north England, an added bonus. And along with the respect and protection that I had acquired through association, so too came entry and special treatment to just about any place my friends and I wanted to go. While I do appreciate this sounds remarkably blasé, being 20 years old in a new city and taking on what felt like a whole new world felt pretty damn cool, I'll admit.

In Bristol, while I was studying at art school, I had qualified to be an aerobics instructor and personal trainer, which I loved doing. Being physically fit and having a tonne of energy, I taught classes whenever I could, which allowed me to make some money in my spare time. I went around to different gyms in Leeds and gave out my details, and it wasn't long before I picked up several classes here and there.

Again, my life became a very strange mix of different worlds. During the day I was at school learning about the origins of ancient Japanese masterpieces and the composition of contemporary lithographs. My degree itself was split into three areas – print, illustration and design – and while in hindsight I would choose differently, doing the course not only allowed me to indulge my creative side but also brought two very important people into my life, Ellie Hansen and Mark Stott, who would, over many years, have a huge impact on me.

After lectures, I would dash off to take an aerobics class on campus, jumping around to 'It's Raining Men'. At night, I trained at Body Balance, and so it went. It was a mad life of culturally clashing worlds and I didn't do anything by half. I was totally immersed in both the mental and the physical aspects of my life, and I loved it. Hurling my body around dancing or lifting weights with a determined force allowed me to connect with what I perceived to be something greater than myself, something that didn't revolve around me using my mind, and allowed me to just exist in a place for a small amount of time. It was peaceful and exhilarating. When I was dancing or doing weights, my mind was completely still and focused on what I was doing. I wasn't thinking about my past or my future or where I fitted in life, or anything else other than what I could do right there in that moment. It showed me what being present is all about, and it's probably the first experience I had of understanding what that really means.

Teaching aerobics on campus was great fun, with many of my buddies in the same degree program and even some tutors joining in to jump around and shake their booties. Despite my love of sports and fitness, I still always chose to study and connect with friends who were creative, musical or artistic. I had no interest in physical fitness being my vocation; it was always more a space and place that allowed me to connect with another part of myself.

One evening I started chatting with a guy at the gym who I'd seen around but never really connected with. His name was Martin and I could tell he was shy, but I'd say hello to him and eventually he started to chat with me. He was muscle bound but a sweet, gentle soul, unassuming, and we became incredibly good friends. Along with training together, we shared stories about our lives and our very different childhoods. The more I got to know Martin and the more he shed the layers of his shyness, the more he exposed his very cheeky sense of humour and revealed himself as a huge amount of fun to be around.

I was close to many of the guys at the gym, but I had never actually crossed the line and spent any time socially with them. Our differences seemed less marked if they were kept in the predictable setting, so it was never really my intention to let my two worlds collide. But then Martin invited me to join him and a bunch of his friends out on a Saturday night at the infamous Hacienda, one of the most controversial night clubs in Manchester and indeed in all the north of England.

I had spent most of my teens hating pubs, with their pervasive stale beer smell, and grungy clubs for the hours I'd have to spend waiting for a friend to also want to go home. I'd often stay far longer than I wanted for fear of looking like a boring git for wanting to go home to bed. Even back then my preference was to wake early and fresh and be ready for the day. But all of a sudden, this whole theatrical underworld of clubs and house music and dancing into the wee hours of the morning in incredible and often rather tiny outfits seemed far more exciting and alluring than ever before.

It was the early 1990s. DJs were like rock stars and the clubs were like Baz Luhrmann *Moulin Rouge* film sets. The rampant drug culture offered a guarantee that even the shyest of people could dance into the night and have the time of their lives. Until Monday morning rolled in, that is.

During this time, my friends and I were going to different clubs around Leeds pretty much every weekend. The club scene was intoxicating. People would turn up wearing the most outlandish, sexy things and nothing was off-limits or too provocative or inappropriate. We were a generation of people trying desperately to express ourselves without any fear of judgment, persecution or inhibition. The freedom I felt was liberating, exhilarating and all-consuming.

London too was buzzing with super clubs like Ministry of Sound and Bagley's but Manchester, or Madchester as it was called, had its own underground club and music scene and the Hacienda was at the heart of it all. The Hacienda was legendary.

It was a big old brick warehouse that had been converted into a fashionable club. Madonna had played her first-ever UK gig there, so it was a real powerhouse.

Despite a huge queue of people lining up to get in, we were waved straight through because Martin knew the doorman. It was massive inside, like an old colosseum, and jam-packed with people jumping, grinding and sweating, a sea of hands in the air. It seemed like everyone in the place was using some type of class A drug, from disco biscuits and E to harder hits of speed and base. Being in the Hacienda was like a crash course in the world of recreational drugs. As with anything that meant having my senses dulled and my wit stifled, I approached it all initially with extreme caution.

Bristol at this time was notorious for its ongoing issues with and never-ending war against drugs. Heroin was a huge issue in the city. Marijuana was everywhere, but I had absolutely no interest whatsoever in smoking it, especially as I'd borne witness to the neuroses that later followed. I knew the risks, so I'd stayed away from it all; it just wasn't my thing.

But the Hacienda felt like the most exhilarating place in the entire world. I found myself surrounded by people saying to me, 'Okay, Vashti, you're going to take a little of this, then this will happen and you'll feel like this.'

It was not unlike your parents teaching you how to ride a bike. Step by step, people walked me through the experience of taking ecstasy, and it didn't feel dark or shady or grubby, and I wasn't the least bit frightened because I was part of what I thought was a caring and nurturing crowd. So when the opportunity to jump down the rabbit hole into a world of happy came to me in the shape of a little white pill, I dived right in. And soon, warm from the influence of my chemical-induced lie, I felt firmly, and foolishly, like I belonged. I danced all night long, at the front of the stage, without even a pause for a pee.

Soon enough, all of my university friends were going to the same places and we were all living for the weekends. We'd study and work hard during the week, and then party hard and fast on the weekend. Because I knew a whole lot of people and had multiple connections, I was often able to get us in past the velvet ropes. I felt like the princess of the party. My new club 'lifestyle' widened my circle of friends even further into the fringes, and I started spending more time with my new club mates and my buddies from the gym. These people were fully immersed in clubbing and really didn't have many boundaries.

By now, I'd moved out of the house from hell, and moved in with a whole new bunch of friends. We rented the top floor of a fantastic old art deco house in Headingley, a really cool suburb of Leeds, and set up an amazing bachelorette pad.

Wendy was an English rose with a passion for Abba songs and pints of beer. Justine was more serious; she had a boyfriend who basically lived off us. He was there constantly skulking around, mooching food out of our fridge. Ellie was gorgeous and clever. I was the wild energetic one.

Our place soon developed a reputation and we became known as the Spice Girls of Leeds. We had a massive, stunning art deco bathroom, almost like a steam room, with emerald tiles from the floor to the ceiling and a huge bath that we'd all get into together on Sunday afternoons. We'd fill it up with bubbles and the four of us would soak ourselves while we chatted and gossiped about our weekend. I adored that time of my life and I loved that house. I had a huge bedroom, beautifully decorated, and not the least bit like a university dorm room. The girls called me the snail because I moved in with everything I owned, a habit from my childhood travelling the globe with every precious possession I owned in my backpack.

On weekends, people would come around and hang out at our house. I'd get home from a club on Sunday morning, stay up all day and go to sleep on the Sunday night. Then I'd get up on Monday morning, go to class and teach aerobics at lunchtime. I was absolutely burning the candle at both ends.

Because I'm naturally a morning bunny, staying up late was really difficult for me, so I started using different drugs to get me through the night and keep me wide awake. I still loved the whole underworld scene of nightclubbing and didn't want to miss out by going to bed early like an old codger. After several months on repeat, however, I realised that what was happening to me and around me was a mild form of addiction, because we did this same thing every weekend. I started to see how messy people were and, although I loved the scene, I felt a bit horrified by it, so I called it quits on the drug use.

There was a vile, nasty side of this lifestyle emerging that I hadn't noticed in all our glamorous fun party days. Most weekends after clubbing, we'd hang at an after-hours place to sober up and come down. There was a grotty old club in a rough area in nearby Bradford that we went to a few times, hazy with oceans of dry ice. We danced through the night and into the morning.

One time, I was on the dance floor at about 5 a.m. and, through the haze of horrid smoke, I saw a young guy with this much older, very messy woman, horribly groping and pashing one another. I recognised the woman as the matriarch of a very rough, scary local crime family and the boy she was smothering was her teenage son's best friend. These boys were very well known in the drug and club scene; they were quite young, and this woman was much older and everyone knew who she was. It was like a scene from Stanley Kubrick's film *Eyes Wide Shut*. At that moment, the reality of the world I was mixing in hit me like a bucket of icy water being poured over my head.

I can quite clearly remember walking out of the club that morning in the freezing cold, the cobblestone laneway blanketed with thick fog. It looked Dickensian and I half-expected a horse and cart to come trotting by. Every weekend, I'd leave these clubs, stumble out onto the cobbles and walk past people going to work. This time, I suddenly realised that time had stood still. I'd pressed pause on my life. I had become so immersed in a world that was not mine, and I was fortunate enough to walk away from it. I was done with it, all of it.

Luckily for me, when I made the decision to stop taking drugs, I was clinical about it. Many others weren't so lucky and a lot of people I knew battled with serious addiction. But I'd made the decision to stop living that life and that was it. I wouldn't go to places like the Hacienda now, but back then, a new chapter was being written in that nineties underground scene. It was an era of abundance and absolute hedonism. And I didn't just live it, I was in the thick of it with some of most amazing characters, and all of us with our stories.

*

By the time we came to doing our degree show, similar to an art exhibition of your work that makes up the final part of your degree, I was questioning what was next. I'd grown out of Leeds and Leeds had grown out of me. I was looking for the next adventure and there seemed to be only one obvious choice – London.

Ellie was considering taking a Master in Design Leadership degree in London and suggested I look at it too. When I began studying art, I knew I was never going to be the one painting the canvas; I wanted to be the one behind the counter promoting and selling. I wanted to work with artists and photographers, so in my head I always thought I'd become an agent of some description and have an incredible storefront filled with magnificent things. So when Ellie suggested we study a master's degree together, I jumped at it.

We were both accepted so, just like a snail does, I packed up all of my worldly possessions yet again and headed off to my next place and space, leaving the dark underbelly of life in Leeds far behind me. My torrid affair with that city and its pulsing clubs and endless nights was over. I was ready to embrace my new bigger, much more sophisticated lover.

Hello, London

6

The Hangover

*We are what we pretend to be, so we must be
careful about what we pretend to be.*
— Kurt Vonnegut, Introduction to *Mother Night*, 1961

L ondon had always felt like home to me, more so than any other place I'd been to or lived in. So when I moved there to study for my Masters in Design Leadership, I felt a strong and instant sense of ease and familiarity.

My grandmother, whom I adored, lived in Hertfordshire on the outskirts of London and my sister Lowri and I had spent a lot of treasured time with her when we were children. I was always excited when the train pulled in to Paddington Station because it meant we were on our way to Grandma's house. She owned a lovely red brick, 1940s post-war house with a pretty little English cottage garden at the front. I still remember John the milkman rattling along the street, and Lowri and I running out to greet him and hopping up on the milk float for rides.

My maternal grandparents were quite wealthy, having been successful in a manufacturing business, and they were very house proud. My grandfather had decorated the house meticulously with beautiful Viennese furniture, opulent rugs and bronze objets d'art. It was very homely and comforting and vastly different to how I lived with my parents. Our home was always put together on a shoestring, and while it was homely and creative, it felt very different to the heavy hand embroideries and gold leaf-framed art works that had been eventually sent across from my grandfather's former home in Austria, prior to the war.

My grandmother, having been my grandfather's housekeeper in Austria, still had that way about her of taking care of things; it was intrinsically in her nature, resulting in a carefully created home that felt inviting and very nurturing.

For years, I'd intuitively known that I would end up in London, so when Ellie and my other best friend Lou decided to move back there, and knowing that my life-long friend Ella Doran was also in London, I felt compelled to join them and relocate to this place that already felt like home. Ellie, Lou and Ella. Three of the true loves of my life, who are still my very best friends and who always, always remind me of who I really am.

I met Lou when I was eighteen at the Art Foundation in Bristol. I was dating Andy Bush at the time and life was pretty crazy. Lou floated into my life, this gentle, feminine presence who only ever brings laughter and a great sense of love and belonging. Lou taught me to accept myself and showed me that it was okay to let my feminine side share equal space with my very powerful, masculine energy.

Ella and I met at the Steiner school, also in Bristol. She is a couple of years older than I am and a wise soul who, like a rudder in choppy water, has always been able to steer me in the right direction. She is a deeply creative being and so intensely passionate about her work that she would often murmur about her artistic projects while sleeping! I often turned to Ella for inspiration for my next move or a check on where I was at in life. Or, more to the point, how far off the beaten track I'd chosen to travel this time.

All three of these beautiful, extraordinary women loved me unconditionally despite some of my crazy life choices. They were always available when I needed a truthful but supportive conversation or some sage advice, and I knew that in each of them I had found a forever friend and we would watch over each other for a lifetime.

Ellie and I moved down from Leeds together and into an average little apartment in North Finchley that belonged to a friend of Ellie's parents. Frustratingly for the three of us, Lou was living in Clapham in the south. We had other university friends nearby, so we already had a little community forming and often I'd bump into someone I knew, which I absolutely loved. I equally adored the anonymity of London, where you could easily lose yourself among a million plus complete strangers.

London felt so alive with creativity and cultural diversity, and with its historic streetscapes framing a somehow familiar backdrop, it often felt as though I was living on a movie set; everything appeared to be ripped from a scene in *Love Actually* or *EastEnders*.

I settled into my familiar routine of study during the day followed by training at the gym at night. At school, I was learning everything from the history of design to how to be successful in the management of a creatively led business. I enjoyed aspects of what I was studying but I found the material far less engaging than my previous degree, this being the start of study that was driven by self-directed learning. The course was sadly lacking in opportunities for interaction with other people, which motivated me to ensure that I continued to work in and on creative business with people who inspired me. It was the perfect opportunity to study and interview my best friend, Ella Doran, and a number of her industry contacts, to discover how they juggled being designers and successful business managers. Before long, I realised that I was beginning to intuitively coach my case studies into being more self-reflective in their approach to business.

I don't know that I fully recognised what was happening at that time as being coaching, but I had discovered a natural, authentic way of working with people. I found myself looking for the potential in their situation, which was always led by a shift in their own approach to doing business and living life.

Toward the end of my master's degree, I was allotted a period of time to write my dissertation. I wanted to focus on my friend Ella's business. She and her then boyfriend Adrian had created Addject Design, a company specialising in fabricating bespoke furniture and interior design pieces. I intended to get right into the detail of the behaviour required to perform multiple roles in one business, especially because their roles were quite different. I wanted to see how they managed to make it work operationally. Their business has grown enormously since then and it's still hugely successful today. They manufacture all sorts of amazing things, including designer giftware, but when they first started out, they functioned not only as marketing and sales directors but also as key designers.

Ella and Adrian invited me to travel to the US with them to assist with trade shows in New York and San Francisco. Of course, I was ecstatic and jumped at the chance. I explained how I could also use the opportunity to study how the two of them created international relationships to enhance their brand and product, but of course what I really wanted to do was hop on a plane and jet off to New York and San Francisco. So that was it! The deal was done and they bought my ticket to the USA.

The San Francisco furniture fair was enormous fun. We worked the fair during the day and then at night we met up with potential buyers and clients for drinks or dinner at the coolest restaurants in town. After we'd packed up the fair, I stayed on for a week and camped on the sofa at the home of some friends of an old school buddy who had a great house on Pine Street just down from Pacific Palisades. Pine Street was quintessential San Francisco, lined with restaurants and a mix of Victorian and contemporary architecture. Walking up and up, it seemed to go on forever, but finally reaching the top, you'd be rewarded with a gorgeous, sweeping vista towards the marina and the bay.

I'd put my joggers on and walk for hours exploring the city, and one of the first routes I did was up Pine Street and then down through The Presidio, the old army base which had these huge pine trees, and then out at the Golden Gate Bridge. It was stunning and I was very quickly falling in love with this beautiful place and its overwhelming atmosphere of diversity. It was clear right from day one that San Franciscans welcomed everyone; this was a city where you could be whoever you wanted to be and that spirit of individuality was absolutely embraced. It was my kind of town.

When my two weeks in San Francisco were up, I knew in my heart I wasn't ready to go back to London. I wanted to stay and explore more of the city, discover all of its nooks and crannies, and soak up more of the energy of the eclectic, creative characters I'd met at the fair. So I deferred my master's program and stayed in San Fran so that we – my new favourite city and I – could get better acquainted.

Everything about this place was super cool. I especially loved The Castro district and its thriving gay community. Every Friday night around 8.30 p.m., hundreds of people calling themselves The Midnight Skaters gathered at the ferry building at The Embarcadero, which is just a few minutes' walk around the Bay from the Golden Gate Bridge, to rollerblade through the city. It was pitch black so people skated with lights on their helmets; it was a massive party on wheels!

The blade runners, as they were called, would weave through the neighbourhood streets and tunnels, along main roads and freeways. It was basically illegal, but there was a sort of unspoken agreement with City Hall that, as long as everyone behaved themselves and were respectful on their route, law enforcement would turn a blind eye, sometimes even closing off the streets to traffic to allow the skaters through. We used to link arms, forming a gigantic chain, and roll through the streets for hours, some nights skating up to 20 kilometres.

The atmosphere was electric and there was a great sense of solidarity; it didn't cost a penny, was great exercise and everyone had a ball. I, of course, loved it! Where else can you do that in a major city? The Midnight Skaters still meet today and it's a must-do if you have the opportunity to visit beautiful San Francisco.

I also joined Gold's Gym and met some fun people who introduced me to the city's crazy club scene, where I was introduced to the drink of choice in 1990s San Fran: tequila. Having not been much of a drinker in my youth, it took me several months of wild nights and dusty hangovers to realise that tequila was not my best friend.

I had started my master's degree to follow in the footsteps of some incredibly inspiring friends who'd become designers, photographers and filmmakers, and to take responsibility for removing myself mentally, physically and emotionally from what had been a rather hedonistic period in Leeds. But like a new lover, San Francisco quickly lured me into her decadent arms and away from my academic focus. She offered a more exciting 'education', and a week of couch surfing turned into a year of wild tales and wonderful adventures.

But it all came to a grinding halt one Sunday morning in December 1997. Back then, long before I had studied emotional intelligence and neuroscience, I simply believed that if I felt something passionately, I should just intuitively act on it. So I did, repeatedly, until one morning, after a night of shenanigans I couldn't recall, I woke up in an unfamiliar place, with a guy whose name I didn't know. It was a massive wake-up call.

I had been at a good friend's party in an incredible old house, a former fire station in the Mission district, complete with the original fire pole and alarm bells. I don't remember a thing about that night except what can only best be described as my own personal version of *The Hangover*.

According to the friends who helped me put the pieces in place the following day, I had made excellent use of that old fire pole. Not only were they were completely impressed by my agility sliding down the pole, which I apparently did multiple times, but were equally entertained by my ability to climb up it.

When I opened my eyes the morning after, attempting to shake the tequila-soaked fog from my head, I found myself lying on a plush beach towel alongside a complete stranger.

My new, and luckily very kind, acquaintance hilariously recounted the previous evening's mischief, which had included me dropping his computer on my toe. And not a paper thin MacBook Air, mind you, but a huge 1990s monitor that could have easily crushed my entire foot. According to him, I had mistaken a part of the monitor for the bathroom door handle and in my haste to get into the bathroom, I yanked and dragged the whole thing off his desk.

Easy mistake, I suppose, if you're smashed off your face. And, fortunately for me, the evening had resulted in little more than an aching toe and a bruised ego.

If that wasn't enough to illustrate that my newfound relationship with booze was unhealthy at best for a girl with a personality overloaded with outrageous, my companion took my hand sympathetically and filled in the details as to why we'd woken up on a large beach towel on the floor. Laughing hysterically, he explained that after I'd crashed his computer, I'd stumbled back to his bed, climbed on top of him and, to my apparent relief, peed like an old nanny goat all over the bed.

Of course I'm not proud of my antics at and after the fire house party. Am I embarrassed? Not really. And to be honest, in retrospect, I love that there are stories to share. But that morning, as the rather charming stranger filled in the pieces of a blurry jigsaw puzzle, I realised that an old pattern was playing out, and as much as I tried to mask it as being my fun, wild and relentless desire to grab life by the balls, even literally, I knew that I had to face up to my darker side. That night was my line in the sand.

My outlandish behaviour and gregarious way of being might have been wonderfully wild entertainment for the other party-goers, but in the harsh light of dawn and with the amnesia from too much tequila wearing off, I was overcome by the unavoidable feeling that, although I had somebody beside me, I was very much alone.

I devoured all San Fran had to offer: the winding streets, the abundance of Californian countryside, the wild nights and the eclectic individualism of that beautiful city and her people. Like the song says, she had stolen my heart, and my head at times too, but living there also made me realise that England, as cosmopolitan as it was, would never be the place that I could again call home.

San Fran marked a release of self-destructive behaviours for me. I had been partying too much, pushing too hard and not being kind to myself. I was determined to make sure that San Francisco was the last chapter in that torrid story, but it was an awakening in many other ways too. I experienced the sense of freedom that came from knowing that there were other places in the world where I felt at home. I realised that I didn't need to live in the country I had grown up in to feel like I belonged somewhere. And with that knowledge came the acceptance that I could venture back to the UK without feeling like I would be stuck there forever. I had found a new home in the US, and a sense of fitting in, buoyed by the diversity and the hard work ethic of the Americans who believe that anything and everything is possible.

When my visa expired and the time came for me to return to England, I felt a sense of peace knowing that there was another place for me and I could come back.

While I was away in America, my parents had moved from Bristol to the south of France. Lowri was now in her final year of university and things were tough for her at home. I felt a strong sense of needing to be near her. I'd been a pretty shitty sister to her, I felt, and it was time for me to step up and care for her. To do that, I needed to go home and regroup.

So I returned to Bristol. I got a job in a local restaurant, pretended to write my dissertation, and worked for my friends who had a beautiful barge that ran up and down the Avon River and under the suspension bridge. For a few months I worked on the boat during the day and spent time with Lowri, until I felt it was time to get my life back into focus and return to London. A stint in Bristol made London seem exciting again.

Now, at 25 years of age, the last decade of my life felt like a series of impulsive, knee jerk reactions. I had spent much of my life overstepping boundaries that I knew existed but hadn't identified due to my extraordinary but conflicted childhood. I felt I had formed some unhealthy attachments, reacting and responding to life according to my impulses and who I connected with in any given moment. As an intuitive and spontaneous soul, this had led me to some wonderful places and people, but it had also taken me into some dark spaces, where love, support, integrity and kindness were less than plentiful.

Right then and there, for some unknown reason, I finally reached a point where I needed to acknowledge that the way I was 'doing' life was no longer working for me. And while I had no real idea of what it was that I needed to change, I knew absolutely that the only place to start was with me, within myself. From then on, I focused on discovering who I could be if I actually recognised and nurtured my authentic, true self. I was both the problem and the solution.

7

Two Worlds Collide

Love is like a friendship caught on fire.
— Bruce Lee

With our first degree behind us, a master's ticked off for Ella and Lou, and with enough wild stories under my belt to – any obvious irony aside – fill a book, we all ended up back in London. Lou was based in South London, Ellie and her boyfriend Mark had gone travelling for a year around the world, and Ella was only a short bike ride away.

I moved into a shared place in nearby Hackney with two other girls, Jo and Nikki. This wasn't just any place: it was three storeys of chic, newly renovated perfection. It was owned by a talented young designer who'd landed his dream job with Calvin Klein in New York and had to move quickly. We just happened to be in the right place at the right time to snap it up.

We had absolutely lucked in! There were loads of things to see and do in Hackney and we had so many great friends, including Lou and Ella, living nearby that we regularly hosted dinners and parties and we'd all hang out on the weekends.

The only thing lacking in our new house was my bedroom – or rather, the amount of livable space in my room. I was the last of the girls to move in, so essentially I ended up with a bedroom the size of a shoe cupboard, barely big enough for my shoes, in fact. My bedroom was so tiny that I ended up commissioning a friend to build me a platform bed so I could maximise my space. The little snail in me emerged once again and I proudly decorated my new cubby with all of my worldly possessions. I had my own furniture, including framed prints, and I attacked that little shoe cupboard like an interior decorator at Kensington Palace, determined to make it the most beautiful and welcoming space possible. I'm sure it was a hangover from my gypsy-like childhood, but I needed my home to look and feel like it had some permanency to it.

On the weekends, I pottered around Shoreditch with Lou or visited Ella, who had become a hugely successful designer and was building a brilliant reputation among the international design community. It was energising being back in the buzz of a city pulsing with creativity and oozing with attitude, with my closest friends all around me. I felt calmer and more grounded than ever before.

London was an electric place at that time. The new millennium was on the horizon, and there was a promise of unimaginable opportunity and change in the air, which I was about to experience in the most serendipitous way when, one particularly chilly

February night in 1998, I was walking to the gym and bumped into a guy I'd met years before.

In my first year of university back in 1992, a group of us went backpacking through Indonesia on our semester break. It was my first summer vacation and Lou, who was studying up at Winchester University, asked me if I wanted to join this big adventure with an eclectic bunch of friends who were all familiar with one another from different times and places. I'd just broken up with Andy Bush, so it seemed like a great antidote to really shake off that unhappy ending.

When we all met at Heathrow, among this hilarious bunch of characters were Lou's university pal Sarah and her boyfriend. They were both lovely. She was a great girl and he struck me as being a sweet, gentle guy. I remember him being tall and super thin and he looked very young. His name was Andy.

In contrast, I was very muscly at that time, a little like an Indonesian water buffalo, because I'd been working out at Ian Harrison's gym in Leeds. Other men looked scrawny in comparison to the blokes who trained there.

When we arrived in Indonesia, we all hung out together for a few days then split off and went our separate ways before joining back up at the end of our adventure for one last hoorah before heading home. In total, I probably crossed paths with Andy and Sarah just two or three times over six weeks.

Most people tend to gain a little weight when they go on holiday. But Andy had caught some sort of dysentery bug or Bali belly on the trip, so by the time we arrived back in Jogjakarta, he was so thin and under the weather that he didn't look at all like the strapping young British backpacker who'd just spent six weeks eating and drinking his way around Indonesia. So at that time, I can honestly say there wasn't the slightest spark with the lovely but too thin Andy Whitfield. There was no instantaneous 'wow, isn't he gorgeous' acknowledgement, no fireworks, and definitely no vomitous 'doves bursting from the sky' moment. In fact, I don't believe we had any real connection at all. But six years later, hustling through frosty Liverpool Station, time definitely caught up with us.

I vividly remember that night in 1998 because it was blisteringly cold. I had my red Northern Exposure jacket zipped up around my neck and I looked toward the glowing street light to offer some hope of warmth and shift my mindset from the dark eerie laneway beside the station to a place where I felt more at ease. A year or two earlier, the thrill of being somewhere unpredictable would have felt spine-tingling and exciting, but on this gloomy winter's night in London, self-preservation was the only thing on my mind.

As I navigated my way through a small crowd of men and women in dark corporate clothes, all rushing around me to catch their train home, someone stood out in the crowd and caught my eye. He was striding toward me in a brown leather jacket, blue jeans and New Balance sneakers, a backpack hanging off his left shoulder: this extraordinarily beautiful, confident and oh-so-familiar man. It wasn't so much that Andy Whitfield was so wildly attractive that he stopped me in my tracks, but more that he stood out because he was a burst of individuality in a sea of boring same-ness.

I'm not sure whether my jaw made a clunking sound when it hit the floor, as my mouth was obviously hanging wide open. But whatever it was, my brain was sending signals all over my nervous system to tell me that something was going on and, whatever it was, it required my immediate and undivided attention.

Coincidentally, not even one week earlier, Lou had mentioned that we should get in touch with her friends Sarah and Andy because apparently they were living nearby. So when Andy zoomed out of the crowd and into my consciousness, I reacted.

When we got closer, I clumsily called out, 'And . . . Andrew . . . ANDY?'

'Yeah?' He stopped.

'It's Vashti, Lou's friend. We met years ago travelling through Indonesia!'

'Vashti, WOW you've changed!'

I chuckled, remembering the brief time I had spent with him and Sarah all those years ago. I was muscle-bound from training and he was ravaged by illness. He was skinny and pale and what I would have described as being a boy on the cusp of becoming a man. Hilariously, I would have described myself at that time as being a woman on the cusp of becoming a man!

As we stood chatting in the laneway, it became apparent that there had been several bizarre near misses for the two of us in terms of reconnecting. The first was that we had both been working out at the same gym for months but hadn't noticed each other. The second was that Andy lived just a few doors away from my friend Ella's design studio, which he walked past about five times a day and that I visited almost every other day.

We also realised that we had not only both grown up in Wales, but had also studied in the north of England at the same time. And currently we lived a scant 20 minutes' walk from each other, which is pretty bloody close in London.

Our conversation was effortless and entertaining and we exchanged goodbyes knowing that sooner or later we'd bump into each other again. We made a loose commitment to Andy and Sarah meeting up with Lou and me, and then I went on my way, not giving Andy much thought in the immediate days following our laneway chat.

The gym I belonged to, or club in London-speak, was a pretty posh place that I really couldn't afford, but it was important to me that I started my 'next phase' in a place that was far away from the 'spit on the floor' type of bodybuilding haunts I'd been frequenting for years before. Having my very own place to decompress, away from everything and everyone, was a priority to keep me clear and focused.

Lou, being the least sporty person you could imagine, would sometimes join me at the gym, and while I bounced around sweating my little heart out at an upstairs aerobics class, she took advantage of the super luxurious changing rooms down-stairs. One weekend, shortly after my chance meeting with Andy, Lou left a message for Andy and Sarah to meet us at the gym for a catch-up. As we poked our heads around the door to the café at the club, we were met by a warm and friendly hello from a solo Andy.

Later that Sunday afternoon, the three of us wandered around Covent Garden and watched a movie at Leicester Square. Andy explained that he and Sarah were spending some time apart; their seven-year relationship had begun to drift. It became apparent, well to Lou anyway, that Andy and I had an awful lot in common. This was largely due to my love of all things adventurous and our shared Welsh history, which was also the brunt of endless jokes.

We adopted fantastic Welsh accents for the afternoon and, along with our too-loud chortling and raucous conversation, were most likely pretty annoying to observers. But we didn't care; it was fast and funny and the dynamic between us was witty and sharp.

Despite our amazing afternoon together, my penchant for making bad choices with men had me completely closed to the possibility that there might be chemistry between us. In a brief moment when Andy had gone to order some drinks at the bar, Lou swooped in, looked me straight in the eyes and said, 'What is going on? You guys get on SO well!'

'Not at all!' I spluttered, completely surprised by her take on what was passing between me and Andy. 'He is SO not my type, he's far too wet for me,' which, in hindsight, only came from my complete lack of experience with men who didn't come complete with a truck load of baggage.

Despite the number of poor decisions I had made previously when it came to men, getting involved with somebody who was still potentially in love with someone else was absolutely not my thing. It felt safe and appropriate that we were hanging out solely as friends with no pretence of anything else developing.

Andy and I started to go to the gym together, often winding up in trouble with other members as we dissolved into snotty, giggling messes trying to outdo one another telling stupid, inappropriate jokes. I was, by far, the worst offender of the two of us.

Over the next few weeks, we took turns introducing each other to our favourite little restaurants after our scheduled gym meets. Andy shared stories about his years studying at Sheffield University which, bizarrely, was only an hour away from where I studied in Leeds. We both thought it odd that we had met six years earlier travelling through Indonesia but, for one reason or another, had never connected. Andy did let slip that he remembered being struck by my green eyes as we sat across the table from one another one night at a restaurant in Pangeran Beach.

We also reminisced about our Welsh childhoods and, despite our vastly different upbringings, we shared similar memories of getting lost in flower-filled forests, making bows and arrows out of ferns, nibbling on blackberries and blueberries picked from the endless hedgerows, and wandering through fields and alongside rivers. We'd each had a childhood in Wales that gave us the freedom and space to disappear into our thoughts. The more time I spent with Andy, the more I realised that I had never been aligned with someone who not only made me feel fully happy, but also made me feel wonderfully at ease. The fact that our relationship had started out as platonic, as he transitioned from a long-term relationship, allowed me the time and space to experience intimacy and friendship that was not influenced by my usual tendency to seek out a sexual transaction.

And there was something new happening for me, too: the development of trust. I remember one time when Andy and I had arranged to meet in the spa near the pool at our gym. As I sat waiting, enjoying the bubbles, a face appeared around the corner of the change rooms. In a manner not dissimilar to someone doing their best Spiderman impression, Andy crawled along the wall, one hand after the other, guiding himself along. For about fifty metres, he crept toward me and then proceeded to slip to the floor, his towel dragging in the water. I nearly peed myself in the spa watching this hilarity unfold, but when he finally made it to the spa and I was able to ask him what in the hell he was playing at, he told me he had accidentally lost both of his contact lenses in the pool, leaving him basically completely blind!

When I stopped laughing, we exited the spa and changed, and I helped guide Andy across London to his optician's to pick up a spare pair of his very Harry Potteresque glasses. As I led him down the crowded London streets that busy weekend afternoon, him gripping my arm tightly, he repeatedly reminded me, half-giggling and half-choking from fear, that he was literally blind and that my wandering off would likely result in him being squashed flat by a London bus.

In that moment, I experienced a profound shift in the way I felt about Andy and knew that we would never return to our simple way of being together as friends. I suddenly felt entirely safe, trusting Andy's vulnerability instead of running from it or judging it.

My childhood role of peacekeeper and pocket-sized conflict resolution expert had seasoned me into becoming a woman who would scare or shoo away absolutely anyone who demonstrated any fragility whatsoever. I'd grown an impenetrable armour around me and I had no appetite for anyone who didn't appear superficially strong, which often painted me as being way too independent and aggressively overpowering.

But for Andy, who'd inherited a fear of standing out, his safe and methodical approach of ensuring that he could almost always predict inevitable outcomes meant that those fiercely independent traits of mine that usually scared other men away were an Aladdin's cave of possibility. He had finally found someone with a sense of strength and bravado that challenged him in a cheeky and playful way, and encouraged him to look beyond the obvious and to question his choices. This allowed him to open his mind to what he was actually capable of and what was possible on the 'outside of safe'.

The vast grey skies, relentless rain and small town mentality of Wales played to Andy's naturally introverted side and encouraged him to go along with life without really questioning what lay beyond the direct influences around him. He didn't make choices outside of his comfort zone, or that were anything less than safely predictable in their outcomes. Years later, Andy would reflect on his childhood, describing his life to me as being comparable to black and white TV: you could still watch all the shows and the storyline was there, but the evocative and awe-inspiring lens that colour provided was absent. 'You do that for me,' he had said, looking straight into my eyes. 'You turn my world into colour.'

As we became inseparable, I felt myself falling in love with this complex man who was as cheeky and curious as he was vulnerable, grounded and calm. And despite his rather obvious passion for spending every free moment with me, I couldn't quite get my head around the idea that he might actually want to *be* with me. Somehow, the old doubts I had worked hard to expel throughout my life were still sitting in the back of my mind, taunting me that I wasn't pretty enough or clever enough, and that if he scraped the surface of this gregarious, powerful, outspoken girl, just below the surface he'd find a rather mediocre human being.

It was now April 1998 and although we had only reconnected two months earlier, the depth and breadth of what we had shared, and the time we had spent together in our insanely close friendship, had brought me to a point where I was completely and utterly confused as to what to do next. I used to call my mum, sobbing about how I was afraid to share my feelings with Andy for fear of losing his friendship, while knowing that what was going on between us was pretty special. It couldn't all be in my head, could it? Being with Andy was like being with a male best friend, an experience that I had never had before and one that I didn't want to risk sabotaging at any cost.

In the meantime, Andy had moved out of his flat and had been alternating between sleeping at a friend's flat and on the sofa at our place. He'd been offered a job in Spain and hadn't made up his mind about whether to accept it or not, so he was in limbo and not wanting to sign a new lease if he was going to head away. The possibility that he was going to move to Spain for work was very real; it seemed, on the surface, like a great idea for a fresh start following the end of his seven-year relationship with Sarah. It was obviously a great opportunity for Andy to further his career as a façade engineer especially because, work-wise, he was stuck in something of a rut in England, getting up at hideous hours of the morning, and arriving at a less-than-satisfactory job after being stuck in his car on the M25. To be able to soak up the Spanish hospitality with its abundance of sunshine and senoritas as he found his single feet again offered Andy the chance to kick-start an exciting new chapter of his life.

I enthusiastically encouraged him to jump on this exciting opportunity, dutifully pointing out the many benefits of living in Spain, including the fun he would have, his newfound freedom and the chance to explore so many other exciting countries nearby. Deep down in my heart I desperately didn't want him to leave, but I did my best to mask my feelings and strategically hide how I really felt. I heard myself selling Spain to him, trying to convince myself that it would be foolish for him not to go. But I was aching inside to share with him how I really felt, what I really wanted and how amazing I thought life could be if we set out to explore it together.

Andy, I knew, was conflicted too. Had this new opportunity presented itself a few months earlier, it might have been the welcome change he was after. But all of sudden London, our friendship and all that was being uncovered for him in terms of how he was beginning to view everything in his life, made the possibility of leaving seem far from anything other than intensely misaligned with what was unfolding right in front of him.

And, despite it not having a clear trajectory, it was the first time in Andy's life that the unknown felt unusually exciting. I, on the other hand, feared losing everything we had. So, here we were, both very much together yet seemingly miles apart, with the inevitable looming and some big decisions to make. As dramatic as it sounds, it felt like the end of the world to me, a clear departure from my usual philosophical standpoint of trusting that all would work out the way it was supposed to.

While Andy pondered a new life in Spain, I was booked to work in New York for a week to represent a designer at the New York furniture fair. I invited the now homeless Andy to stay in my room while I was away. He got on well with my two flatmates and he'd definitely outstayed his welcome at his friend's place. We had already discussed him moving in for the short term because one of the girls was vacating our gorgeous house to move in with her boyfriend.

The night before I was due to fly out, Andy asked if he could drop his stuff over and sleep on our sofa. He also offered to drive me to Heathrow airport in the morning. As fate would have it, we had other guests staying the night at our flat and Andy found himself without a place to sleep. I indicated to Andy that if it wasn't too frightening an offer, he could sleep with me in my bed. By appearances, I reasoned, it was no different to a girlfriend sleeping over.

That fateful night, in all of its glorious intensity, hilarity and sheer ridiculousness is permanently etched in my heart and mind. The first fifteen minutes of us trying to settle beside each other without being too snug for 'friends' became the most hysterical comedy of errors one could possibly imagine. My platform bed, remember, was only half a foot away from the ceiling and barely the width of a small double. I did my darndest to avoid any awkward leg touching, and to find an innocent place to put my hands.

Wriggling to give each of us space on the tiny mattress, I felt myself slipping off the side of the bed. Andy, being right there, leaned out to grab me. I nearly pulled us both off the bed but we somehow, miraculously, avoided crashing to the floor as I lurched up and over like an acrobat, landing on top of him and leaving us both laughing so hard that we cracked our heads on the ceiling!

We eventually surrendered to the confines of my miniature sleeping quarters and strategically snuggled in beside each other, Andy nestling into my back and me doing my best to appear relaxed in light of this not unwelcome turn of events. My heart was beating so fast that I thought I might have a panic attack. I angled my by now fully alive body parts away from him, feeling enormous relief that I wasn't the one with a willy which would have given me away in a heartbeat, because at that particular moment, a platonic friendship was the *last* thing on my mind!

I suddenly found myself curled within the embrace of a man I was utterly crazy about, his soft nose so close to my ear that I could hear him breathe and his hand tenderly, if not intriguingly, resting on the top of my hip and cupping the front of my pelvis. The intensity of flight or fight accompanying my new sleeping arrangement made me almost want to pass out. My mind raced with possibilities and options and confusion. Should I do my best to go to sleep and not make the positioning of his hand mean anything more than the safest place he could rest his hand without running into tricky territory? Or should I totally 'go for it' and act on my passionate, intuitive impulses, taking the risk that he might recoil and push me away, or off the bed again, indicating that I had fully and completely misread the entire situation?

I contemplated the benefits of proudly abstaining from my usual destructive behaviour and in demonstrating huge respect for the uniqueness of our platonic relationship. Previously, my experiences of intimacy with the opposite sex had only ever dissolved into rather empty and meaningless exchanges, so I was intensely mindful that if this monumental thing were to happen it wasn't going to be me who initiated it.

My head was spinning and I could barely breathe. In the end, choosing heart over head, I went with Plan B and released myself into the incredibly delicious moment that it was. I turned my body to Andy's, snuggled into him and wrapped myself around him, pressing my lips against his, allowing the incredible love and insane passion I felt for this beautiful human to melt right out.

And that is how Andy and I began as a couple, as a partnership – two imperfect beings each finding their missing piece.

Just for the record, while I realise I have painted myself as some sort of life sucking Dementor from a *Harry Potter* movie, and that you might be thinking that Andy had quite possibly been strategically trapped in my ridiculous platform bed, as the night unfolded, Andy shared his own fears of being rejected by me, of jeopardising our friendship and of potentially losing the first person in his life who had allowed him to see that life wasn't just a straight line. He also told me that he was worried that he wasn't exciting or interesting enough to be considered as a boyfriend or partner for me.

We talked well into the early hours of the morning, both unclear about what would unfold next and how, but wrapped in Andy's arms it didn't matter. I drifted off to sleep in the delicious comfort of knowing that for the first time in my life I had found where I belonged.

Part Three

THE BOOK OF ANDY
AND VASHTI

8

A New Beginning

All this time I've loved you and never known your face ...
Wanna stay right here until the end of time ...
I've found the one I've waited for.
— Lamb, 'Górecki'

August 1998

After just a few months of officially going out, Andy and I moved in together. Well, technically he didn't really move in; Andy stayed the night and never moved out!

We were living in East London. Andy was doing façade engineering and I was working for two different design companies that belonged to my friends. Andy wasn't really enjoying his job; he was still getting up in the dark at all sorts of crazy hours – most mornings it was around 4.30 a.m. – and still spending way too much time stuck in traffic on the M25. But otherwise we were crazily happy and settled into a lovely life together.

Even though we were still finding our way in this relatively new relationship, there was such a sense of complete comfort with one another, it felt like we'd been together for a long time. I knew that having Andy in my life somehow made me connect with myself better; when I was with him I could be the person I really wanted to be. Andy made me feel like I was inspiring, and that was very flattering. He made me want to honour my true self and use my fearless, impulsive side to make choices that led to positive adventures and opportunities, rather than self-destruction.

Andy had a far more sensible approach to everything. He would say he was dull and sedate, but he was anything but that. He was calming, which gave me the head space and quiet in my mind that I needed to stop and reflect not only on what I was doing but also on who I was being. For a long time I'd been caught in the thought that I was unlovable and closed myself down to the possibility of letting love in. Andy not only opened up my heart but taught me that I was a worthy partner.

Life in London was vibrant and fun, but best of all – and for the first time in my life – I was sharing everything with someone. When Andy woke up at his ungodly hour, I'd get up too and make him breakfast. And when he headed off to work, I'd go for an early morning jog along the canals.

Back then, London's canals were not the most picturesque or safe place for a young woman to be jogging on her own before dawn, but I liked the grunginess of the area and the interesting paths and I felt like I was shaking the cobwebs off before heading to work. The canals today are totally different; not only have they become a tourist destination, but also they are alive with the buzz of cyclists, runners and countless London hipsters on their way to one of the many cool cafés that line the waterfront.

I was working for two design companies, both owned by friends, doing PR and getting their work out into the market place. I also did a lot of styling and arranged photo shoots. The design scene in London was really emerging then; it was very cool and I immersed myself in it. We'd regularly head off to Milan or New York for furniture fairs, which was very glamorous. And I loved being with such creative, clever people. There was always a lot of networking involved because we were trying to get our products distributed, so we'd do drinks and dinner at the super chic restaurants in these very cool cities. It was great fun.

I have always loved design. I fell in love with the colours, textures and shapes of fabrics when a child travelling through India, so it's probably no surprise that's what I ended up doing. Being confined in a campervan for four years definitely had an influence on my vocation and eye for aesthetics! I hate being stuck in clutter, and a lack of organisation and space drives me bonkers.

On the weekends Andy and I would hang out with friends, and most Sundays we'd go to the beautiful parklands of Hampstead Heath for a picnic or a wander through the grounds. It was a wonderful time to be in London. East London had become a very edgy design sector, a real hub for the arts and media scene. Places like the now famous Electricity Showrooms had opened up, along with the White Cube gallery which I loved, although sadly it's no longer there.

Hoxton Square was on our cycle route and had grown from grunge to cooler than cool. We were quite close to the Shoreditch markets, so Saturday mornings we'd go and get our fresh veggies and flowers for the apartment, and potter around together. It was London life at its absolute best for two besotted lovers who could make just walking down a brick lane an amazing shared experience.

My work took me to some really cool places. I travelled to New York quite a few times, taking ranges across to show to buyers at department stores like Barneys. During the day we'd have back-to-back presentations with buyers and it was bonkers busy, but at night I'd get to catch up with some of my besties who were living there and they'd take me around the newest grooviest bars and restaurants. I loved New York, I still do, and I feel very much at home there amid the chaos.

In August 1998 I went across to a trade fair and after work one evening I caught up with one of my dearest university friends. Mark was originally from the north of England and had this beaming voice and deep Mancunian accent, which I loved. He'd been going out with my best friend Ellie and when we all finished our master's degrees, the two of them took off together travelling. They'd been right around the world and had just returned via Australia. Their relationship didn't last the journey, but we'd always stayed friends.

That evening, in his most delicious accent, Mark said, 'Vash, maaate, you should go to Sydney. It was made for you, you'd bloody love it. Everyone is outdoorsy. You can be running on the beach in the morning, then go to the office, then back to beach in the afternoon instead of running in the dark and the shadows with the rapists. You have to go!'

I had to admit the canals were pretty awful, but I always backed myself that I was fast enough and fit enough to get away from anyone – still, not ideal.

Although my childhood had stamped on my brain a need for sunshine, blue sky, wide spaces and the stimulus of unpredictable cultures and landscapes, Australia had never really been on my radar. The only thing I really knew about it was *Neighbours*, and the image in my mind was of red brick suburban homes or hot dusty desert places like Alice Springs. I thought of barbecues and the funny way Aussies pronounce words like cappuccino, you know 'capo cheenoooo'!

Mark rattled on about his love affair with Australia, about these amazing places he'd seen and the incredible weather he'd soaked in. I mentioned *Neighbours*, but he quickly set me straight.

'No!' he enthused. 'It's not all like that at all. It's ocean and surfing and people turning up for work after they've already been up for hours swimming and surfing. It's sunshine and sand. Vashti, it's so you.'

And so the seed was planted.

Mark and I had a liquid dinner of dirty martinis that evening, probably too many. His travels with Ellie sounded amazing, but when I put my head on the pillow later that night, a little worse for wear, I wasn't really thinking about Australia. All I could see was Andy's face in my mind and I couldn't wait to get home to him the next day.

When I woke up, New York was at her finest. It was early, the summer sun was up and I grabbed my joggers and went for a long walk before I had to pack and head out to JFK airport. That really gorgeous New York morning has remained etched in my mind. The sun was warming my back and the steam was rising out of the subway grates. I could just make out the shadow line of the water towers on the tops of buildings. It was a quint-essential New York day.

I wanted to get Andy a present and came across a little flea market setting up near SoHo. There was a bunch of stalls with a large book stand. I love books, I'm a huge collector and over the years Andy and I often gave one another books with little messages written in them. Today I have shelves full of books and if you pull one out most likely there'll be a note from one of us to the other; I absolutely treasure them.

The first thing I saw at the book stand, sitting on top of a pile in front of me, was a striking photo that caught my eye. It was of a guy diving into the bluest of blue water you could ever imagine. The shot looked like it had been taken from below the surface so you could see the ripple of the plunge and the white water melting away. The title of the book was simply *Australia*, and it was a collection of images taken over 24 hours in Australia. It was a huge book, so big it was a challenge to fit onto a book shelf, but it was absolutely breathtaking and I literally thought 'Oh my god' when I picked it up.

The book was published in the 1970s and had photographs of a whole lot of different places in Australia. The shots had the most vivid colour and every page was a feast for the senses – red deserts, white beaches and so much blue!

Here I was, bizarrely staring at what I felt was the most incredibly gorgeous country, gaining insights without actually being there. I grabbed the book and held it to my chest. A chill of excitement rushed through my spine. Somehow I knew this book was meant to find its way to me. This was the universe's way of saying this was where my focus with Andy should be. After my conversation with Mark the night before I felt like it was a real sign that Andy and I needed to go to Australia, so I bought the book for Andy and wrapped it up ever so carefully in my hand luggage.

I couldn't relax at all during the flight home. I was so excited and had so many thoughts running wildly through my mind that I felt like I was in a constant state of fight or flight. Butter-flies were doing tumble turns in my tummy at the thought of seeing Andy, but I had a mixture of emotions because I was terrified Andy might not embrace the idea of going to Australia like I had, and this might impact on our relationship.

I'd never felt more excited about what lay ahead. Or more agitated. On the one hand was the impulsive side of me. On the other, the nagging self-doubt side was thinking, 'Run away as fast as you can.' This side was saying that I should leave Andy because then he couldn't leave me if he said no. My self-defence mechanism was up, and he wouldn't be able to break my heart. My head was emotional soup.

My plane landed at Heathrow at the same time as a massive jumbo from Karachi, and it was quite a hilarious scene. I was in the middle of a sea of Indian families and I could just see the top of Andy's head bobbing along like a cork on the wave of people. He scooped me up out of the middle of the human froth and gave me a lingering kiss. My aching heart and crazy head were a little overwhelmed by the surreal experience of being met by this person who actually seemed to love me. As he held me, I almost wanted to cry with the relief that this was all really happening. We were in this together. For the first time, I no longer felt that I was on this journey through life alone.

Andy had packed a gorgeous picnic and we went off to Hampstead Heath for lunch. As we lay in the weakening summer sun, I gave him the incredible book that I had bought, hoping it would inspire his curiosity. While he was flicking through the pages I very sheepishly said, 'What do you think about going to Australia together?'

He looked a bit puzzled and asked, 'What do you mean?'

I blurted out my bold plans for us to take off for a year or so together.

'What do you think about us just going and seeing what it's like? Why don't we go and see where it takes us?'

'I'm in!' he beamed. 'Absolutely! I'm in.'

He was genuinely excited, so we went home and immediately started planning our big brave exciting new adventure – and I breathed an enormous sigh of relief.

I've often thought about that day, it really sticks in my mind. Andy had come from a very conservative Welsh background, and the thought of giving up a 'good solid' job to head off into the unknown, with no job, no home, no family or friends to connect with, was a huge leap for him, given the stream of values that had been passed down to him which were based on security, safety and reliability.

But I honestly think he was so ready to embrace me and a new life together that if I'd said, 'Let's run away to Serbia and join the Peace Corps' he probably would have!

When I look back now, what was most insane about that moment in time in that New York flea market, with the warmth of the morning sunshine kissing my cheek and the curated set of photographs of life on the other side of the world in the palm of my hand, was that I knew so deeply and profoundly that just as everything lined up in order for me to reconnect with Andy, right here in this very moment that same kind of crazy 'meant to be' magic shit was going down!

Because little did we know that on page 23 of that book was a full page bleed of an aerial view of two little streets in the Sydney suburb of Paddington, which we would not only call home one day in the distant future, but where we would also create a life and legacy of the extraordinary!

9

Finding Home

If you look on every exit being an entrance somewhere else.
— Tom Stoppard, *Rosencrantz & Guildenstern are Dead*

At the ripe old age of 27, Andy was too old to qualify for an automatic visa, so we sent off a very sucky letter to the Australian embassy, hoping to twist their arm to let him in.

It went something like, *Dear Sir, My name is Andrew Whitfield and I am writing to apply for a visa to travel to Australia. I would like to go to Australia because I have a deep love of architecture and I am wanting to explore unique Australian design. I am also a façade engineer and all I have ever wanted to do in my life was travel to Australia to see the engineering structure of the Sydney Opera House. I have not had the opportunity to travel previously due to study and I'd like to spend a year learning the crafts of Australian architects and exploring your magnificent country. I do hope you can assist me in making my dream come true. Yours sincerely, Andrew Whitfield.*

Of course we failed to mention anything about a huge desire to spend long lazy days in the sun, surfing and drinking margaritas! My prose worked perfectly and Andy was granted a visa, so we booked the tickets and three months later we were off to Oz.

Andy and I were at the beginning of our relationship and this trip was about us wanting to write our own chapter together, to do something that was uniquely about us and for us. But I don't think either of us ever thought we'd end up staying!

Our relationship was growing in London, but there were always influences in the background that tugged at us. Andy had his old friends and I had mine. His friends were great guys but they were still getting pissed at the pub every weekend and Andy was becoming far more excited by the idea of waking up fresh to all that was out there to explore together. My friends were all very creative design types, far more interested in dinner parties and Danish furniture. I could see that a line was starting to appear between our two past lives. It wasn't an either/or but more of a misalignment in what our respective friends did to enjoy themselves.

I thought we could either continue on doing the same thing and maybe the relationship would fizzle out, or challenge ourselves and do something amazing, and if I had an opportunity to push life to the brink I did. We had established a lovely routine but it was time to start forging a path just for us, to test the strength of what we had outside our comfort zones in London.

I know that being with me made Andy question what he was doing with his life, where he was going and why he was clinging on to things from his past that didn't make him happy. So when I came to him with the idea of travelling to Australia it was like giving a hungry kid an apple. We offered each other the chance to step way beyond our comfort zones and to try things that perhaps, alone, we didn't have the balls or the inclination to try.

We wanted to create our own history together and I think we both really knew in our hearts by then that we'd found the person we could stand beside and take gigantic leaps with. This was about trusting one another to do that, and it was about sharing the experience and the belief that together we could do anything.

We were writing 'The Book of Vashti and Andy' and we had to start with our own chapter. When you're with that person who gives you the confidence and the energy and the will to achieve anything you put your mind to, it really is magical. We were a powerhouse together. But best of all, we didn't really care how any of it turned out. As long as we were together, we were right where we were supposed to be.

There's a beautiful moment in the *Be Here Now* documentary. Andy, who was very close to death, was reflecting on his life. He said, 'I look at my life and I don't regret any choices I've made, but to be honest I don't think I'd look at my life this way if I hadn't been with Vashti for the last twelve years.'

When I hear him say that, it reminds me not only what a force we were together but also how easy it can be to remain stagnant and a little bit safe. We refused to stay in that safe place; we took life by the horns and were always ready to catch one another if something didn't go according to plan.

So on 30 November 1998, with our little backpacks over our shoulders and our worldly possessions in the luggage hold, we boarded Qantas Flight 1 bound for Sydney, Australia. The thing I remember most vividly about that flight was the captain's very deep, very Australian voice waking us from our sleep saying, 'We are now flying over Australia.'

Hooray! We were so excited. I got my bag out and raced to the bathroom, put my lip gloss on, brushed my teeth, although not quite in that order, and prepared myself to land. And five fucking long hours later we were still flying over Australia! Suddenly I understood how vast Australia really was and I realised that we were landing in a foreign place that we knew absolutely nothing about. We arrived on 1 December 1998, which will always be a very special day for me.

The first thing that struck me when we got off the plane was the humidity. We'd left behind a bleak winter in London and stepped into wide blue skies and sunshine like I'd never seen before – as well as stifling humidity. That day, the sheer space of Australia made the biggest impression on me, and it still does today. I love that you can see sky everywhere. It's not like London or New York where you look out and you see the tops of buildings or shadowy streets or there's someone in the way rushing past you. Wherever you are in Australia, even in the biggest cities, you see sky and space: open, wide, stunning, precious space.

That December would become unseasonably wet. One day, a few weeks after we arrived, a huge thunderstorm dumped hail stones the size of tennis balls, without the slightest exaggeration. Andy and I stayed huddled in our flat, peeking out through the curtains; we'd never seen anything like it.

My gorgeous friend, Ellie, who I'd lived with while I was at university in London, was at the airport with her new boyfriend to meet us; we were staying with them until we got settled. They were so excited to see us and took us straight to a gorgeous little café for breakfast; I remember the smell of the coffee like it was yesterday. Yes, Australia, you are responsible for my beloved morning coffee addiction. A drink I loathed until 1998, by the way.

Andy, with his very distinct soft northern accent, asked the waiter for a croissant. When you pronounce it with the proper French accent, it sounds like 'qwasson'. This very handsome barista replied, in the most brilliant Australian voice I'd ever heard, 'I think you mean cross-ont, mate.'

We all giggled. He genuinely believed that he was educating us!

Ellie and her boyfriend had a cool little apartment in Newtown which was, back then, an alternative, kind of grungy, rough-and-ready suburb with a great pub culture. It wasn't really my thing and seemed far too similar to what we had left behind in London, with no sign of sun, surf or the incredible beaches we had read about. Ellie and her man were still in celebration mode and were having a great time boozing and partying hard. It was the first time ever in Ellie's and my friendship where I felt distant from her. It had been a good few years since we had seen each other and finding Andy had brought a calm to me that was not aligned with Ellie's expectations of where my expected boundary-less attitude would lead us. I'd left those wild ways behind a long time ago, and the Newtown scene wasn't Andy's thing at all, so it all felt very out of sync. Honestly, there were moments when I thought, 'What the fuck have we done?'

I felt bad because I'd taken Andy all the way to the other side of the world to arrive back in the same place we'd left behind. But one rainy afternoon a couple of weeks after we arrived, we took a bus over to Tamarama and Bondi Beach. When we stepped off the bus, all we could see was this enormous beach stretching out forever. Being in such a big urban city with a beach was unusual, but this was spectacular. We walked down onto the foreshore at the south end of Bondi, scrunched our toes in the sand and let the ocean lap over our feet. And there, against the blue sky and blinding sunshine, we realised life would never ever be the same again. Together, we had found our way home.

We got ourselves a tiny studio apartment just up the road from Bondi Beach, opposite the famous chocolate shop and Laurie's vegetarian restaurant. It was a skanky, crappy, tiny place with a never-ending stream of cockroaches, but it was ours. We had a scant $300 to our name, so we did the logical thing and went to Ikea on a bus and bought garden furniture and some fairy lights to make it feel like home.

We didn't really know how long we were going to stay in Australia; we just thought we'd get ourselves set up and see how things went. So sitting on plastic garden furniture felt like a perfectly good idea at the time.

Andy had brought his push bike over from London and I bought a mountain bike when we arrived, so we cycled around quite a bit, exploring the city and getting familiar with our surroundings. After about a week of sun, surf and friendly faces everywhere, we knew that Sydney was going to be our first and last stop on our 'discover Australia' tour, so Andy put together a plan. His steadfast childhood training in how to secure a job meant that he didn't mess around: as soon as we had the keys to the apartment, he was out job hunting. He'd get on his bike in the morning and cycle around, looking at major building projects and huge structures, stopping to chat with workers and make contacts. He found the two major engineering companies in town and managed to get a meeting with the guy who headed up part of the global engineering group Ove Arup, the company that looked after the Sydney Opera House.

He went for a meeting with Kevin, a handsome, silver-haired man who really liked Andy. Kevin had been leading a new division of the company that constructed façades and they needed employees who could abseil. Abseiling to check the façades of buildings for cracks or structural issues was quite cutting edge back then and Andy loved the idea. He was very outdoorsy, and he was a really great abseiler and climber, so he was perfect for the job. Kevin offered Andy a job and provided us both with business visas for two years. So within a few short weeks of touching down in Australia, Andy had landed his dream job and secured visas for us. We were a great team: I pushed Andy to the starting line of whatever crazy idea we had, then he'd take the baton and run with it. That's how we lived our lives.

For a little while, until I got myself established, Andy was supporting us both. I'd never been taken care of! This was the first time a man had said, 'I'll look after you until you work out what you want to do.' It was a lovely feeling, although short-lived. Andy had also inherited a very fear-based relationship around money, and soon told me that I should probably get off my surfboard and look for work to tide us over. He also taught me that I was now very much part of a partnership and that meant stretching myself in equal proportion to him. So where a credit card might have come in handy in the past to prolong some time in the surf, I learned a lesson about having the best of both worlds: sun, sand and a regular income.

I found the opportunity to do what I did best pretty quickly by doing some personal training and teaching some aerobics, and I began working in Orson & Blake's fabulous new Queen Street interior and homewares store, which I loved. The stores were owned by the incredibly talented David Heimann and his gorgeous life partner Bridget. They were both very connected to Sydney's fashion scene and had multiple stylists coming into the store to hire items, so it was an amazing opportunity to make some inspiring new creative friends and to mix with many a stylist, which made me feel closer to the creative side of myself, the one that I'd left behind in London.

I continued on with this work for about eight months until Andy and I had a conversation where he laid it on the line for me. 'Now it's your turn to find what you want to do here and what you want to do with your life,' he said.

He reasoned that I could easily float around in a leotard for the next few years, or work my way up to building my own business as a stylist, both of which would be fine if that's what I really wanted to do in my heart. But that's not what we had come to Sydney for. We both knew that this was our time to look beyond the obvious and take a giant step outside of our comfort zones.

A dear friend, whom I loved and who also worked at Orson & Blake, Amy Levack, was visiting our apartment one morning. 'Vashti,' she said to me, 'if you could do anything in the world, what would you do with your life?'

I told her that, as crazy as it sounded, I wanted to be paid to inspire people to live up to their greatest dreams. I wanted to earn an incredible living being nothing other than my larger-than-life self, teaching people how to unlock their potential. It really was – and still is – what inspires me most!

Coincidentally, later that morning, I opened the *Sydney Morning Herald* newspaper and came across an ad that read: 'Do you want to become an executive coach? If you've always wanted to inspire others to pursue their life ambitions, train to become a coach.' Bang! There went the universe once again, bringing together those inexplicable moments where everything aligns. Amy and I burst out laughing because we couldn't believe the synchronicity about what we'd just been talking about and what was in the newspaper.

I signed up and trained with Result Coaching Systems to become an Executive and Performance Coach. It all flowed so easily to me after the work I'd done for my master's, the structure and accountability I'd learned from being a personal trainer, and my innate curiosity in human potential; this really was a natural next step.

By the end of my initial training course, I had a full diary of clients and it was fantastic. But soon after, through additional advanced programs I took, I realised that I loved working with groups even more. My visual mind was also very good at taking teaching points and processing them into cohesive and clear models. Six months after I began coaching, I also began designing, writing and facilitating coach-training modules and programs with the same company that trained me, and facilitating training in New Zealand, Singapore and all over Australia, teaching leaders to become coaches.

I had the pleasure of working closely with David and Lisa Rock, the directors of the company, to fine-tune the various coaching programs. And while our relationship was feisty and challenging, we pushed one another to create something really meaningful that made a difference to others.

My clients were an eclectic mix of people – from barristers who wanted to career transition into producing films to authors trying to follow through on completion of their next book, from talented young actors wanting to break through to the American entertainment market to senior executives looking for support and co-creation in whatever their next chapter in life might look like.

Often my clients wanted to achieve more in their lives, but actually do less. Some were desirous of transitioning to something more meaningful, others wanted to stop and look at their lives to see if what they were doing was what they actually wanted to do. For many people who have been on the treadmill of life unhappily, it's quite difficult to suddenly come to a full stop and head in a different direction. I helped them clarify their vision and define their goals, and collaborated with them as they navigated their plan and their weekly actions. But most importantly of all, I supported them to craft a new way of operating and thinking, and to form new habits in the way they approached life and support structures that would encourage and support sustainable long-term change.

I loved my work and I loved my life. I'd put the steps in place, as Andy and I had agreed we'd do, and I was doing what made me happy, while making a difference to others. I was absolutely in my element.

We'd only been in Australia a few weeks when we got to enjoy our first Aussie Christmas. We were totally skint, really didn't have much money at all, so it was a very low-fuss day but it remains one of the best Christmases I've ever had.

It was hot, of course, which for a couple of Pommies was absolutely bizarre. To be truthful, it actually didn't feel like Christmas at all because the sights and sounds and smells were so foreign to us. Sun and barbecues on Christmas Day – what the . . . ? The thing that kept reminding us it actually was Christmas was the relatives ringing from the UK to wish us a Merry Christmas.

We didn't decorate a Christmas tree or anything like that, but in the morning we exchanged gifts, which were books we'd gotten one another. Then I made a yummy goat cheese and chicken salad and we walked down to Mackenzie's Bay, near Tamarama, for lunch. We climbed the rocks and spread ourselves out on a blanket, lying in the sun. We spent the whole day in the sunshine, reading and having the most fabulous time, giggling to ourselves at the pasty white Irish backpackers who sporadically wandered past, wearing just underpants and those strappy Velcro thongs, with Santa hats on their heads and a dose of painful looking sunburn.

It was so strange to be at the beach in my bikini on Christmas Day; it was unheard of back at home. Andy and I had never experienced anything like it. It was a bit like *The Truman Show* where somebody was telling us it was Christmas so we were just going along with it. Of course it felt so strange and different from what our families were doing in Wales, but we were in heaven! Honestly, it was like winning the lottery. Who'd ever have thought you could get up and go for a swim at the beach before Christmas lunch? The only downside to our magical day was coming home to our shitty, tiny, cockroach-infested apartment.

I was walking down the stairs one day in late May 1999, about six months after we'd arrived in Australia, and saw that one of the apartments behind us was open. It was being renovated, so I lingered for a bit to get a good look inside. It was a spacious, beautiful place with enormous windows facing towards the harbour and the views were stunning. It was a one-bedroom but it was so much bigger than the hideous place we were living in. I conned one of the tradies into letting me take a sneak peek inside and as soon as I walked in, I fell in love with it. I called the real estate agent and asked if it was coming up for rent and she said it was.

When Andy came home that night, I was bursting with excitement. He went and had a look at the apartment and loved it as much as I did. 'I'll ring the real estate agent and see what we can do,' he said.

But then I didn't hear anything more about it.

It was my birthday early in June and when I woke up on the morning of my birthday, Andy had placed a present on the end of our bed. Inside a beautifully wrapped little parcel was the key to the apartment. So, for my birthday, we moved downstairs into this gorgeous apartment. It was the best birthday present I could've imagined.

We still hadn't bought any proper furniture, only the Ikea garden furniture, so the following weekend we went out fossicking around vintage furniture stores. By then we'd both realised we were going to stay in Australia for a while. In one shop we found two beautiful wooden benches and a huge antique school desk, which was so expensive, and realistically we probably couldn't afford it, but it was perfect. So we went to the bank and got a little loan – our first-ever loan together – and we got our furniture. I still have that desk, it was so big that we used it as a kitchen table and it's still our kitchen table at home today.

Andy and I were ridiculously happy and although it can sound clichéd, we really were the perfect little team. He was doing some amazing work, scaling down these huge buildings like the best-looking Spiderman you've ever seen. He climbed the Sydney Opera House a dozen times. Can you imagine what the view was like from the top of those brilliant white waves? Only a handful of people in the world have ever witnessed it.

I knew that Andy was an incredibly good-looking guy, and hilariously, some days he'd come home and drop a handful of business cards on the bench from secretaries who'd spotted him sailing down past their windows. I don't blame them! I would've done the same thing, but I reckon there were more than a few ladies who didn't get much work done the day Andy was scaling their office.

Among many memorable experiences we shared in those first years was celebrating the Olympics in Sydney in September 2000. The eyes of the world were on our new home and the whole city buzzed for two weeks with a palpable party atmosphere. Everywhere you went, people were happy and there was a sense of elation and pride. The streets were filled with tourists from eclectic nations and it felt like a melting pot of fun.

I have one very distinct memory from those Olympic Games: discovering I was pregnant. Andy and I were both a little stunned at first, but equally quite amazed that we could make a baby. Once we got over the initial shock, the reality of having a child weighed heavily on us. In our hearts we knew that it was too early in our relationship and not the right time for us to become parents. We had just started to get ourselves established and neither of us was ready to be parents to another human being.

We talked about it a lot, and we both felt that the timing wasn't at all right. There was so much to create and experience together before we became parents. This was a conscious choice for the both of us, not just me or Andy individually. One didn't persuade the other; we discussed it together and we made a decision together. We were totally on the same page.

The day of the procedure, Andy arrived home with a beautiful bunch of tulips for me, and he snuggled me up and made sure I was okay. But we were completely aligned and comfortable with what we'd chosen. We thought as one.

Later on, when we were actively and intentionally trying to start a family, we struggled, and I thought a lot about that.

But I now wholeheartedly know that children find their way to you if they are meant to be.

A year later, almost to the day, we were climbing the stairs to our apartment, carrying the shopping after a Saturday morning trip to the market. We started having a conversation about weddings because one of my best friends was getting married and having this very cool contemporary London wedding.

'I hate weddings!' Andy said. 'They're so boring. You end up sitting next to someone you don't like, eating bad food.'

And I was like, 'You haven't been to the weddings I've been to, because they're nothing like that!'

So we were having this mock argument when I asked, slightly more seriously, 'Don't you want to get married?' We'd actually never had the 'M' conversation before.

Andy replied, his voice etched in my heart, 'I'd love nothing more than to call you my wife, Vashti, but I don't want a stupid wedding that's all about other people.'

Being a seriously handsome guy, Andy often got asked if he had a girlfriend, which was flattering but it kind of irritated him. As he explained to me, saying you have a girlfriend doesn't really mean much because most women would think they still had a chance with him. Besides, the title 'girlfriend' didn't in any way convey the depth of our relationship and what he felt about me. We lived on the other side of the world together, we were making a life together, and we were so much more than simply a boyfriend and a girlfriend.

Half jokingly, but also half seriously if I'm being honest, I asked, 'So what about something crazy like a wedding in Las Vegas with just us and Elvis?'

And Andy said, 'Yes!'

So we ran upstairs, threw down our shopping on the kitchen bench and started planning. We were effectively engaged!

We were due to fly back to the UK for my friend's wedding, and we'd planned to go on and have a holiday in New York before coming back to Sydney. We were able to schedule the flights so that we could fly from New York to Las Vegas, then back home. We booked in at the Luxor, the hilarious Egyptian-themed casino that was pyramid-shaped. Thinking about it now, I'm sure Andy would've loved to have abseiled down that façade!

Then we booked a drive-through Elvis wedding where the driver was the witness. Our plan was to fly into New York on Saturday 8 September 2001, have a few days in New York to look around and shop for our wedding outfits, then fly to Las Vegas on Tuesday 11 September. By that afternoon, we pretty much had every detail of our itinerary planned. We did it in about an hour! We had the whole thing arranged, done and dusted.

Landing in Las Vegas, we'd head straight to the registry to get our wedding licence. We'd then go to the hotel and get ready. At 5 p.m. the limo would arrive to pick us up. The driver would take us to the Little White Chapel Tunnel of Love (true!) for the drive-through ceremony. Then we'd go out and celebrate, staying up all night before flying back to Australia the next morning as Mr and Mrs Andy Whitfield.

We didn't tell a single soul, and not because we didn't want our friends and family to be there, but we were in Australia, far away from everyone we loved and trying to get them all together was impossible. If we'd waited until we could do that, we would've been waiting another ten years. We also wanted this to be about us, just us, Andy and me. So we thought we'd marry and then get everyone together to celebrate at some point later on. It was early June and our secret September wedding was all planned.

10

September 11

There are a thousand ways to kneel and kiss the ground;
there are a thousand ways to go home again.
— Rumi

We flew into John F. Kennedy airport on Saturday 8 September 2001. We arrived early in the morning and it was already looking like a gorgeous New York day. The autumn weather was unseasonably warm in The Big Apple, although to be honest, most places feel warmer after you've been in London! Andy and I were so excited: it was his very first trip to New York, and, given its wow factor and the fact that we were being married in a few short days' time, resulted in sensory overload for both of us.

Our wedding was still a humungous secret; neither of us had breathed a word to anyone, even after weeks of planning and remaining tight-lipped, which was increasingly difficult to manage. I really wanted to shout to the entire world that I was marrying the love of my life. I was relieved that we were finally able to release some of the pent-up excitement about our big day and I had planned to fully enjoy the next few days of living absolutely in the moment, minus any of the pressures or expectations that normally accompany a wedding.

Although I knew our family and friends in the UK would be disappointed that we hadn't included them, it felt right for our ceremony to just be about the two of us, and I hoped that in time they would all understand that this was exactly how Andy and I wanted our day to unfold. It was entirely about the two of us being able to honour one another without any of the usual fuss or fanfare.

We spent the rest of our weekend soaking up as much of Manhattan as we could: we dined at amazing restaurants, sipped cocktails in the coolest bars and dived right into the atmosphere of that amazing city. Andy was obsessed with New York's architecture and loved the huge towers and amazing, iconic designs of the Flatiron Building and the Chrysler Building. People-watching was one of our favourite things to do, so we lingered over coffee and drinks with our eyes glued to the bustling streets and the colourful characters rushing past, like spectators at the world's largest human parade.

On Monday morning, over breakfast in SoHo, we agreed we should abide by one wedding tradition and keep our wedding outfits secret until our ceremony. According to some old wives' tale, it's considered bad luck for the groom to see his bride before the wedding, so we added our own modern twist and decided to spend the afternoon on our own, shopping for our outfits. We were flying out the next day and it was our last chance to do some shopping and take in a bit more of the city.

I remember having the most fantastic day. I spent my time moseying about SoHo, discovering eclectic and interesting little boutiques with quirky curated lines that were a bit off the beaten track. I had no preconceived idea of what I wanted to wear to my wedding, other than the complete confidence that I would not arrive looking like a huge fluffy white meringue! I wasn't sure, however, what one was supposed to wear to drive-through nuptials. I guessed there was no particular dress code for the bride when being married by a complete stranger wearing a white leather Elvis costume.

I loved fossicking around the little boutiques of SoHo and felt sure I'd find something special, tucked away on a rack in a gorgeous little store. I had faith that somewhere in New York, the right thing would appear. As I wandered, I came across a very contemporary boutique stocking pieces from young New York designers. I loved the look and feel of the little shop with its independent labels; clearly, the owner had a great eye for beautiful pieces made from unique, colourful fabrics.

Hanging near the back of the shop, I spied a pretty little poppy-red dress that had rubies hand-stitched down one side with a very delicate nude-coloured slip underneath. It was so finely put together that it looked and felt like a couture dress. It was shin-length, so not too casual or too formal, something between haute and a bit beachy all at the same time.

I tried it on and fell in love with it. The shop attendant, a hilarious gay New Yorker with no eyebrows and a deep drawl that absolutely belied his rather feminine appearance, squawked at me, 'Darling, it's fabulous, but it would look better with these!'

And he shoved a pair of chicken fillets, those awful fake plastic boob inserts, under my bra. They worked, of course, but big boobs were not something I was genetically blessed with, so I took the dress and left the implants.

After another perfect day of hanging out in New York, our last, we went out for drinks that night and chatted about the people and places we had seen in our separate travels earlier in the day. Andy was so vibrant and I felt that we were in complete alignment in our collective love of The City That Never Sleeps, the place that had always represented, for me, the concept of really feeling *alive*. We were both totally energised by crazy, busy Manhattan rushing around us, and the electricity of the city. By her very being, New York gifts you the unshakeable feeling that everything is possible.

The next morning, we woke early and went for a jog around lower Manhattan. We ran down Broadway Avenue to the bottom tip of the city at Battery Park, then looped back up past the Museum of Jewish Heritage and along the edge of the Hudson River on the esplanade before cutting back across the south bridge and through to the World Trade Center. We stopped at the Twin Towers to catch our breath and take a good look at those imposing structures. Andy was quite taken by their height and I'm sure he was weighing up the challenge of how a façade engineer would abseil down those enormous monuments.

I remember noticing how brightly the sun was reflecting off the shiny metallic-looking windows that stretched so high they seemed to pierce the sky.

People were rushing into their offices, coffees and donut bags in hand – typical New Yorkers with their arms so full they crushed their phones between an ear and a shoulder so they could talk and run to work at the same time. It seemed that if you stood still long enough during a New York morning rush, the sea of pedestrians would pick you up and carry you along with them to work.

We looked around for a few minutes and then I hurried Andy along, because we had to get back to our hotel to shower, change, check out and get to the airport. That afternoon we were flying to Las Vegas.

We were about six blocks away from the Twin Towers, heading uptown, when we noticed the sky turning a strange yellow colour and became aware of a sudden increase in the noise level around us. It was almost as if somebody had switched up the volume on New York City. Sirens, alarms and bells began going off around us; it was noise like we had never heard before.

'Something is going on in the city, Hon,' I puffed.

And as though we had been thinking exactly the same thought, we picked up our pace in tandem. We ran as fast as we could all the way back to our hotel, unaware of precisely what had happened but fully cognisant that something was terribly wrong in Manhattan. All the while, the noise was increasing dramatically and the smell of things burning was overwhelming. It was so unsettling.

Back at the hotel, we immediately turned on the TV to see if we could find out what was happening, thinking there'd been a massive fire or something similar. Flashing across the screen was the image of the first plane that had flown into the north tower of the World Trade Center. It literally stole my breath away. We had been standing inside the plaza, in that exact place in the World Trade Center, only twelve minutes before.

I felt my knees give way, my body buckling like when someone kicks you in the back of the knees and you can't stand up. I heard Andy's breathing change. We were utterly shocked. We both slumped onto the end of the bed, eyes glued to the television. At that point, only one tower had been hit, but a few minutes later we watched as the second plane flew into the south tower. I slid down onto the floor, feeling like I was going to vomit. My whole body was sweating.

We watched all of this unfolding on the screen in front of us, and just a few minutes' run away from where we were sitting. It was a confusing time. No one seemed sure of what was really happening. It felt like the city was under attack.

There was a palpable sense of panic around us. We heard people screaming in the streets, and others were rushing around the hotel, doors banging along the corridor. It was an awful feeling of our lives being completely out of our own control. For that brief period of time, we had a tiny taste of what it must feel like to live in a war-torn country where bombs randomly and unexpectedly go off around you and nowhere feels safe.

In those few moments, everything we knew as safe and normal had totally evaporated.

Our bodies had naturally slipped into fight or flight mode by then, because we didn't know what was going to happen next. By this time, the news broadcasts were saying that it was a likely terrorist attack and that the government had closed the airports in and around New York, and in other parts of the US as well.

We were due to check out, but there was no way we wanted to end up on the street with nowhere to stay, so we went downstairs to reception to see if we could have our room for another night or two until we figured out what was going on. We weren't the only ones. There was a line-up of terrified, anxious guests and others trying to find a safe place to bed down for the night.

'I really don't know that I can extend your reservation because other people are booked in, so at the moment, I can't,' the clerk told us.

Everyone around us was freaking out. We walked up to Union Square and went into a grocery store and it was insane; people were queuing for miles, buying everything they could, from bottles of water and cans of food to toothpaste and flashlights. They were stripping the shelves like the country was going to war. People were outright panicking and I can remember standing in that line thinking, 'I have no idea what I should buy!'

We bought giant bottles of water, then went to a bar and ordered huge gin and tonics. By midday, we were sitting in a sports bar watching the news unfolding on the TV. The thing that struck me was how quiet it was. This was normally a pretty rowdy, lively sports bar but an eerie silence had descended on New York. As the barman poured our drinks, and we stared at the screens with tears streaming down our faces, we saw people emerging from downtown New York like zombies floating along the street, ghost-like, covered in ash and dust, scraped and torn from flying debris.

Honestly, if you didn't know better you'd think you were on the set of some Ridley Scott Hollywood blockbuster. It felt unbelievable, unreal. Some people had sleeves ripped off and bloody, cut arms; others were still in their business suits but they were covered in soot so thick you couldn't distinguish whether they were men or women, white or black, injured or not. It was the most bizarre and horrifying thing I've ever seen and those ghostly figures just kept emerging out of the dusty haze.

We saw hundreds of people walk past the bar in a trance-like, traumatic state. Most of them wouldn't have yet seen the news and would've had no idea what was going on. As we walked back to our hotel, we passed two people sitting on a park bench. They were sitting so still and were covered in so much dust they looked like a bizarre art installation.

Shockingly, as we learned later, the tragic events in New York weren't the only ones to have nearly ended our time together. We were due to fly to Las Vegas that same day on United Airlines Flight 93, which normally would take off from Newark, bound for San Francisco. The plane we were due to catch was the last to take off that morning and it had crashed into the Pentagon, killing everyone on board.

We knew our parents would be terrified for us, but all of the phone lines around New York were jammed and lines were going down right across America. I managed to get a call through to my best friend in San Francisco, who called my cousin in Berkeley, who called his cousin in Israel, who then finally managed to get through to both sets of our parents.

We were able to extend our stay at the hotel for one more night, which was a huge relief. Then, our gorgeous friend

James Houston, an Australian photographer whom Andy had met through modelling, took us in for the remainder of our stay in New York. Luckily, he was house and cat sitting and had space in this alternate location, as his own apartment was now unreachable for the time being.

At night, we walked around Union Square to stretch our legs and get a feel for what was happening around the city. There wasn't a surface anywhere not covered in posters of people missing since September 11: a pregnant woman looking for her wife; parents seeking their children; sons, nieces and fathers – all missing. It was an extraordinarily heartbreaking experience to be caught up in. I remember seeing two hospital workers embracing and crying on the street, the sense of the irreversible damage done, all-consuming.

People were holding candlelight vigils on street corners, praying, crying and hugging strangers. And there was still a great sense of worry and unease among New Yorkers that something bigger might still come. Andy and I, along with everyone in NYC, were together sharing this extraordinary experience, and it was one of those times when you realise that there is nothing to be done if it's meant to be.

Obviously, our wedding plans were shelved and we ached to be home safe in Australia. Every day, we got on the phone and listened to whatever message told us, 'We're sorry but this flight is not going today.'

On 16 September, after seven days in New York, we found a flight to Sydney. The airline informed us that we had a connection in Los Angeles airport and, if we missed the connection, we wouldn't make it on a flight to Australia for another three weeks.

September 11

There were barely minutes between our flight landing in LA and the flight to Sydney taking off, so when we arrived at LAX, we bolted off the plane and sprinted the entire length of the airport. Andy and I must've looked quite mad, but we were not missing that flight!

We collapsed into our seats and jetted away in the most turbulent take off I've ever experienced; it was awful. I closed my eyes and gripped Andy's hand firmly, wondering if maybe this was the time we were supposed to perish. We'd had a close call with death once already this week, maybe this was going to be our end.

We didn't sleep at all the whole way home. We were full of adrenalin and couldn't relax. I remember *Moulin Rouge* playing on the screen and everything feeling so surreal. It wasn't until we got into a taxi at Sydney airport and began the drive toward home that I felt the sick sense of fear starting to leave my body.

As the taxi neared Moore Park Road, I saw a guy, a fireman, who ran the soft sand at Bondi Beach with me every day, riding his bike on his way to the fire station to start his shift. Seeing him made me feel like we were truly back home and safe again.

It was a very poignant time in our relationship, for being present and celebrating the moment, one of those remarkably 'saved by the skin of your teeth' experiences that changes lives. September 11 is forever etched into my soul, as I'm sure it is for so many others. Everything Andy and I experienced in that short time will stay with me for the rest of my days. Exactly ten too-short years later, on 11 September 2011, my beloved husband passed away in my arms in Sydney, Australia.

*

I was cleaning out my storage cupboard with my daughter Indi recently and she came across my poppy-red wedding dress. She asked me what it was and when I told her, she flipped out.

'That's a bit inappropriate for a wedding,' she said.

'Says who?' I replied.

I don't generally get emotionally attached to things, but I did keep the dress for Indi, thinking one day she might cut it up and do something very clever and creative with it.

11

Till Death Do Us Part

*If you live to be a hundred, I want to live to be a hundred
minus one day so I never have to live without you.*
— Disney's Winnie the Pooh

I t was a rather strange mixture of emotions that we felt
when we landed back in Australia. We were so grateful to
be home and we both had an overwhelming feeling that
this really was our home now; we were settled, and our future
would be here. It was probably the first time either Andy or
I had openly acknowledged that Australia was where our life
would be; we'd made a life here that was so much more than
an expat visit. Australia was where our friends, our careers
and our hearts were. We were thankful to be back in a place
of peace and friendship, and it really struck us how free and
secure Australia was after our 9/11 experience. We were
incredibly grateful, and I always will be, for this faraway sunny
island that welcomed us with open arms. We were so aware

that so many people risk life and limb to find a safe place to call home.

But we also felt a slight disconnect from what we had just lived through in New York and the way this was portrayed in Australia. It was singularly the most shocking event I have ever lived through; the grief and the fear, the horror and the emptiness we felt in New York was something that would change the way Andy and I both thought about life forever. And yet back in Australia, the sun still shone and everything went on, just as usual.

While our world as we knew it – our Western, white, safe, secure world – had been rocked off its hinges, 9/11 was also the most grounding experience I've had. Andy and I both felt that in some ways this must be what it is like to live through war, to go to bed terrified of what might come, to rest your head on the pillow feeling totally unsafe. We only had a few days of that but it gave us a horrible taste of what it must be like for people in countries where this is a reality every day of their lives – the very countries that I had adventured in quite freely as a child.

I suppose our close proximity to this event, and the very real 'sliding doors' feeling that if it had happened a few minutes earlier we could've died, really affected how we felt about it and we were very sensitive to it because it was so profound. I suppose to some extent, too, watching the images on television in a country far away never really captures the emotion and grief that we experienced at ground zero; it felt like they had physically seeped through to our bones.

A friend in Sydney had sent me some flippant joke about Bin Laden, which was probably quite witty or funny to others, but I couldn't find any humour in it, I was totally disgusted. I get that Australians like to take the piss, and do have a rather laconic and sometimes black sense of humour, but it really hit the wrong nerve with me and was probably the first sense I had of being so far away from the rest of the world. I guess it was what you could call an awakening to the realisation that it would be all too easy to get lost in the bubble that we were living in and that moving forward was of vital importance to make sure that we both educated ourselves as to what was going on around the rest the world and how in some small way we might be able to make a difference to someone, somewhere.

The images of the faces of lost husbands and wives, sisters and mothers and daughters, brothers and fathers and sons, on posters pasted up on every available inch of space around New York were incredibly moving. It all happened so fast and yet for some people it would take forever to forget. The shabby photocopies, home-pasted collages or old family photos pinned on lamp posts, bus stops and mail boxes, turned the city into a candlelight shrine, where the righteous became humble and the bold became tame.

How can we ever really understand the horrors of not knowing where your child might be or if your husband or wife will come home from work? Or when the next building might fall. My brain couldn't fathom what it must have been like to watch as quite possibly your son or your husband or your wife or your daughter hurled themselves from the heights of the towers, to avoid whatever unknown terror awaited them. The images of those flimsy bodies, falling like origami birds through the sky, will forever be burned into the walls of my memory.

Strangely, there were many positive things that came out of our experience. But the greatest gift of all – and the one so many were also so fortunate to experience – was that it reiterated that you really do have to live in the moment. You never know from one minute to the next where life may take you or when you'll be dealt a curve ball you can't catch, however clever, talented, wealthy or brilliant you are. It cemented for us that you really don't know how long you have with each other and that you need to make the most of every minute. And it also absolutely cemented for me, as it did for Andy, that the person who mattered the most to me was standing right beside me.

On the morning we arrived home, I became so much more aware of everything around me. My senses were totally heightened. Spring was in the air and the wisteria was glorious – I'd never truly noticed how magnificent those purple blooms were and how stunning a picture it was of the trees in full bloom, gigantic bouquets mirrored by the purple of the fallen blossoms beneath. It was utterly beautiful, a little slice of heaven. Sydney was majestic and I now had a new appreciation of this peaceful city that had welcomed us with open arms.

Of course, we didn't actually get to achieve the main thing we went to America for and that was to be married. We were so raw with emotion when we got home we weren't really in the head space to think too much about it, but we had a very firm resolve that we wanted to be married sooner rather than later. And we weren't in the mood for anything frivolous;

we wanted to celebrate being together in a very real and meaningful way.

Andy and I talked about what we could do and we had lots of different ideas. But I said to Andy, 'You know, all I want to do is to stand in front of the people we love and care about who are here in Australia and tell them what I love most about you.'

So that's exactly what we did.

On 1 December, the same date that we had arrived in Australia three years earlier, we were married. I hold that date very near to my heart; it is a day of many new beginnings.

We wanted to be married in a place that was special just to us, that had been a part of our lives, somewhere unique that we treasured. We came up with the idea that we'd get married at the newly opened Gertrude and Alice, a little book store in Hall Street, Bondi. It was one of our favourite places and we went there all the time to search the big old wooden shelves for treasures.

Gertrude and Alice was like a Seattle book store. It had old wooden floors that would have been glorious a long time ago but had weathered beautifully, with floor-to-ceiling book shelves and big old wooden ladders that rolled along rails so you could reach the books on the top. The shop was a bit like a cosy private library, and the books were almost falling off the shelves with a cluttered sense of randomness, when in actual fact there was no randomness to it at all, this was a perfectly curated treasure trove of brilliance. In nooks and crannies there were big sofas with people reading books and having cups of tea, or quirky bright red velvet antique chairs that you could sit on to soak up the words around you.

This book store was the first one of its kind in Sydney and it had a lovely old school feel about it. There was a beautiful story behind how the store was named, which was after Gertrude Stein and Alice B. Tolkas, two Jewish-American women who met and fell in love in Paris in 1907. They were writers, artists and academics, and they forged a life together despite the challenges of being gay at that time. They were rebellious, stubborn and determined to live their lives their own way and that appealed to me enormously.

On the day of our wedding I got up at 4 a.m. and went to the flower markets with my girlfriend Heidi, who'd offered to do all of the flowers for us. We wanted them to look like a wild meadow, unpretentious and familiar. Then Andy and I went to our beloved little Redleaf Pool, which is now called Murray Rose after the Olypmic swimmer, at a harbour beach in Double Bay. We lay curled up next to each other and wrote out our vows, which were the five things we most loved about one another. Which, by the way, we weren't going to share with each other until the ceremony.

Funnily enough, a few years later we bought our first apartment right across from this beach, with views of the harbour and its sunsets. We were also awarded our Australian citizenships. How lucky we were.

Heidi and I had chosen an eclectic combination of flowers – blue cornflowers, that felt like they brought Europe into the space, and lots and lots of wild roses and country flowers to bring our pasts into the present. Jane, who owns Gertrude and Alice, told me that the perfume from the flowers lingered through the shop for days.

With a small budget, our menu was inspired by a giant Tuscan picnic. We had all sorts of beautiful cheeses, including giant wheels of ricotta and parmesan, a huge clove-studded glazed leg of ham, fresh figs with honey, Portuguese tarts, and cherries, redcurrants and pomegranates overflowing from bowls full of fresh fruit. There were huge hunks of handmade chocolate and handfuls of yummy treats to grab as you walked by. It was kind of Tuscan feast meets Santa Barbara with a touch of the dining hall at Downton Abbey! With all of it set on a huge old wooden table, it looked just like a renaissance still life painting. Did they have chocolate then?

At 3.40 on the afternoon of 1 December, which was a Saturday, our gorgeous Scottish friend Anna, as she was known, picked us up in a beautiful old white vintage Stag and drove us to our wedding. Andy and I were greeted by about 50 of our closest new friends, who clapped and cheered and whooped as we made our way into the store and gathered underneath the huge window that looked out on to the olive tree that still stands there today, and that was where we shared our marriage vows.

Andy reached for my hand as we took turns sharing our five favourite things about one another. He said he loved how I always said yes to any opportunity or offer that came our way, that I was always the one that said 'Let's just try it', and he wanted to spend the rest of his life with someone who wanted to try life and not be afraid of stepping out of our comfort zone. He also said that he could imagine running along the beach with me every day and could see himself running along behind me when I was an old wrinkly granny, still wearing the same bikini that I wear now! He loved the idea that we would grow old together and be totally comfortable in our skin. He also said that he loved the way that I acted when I bought something new! He joked about how he'd ask me, 'Is that new?' Then he put on this very funny voice to mimic my response, which was always 'This thing? No, had it for ages. You just haven't seen it!'

I said one of the many things I loved about Andy was his empathy. If something was at all emotionally moving or touching, even if it was a television commercial, I'd turn around and Andy would be crying too. He felt so deeply and had such a high level of empathy and he wasn't afraid to show it. If I was feeling something emotional, I knew he was feeling the same way.

There were many precious moments and genuinely hilarious things which formed our unique wedding vows, like Andy saying that one of the other things he loved so much was that we had the same size feet – I have giant, hobbit-looking feet – and he could run out the door in my thongs!

As I snuck a look at everyone around us, I was struck by how engaged they were. Whether they were laughing or crying, holding their partner tight or nestled up to one of their buddies, they were all so present. Bar perhaps one friend who I am sure had smoked some wacky tobaccy beforehand and devoured about twelve Portuguese tarts while we spoke! You know who you are.

We both wore the outfits that we had bought in New York, as not only did they have a special significance to us, but they also brought in their physical form a symbol of life, love and loss, which was something we both spoke about at the end of vows, to our friends, a number of whom had lost close friends in the 9/11 attacks.

Andy wore a beautiful black and white suit with a pink and white striped Paul Smith shirt, just pink enough that it had that quirky Paul Smith feel to it. His blue eyes against the pink of the shirt were blazing, especially with the constant flow of happy tears that kept tumbling down. The poppy-red dress that I wore took everyone by surprise, but it very much affirmed the feminine, soft side of me that Andy allowed to emerge.

Our vows may sound flippant or silly, but they weren't. They were ingrained in something much bigger. The horror of 9/11 was still with us, so my final message to all of our wonderful friends was that in this crazy time of unexpected loss, it's so important to honour the people you love the most. It was a moment of real love for us, with the people we cared about in Australia.

I'm stressing that these were the people we cared about in Australia, because our family and lifelong friends weren't there, and my parents were devastated. Andy's parents, Pat and Rob, came around to it even though they were disappointed too, but Dad never forgave me because they felt so excluded. But it wasn't because we didn't love them. We just wanted to keep the whole thing very simple and informal and about us.

When Andy and I finished pledging our love for each other and completed the formal part of the marriage vows, we were presented as husband and wife. Andy leant in and gave me a lingering kiss and for a moment I was completely lost in time. When I looked up everyone was crying! I think that more than anything they were touched by our authentic show of love, and they felt privileged to share the occasion with us.

But then the party started! Our Tuscan feast began, and there was lots of champagne to drink and lots of celebrating to do. We had a tarot card reader, a gorgeous young actress from *Home and Away*, tucked away in the back room, and people queued up to sit with her and have their cards read.

Andy and I stayed until about 7 p.m. and then snuck off! We wanted to be together to soak up what we had just shared with one another. So we left everyone to eat and drink and dance and have a great time, and by all accounts that's exactly what they did.

When we arrived home, we found that Heidi had somehow got into our apartment and scattered handfuls of beautiful wild rose petals all over the stairs and in our bedroom. She'd even layered petals all through our bed! It was hilarious, cheesy and took hours to clean up. But the love, thought and care that went into it was what we bathed in. We snuggled up and – contrary to what most newlyweds do – fell fast asleep.

The next morning, still in a haze, we threw some clothes in the car and drove down to Jervis Bay, where we spent two days together, hanging out in a little cabin on the beach and soaking up that we were husband and wife.

Mr and Mrs Andy Whitfield, till death do us part.

Part Four

WE ARE SPARTACUS

12

Not Just a Pretty Face

And the day came when the risk to remain tight in a bud
was more painful than the risk it took to blossom.
— attritubed to *Anaïs Nin*

One gorgeous Sunday morning as Andy and I were huffing and puffing our way along the Bondi to Bronte walking path, a lady running towards us abruptly stopped us in our tracks. She introduced herself to us as Helen White, and she was a gregarious, chatty kind of woman. She got right up close to Andy's face, staring at him quite intently.

'You are so beautiful,' she said. 'Do you have an agent?'

Her eyes were studying every detail of his face and I could see she was quite taken by him. Andy burst out laughing. I mean, here we were in our sweaty exercise clothes, hardly the picture of glamour, being bailed up by a complete stranger. I think he thought the whole thing was some kind of joke, but I was quite curious.

He was being very polite and sweet, and out of the corner of his eye he glanced at me before very cautiously saying, 'Um, no!'

She explained that she was an agent and thought Andy could have a career in modelling. She asked if he'd like to do a shoot.

Andy, smiling, said politely, 'No thanks.'

But I butted in very enthusiastically and said, 'Yes he will!'

What harm could it do? You hear stories of people being 'discovered' while walking along the street, plucked from obscurity and off to stardom, but you never imagine it's going to happen to you.

A week or so later, Andy went along to the studio to do the photo shoot, not entirely certain of what I'd pushed him into, but – probably more to his surprise than mine – he found he really enjoyed it. I think it was a bit of fun in comparison to the pretty serious physical work he was doing scaling up and down buildings.

Helen did some tests shots and signed Andy up with Shoot Model Management. I don't think he ever really thought much would come of it, but I was so proud that he was willing to give it a go. It would've been very easy for him to retreat to the default position of shyness and his comfort zone, but he pushed himself out there and very quickly began to get calls to do modelling assignments, fashion shoots and ad campaigns for all sorts of brands. Helen saw something in Andy that we'd never contemplated – and she was right.

Andy was quite a shy person and would never have dreamt of pushing himself out there for something like this, but there was no doubt he was a beautiful looking man. He had a chiselled face with very feline, squarish features; his face was very structured and asymmetrical, and his eyes were a piercing blue. There was a ruggedness to him too, but a refined ruggedness; not that Russell Crowe sort of sheer brutishness, but a Calvin Klein style of Adonis sophistication. He was also in great shape, not only from exercise but also from the physicality of his work; he seriously had that kind of Leonardo da Vinci anatomical diagram body, with a great butt and washboard abs.

I wouldn't say that Andy absolutely loved modelling work. He wasn't the clothes-horse type who'd enjoy standing around all day being fussed over. But nevertheless it was fun and it paid well, and it exposed him to other opportunities. Those high fashion shots for magazines like *GQ* really opened doors for him, including work filming television commercials.

What he did love about modelling though was the fact that for the first time in his life, he was no longer quite so terrified about being the centre of attention. It was a huge breakthrough for him in gaining confidence in himself, and later on this would open up a whole new world of possibility.

The first big opportunity was when Andy was cast in a television commercial for Jaguar. He was offered the chance to fly to New Zealand to film this amazing ad, which was almost cinematic in its style, and he got paid big bucks for it! His first ever well paid TV commercial.

Television commercials were a whole new and exciting world for Andy. He loved being on set and he loved the camaraderie of the shoot crews. He loved being around a large group of creative people and being able to work with a team who collectively produced. He wasn't particularly interested in standing around looking pretty, that wasn't Andy's thing, but he was really interested in shooting commercials and began to take a keen interest in the cameras and how they work and the whole process of filming and editing and the machinations of motion picture.

Andy had always loved photography and that first day on set filming for Jaguar sparked a real curiosity about the technical side of production, opening his eyes to an area he'd never considered before. He'd never wanted to stand out, but he had a great sense of wonder and his attitude was 'Well, what would it be like?' And so his passion for acting was born.

For Andy, pursuing acting was never about being famous, quite the opposite. He never wanted the limelight – in fact he still felt quite uncomfortable being the centre of attention – but he wanted to be part of something. He had a strong creative side that he wanted to tap into and he wanted to push himself to see what he was capable of achieving. He also loved being part of a team and a crew, and the camaraderie he'd experienced filming ads, particularly around blokey camera crews, was what he enjoyed.

He started to make a name for himself and filmed quite a few television ads, but one in particular stands out in my memory. Andy did this hilarious ad for the breakfast cereal Special K. He had to bleach his hair peroxide blond and then it was dyed the red colour of the Special K logo! He was walking around with very strange coloured hair for a few weeks. He must've looked ridiculous back at work, like a strange kind of skinny Ronald McDonald scaling down buildings with bright red hair.

As more ads came in and his interest grew, he started taking acting lessons with On Camera Connections in Sydney.

Sandra Lee Paterson who ran it was legendary in the film and television industry, and she was a real character. From day one, Sandra really encouraged Andy; she saw something in him and was so supportive. Even if originally it wasn't his acting skills, there was something about him that had potential beyond what we knew. There was a charm and authenticity in Andy that was worth investing in.

Every week he went to lessons, and they weren't just in acting. He was also learning how to move in front of a camera, which can be quite tricky. He met other people wanting to learn the craft of filmmaking and behind-the-scenes production too, and people who were going off to pilot season.

Pilot season wasn't a concept we were familiar with at all. It's basically the one time of year in LA when actors from all over the world gather to audition and film potential shows. It's the best possible chance to show off what you can do and hopefully catch the attention of someone who can do something about it!

By then, Andy had done enough commercials and filmed enough test footage with Sandra to make a decent show reel. Sandra was a brilliant mentor to him and inspired him to absolutely go for it. He was still juggling his engineering work at this time, but our attitude was to see where acting took him and whether something happens or not, it's all part of the journey.

Through Sandra, Andy met the actor John Noble and on weekends John would invite a group of young actors around to his house for The Parlour Group, as they called it. It all sounded very 1920s. They'd meet in John's living room and perform little acts or share pieces of writing without any fear of judgment. They'd help one another grow creatively and Andy was very inspired by John. John has built an amazing career. He's performed in a huge number of Australian TV shows like *Rake*, *All Saints* and *Miss Fisher's Murder Mysteries*, but he's also had huge success in the US, landing roles in *The Good Wife*, *Fringe*, *Sleepy Hollow* and Peter Jackson's *The Lord of the Rings*. Andy looked up to John and I think he was quite a mentor to him. As a young guy starting out in a very big and unfamiliar industry, Andy was so lucky to have these incredible people take him under their wings and nurture him along the journey.

The modelling jobs were coming in regularly and Andy was beginning to get little parts in shows like *All Saints*. They'd only be one-off episodes, but he was auditioning well and landing roles which whetted his appetite and gave him a taste of more to come. I could see Andy really growing through his on-camera work. For him, it was all about self-awareness. I was doing a lot of ongoing training and learning for my own work, and Andy followed suit. He was open to anything that would unlock his ability to grow – as an actor, as a man and as someone who felt responsible to make a difference to the world in some way.

He attended the controversial Landmark courses, the legendary racing car driver, Sir John Whitmore's transformational coaching programs, and also Faith Martin's Breakthrough workshops for aspiring actors. He signed up for whatever he could to challenge himself to push beyond any old self-limiting beliefs that he saw as standing in his way. He had his own coach, and attended therapy for a while; he wanted to relinquish any fears that stood in his way. It was about facilitating a higher purpose in life and letting go of the things that hold you back.

Andy was often caught in an old habitual pattern of thinking, which anchored in him an illogical fear of being humiliated. He later realised this was left over from his rather harsh experience starting in a Welsh-speaking school as a shy little four-year-old. It was still his biggest weakness and often held him back from having a go at things.

One of the wonderful things about our relationship was that, because it was so based on trust and commitment to each other, neither of us had a problem holding the other one accountable. Whether it was Andy reassuring me that despite my being new to my field I still had the right to bill myself out at a higher fee, or me being able to see that he was getting bogged down in an old pattern of thinking, like worrying about whether or not he was good enough to go for a TV audition. I'd make him push through it, so long as he was up for the challenge, and make him confront whatever fear was holding him back. And at the end of the day if words didn't work, a run in the sun, a swim and a cuddle would reassure him that I believed him capable of anything.

Andy came from a very small town in Wales and his parents were two very loving, humble and gorgeous people who wanted to fit in with their environment and not stand out. So Andy came from this environment of never stepping out of his comfort zone; in fact, he did everything to avoid it, so sometimes I had to give him the shove he needed.

Andy was still engineering and Ove Arup were amazing, giving him time off when he needed it to do a shoot, But the more he threw himself into acting lessons, the more he realised that if he was going to be taken seriously as an actor, he had to give up modelling. Which was a bit of a bugger because the modelling jobs were very well paid! We had a long conversation about it and agreed that I would step my work up a notch to allow him a little more freedom to pursue this. Suddenly his engineering work was the bread and butter, a necessity, and to be faithful to Ove Arup and loyal to them for the flexibility they'd given him, he worked twice as hard. This was a real commitment the two of us had made and we put everything into it.

Those early years after we were married we'd been living a wonderful life. Andy was doing modelling on the side, as well as TV ads and stuff, and my career coaching and facilitating was going from strength to strength. We had a lot of fun. It was absolutely carefree; we were living in Sydney in the sunshine, the polar opposite to London, and savouring the Californian-like lifestyle that Sydney gave us. It was a time of great love and companionship and friendship, and it was one of the happiest times of our lives. We had no obligations other than to one another and we could pursue our dreams. Now, all of a sudden, Andy's career was taking off and I was doing what I loved with work that was taking me all around the world. 'Wow, we've really made this happen,' we thought to ourselves.

When we flew to Australia we had little more than our backpacks and a dream to enjoy all that life had to offer us as a couple. But with the sun on our backs, and a huge amount of love and trust in our hearts, we'd achieved all of what we dreamed of when we boarded QF1 on that cold London evening in November 1998.

13

The Lioness and her Cubs

Whether or not it is clear to you, no doubt the
Universe is unfolding as it should . . .
— Max Ehrmann, 'Desiderata'

In the middle of 2003, my sister Lowri invited us to her wedding in England. It was early August, perfect for a beautiful summer wedding, and the perfect time too for Andy to skip a Sydney winter and fly off on his first solo mission to a busy summer in LA.

His friend Karin Catt, the fashion photographer, had set him up with a good handful of connections in case he needed a place to stay and some moral support. If all else failed, there would at least be a few familiar names to get in touch with. His plan was to get his face in front of as many managers as possible and dip his toes in the pool, which was colossally larger than the tiny pond he'd been swimming in.

Andy had been picking up lots of little roles that really validated that there was the potential for him to pursue acting as a career, and with Sandra's help he pulled his show reel together and bought his ticket for LA.

This was a huge experience for Andy, heading off on his own to a country and industry that he had little to no experience in or of. But keeping the vision we had created together front and centre, his intention was to try to land a few auditions and sign an agent who would help him take the next step forward. He was right out there on the edge of his comfort zone and, while he was terrified, he felt more alive than ever.

We flew to Bristol, where we would reconnect with my family and celebrate my gorgeous sister marrying her long-term boyfriend. Then we were going our separate ways. Andy was heading off to the States and I was spending some time with my fabulous lifelong friends in London, before flying home.

A week later we found ourselves literally clinging to each other and sobbing at Paddington Station. Andy said goodbye and jumped on the Heathrow express to catch his flight. A little tear rolled down his cheek and I bristled with an unfamiliar wave of fear at the thought of us being apart for such a significant chapter in his life. It was the first time we'd been apart since we started going out back in 1998 and it was absolutely bizarre to know I wouldn't be waking up beside him the next day. Whenever there'd been an adventure of any sort, we'd done it together, and it felt very strange not being with Andy on this particular part of his journey, which was so huge and exciting. But deep in my heart, as sad as I was to farewell him, I was equally as excited about the opportunities that lay ahead for him.

Through his old modelling connections, Andy had organised to stay with some friends of friends in Los Angeles, two really lovely female German models, identical twins, who were in the United States modelling. I know at this stage you might be thinking, '*What*, the love of your life is heading off to stay with twin models?' But just for the record, Andy was more monogamous than a swan and it literally never ever bothered me. Besides, let's remember, I was the one with the rather shadier past.

The girls were staying in a huge old Californian mansion on their own. I have no idea how they came across this place, but it was so dilapidated it should've been condemned. The electricity only worked in one corner of the house, which was literally falling down around them. Worse, when Andy arrived the girls told him they were certain the house was haunted. Adventure was what we asked for and adventure was what we got!

Andy had a room to himself with peeling wallpaper and a strange sword mounted on the wall. He is not the sort to be easily spooked, but he said the room had a real eeriness to it and he often felt like there was some sort of presence around. One night he woke up quite suddenly with the feeling that someone was standing over him; he was all sweaty and hot and quite shaken by it. Wide awake, he rang me.

'Vashti, I'm sure this place is totally haunted,' he said.

He was half joking and half terrified at the same time. I talked to him for a while and we laughed about the craziness of it all, until he went back to sleep.

Andy didn't have a great deal of down time to think about who or what he was sharing the house with, because he had such a crazy schedule of auditions and meetings with potential agents that he barely had a moment to breathe. His focus was very clear.

Although the girls were around sometimes, Andy didn't see them that often, because they were working during the day. They were very sweet, gentle souls who in their spare time fostered puppies that were on death row. Andy would come home and there'd be dozens of dogs running around. The girls would feed them and walk them and look after them for a few days or a weekend before the pups went back to the pound.

The twins made him feel incredibly welcome, but other than weekends he barely saw them. He was very much alone, living on a shoestring budget, trying his best to be seen and heard and stand out from the crowd of people trying to be seen and heard!

Being away from Andy for the first time brought up some strange and very familiar feelings for me. I began to think about all that lay ahead for him and as I thought about his potential and all the exciting, creative people he would meet, I began to think about what else I really wanted for us. Having this time apart gave me a chance to reflect on our relationship, where we were headed and what our future was, besides pursuing our inspiring vocations. We were both pursuing amazing careers, but what was next for us as a couple? Deep down, I was beginning to think about having a family. I was 30 and Andy was 32. Maybe it was time to start factoring this into our lives.

During one of our long phone conversations between LA and Sydney, I tentatively broached the subject with Andy.

'Darling, there's something that's been floating around in my head a lot while you've been away,' I said, very gently but with just the right amount of enthusiasm. 'And that's when . . . not as in right now, of course . . . but when we might consider making babies.'

There was a long silence down the line. Andy was gobsmacked, which is probably no surprise given I'd tossed this little bomb-shell at him at the least opportune or expected time! When he started to speak, I could hear by the tone of his voice that he was a bit stunned.

'Vashti, do you have any idea what I'm trying to deal with here? The thought of making a baby is the furthest thing from my mind right now.'

And so I very wisely read the state of play and pressed pause on that conversation for the time being. I momentarily snapped into one of those 'Vashti self-doubt' moods that had shadowed me all through my younger years, thinking, 'Oh my god, am I in this on my own?'

It was nothing to do with Andy, it was my emotional safety valve. That's how I used to operate, with me almost trying to push him away for fear of *being* the one pushed away. Poor Andy was on one side of the world working his guts out to build our future, and I was on the other side, desperately missing him and filling my head with old thoughts that deep in my heart I knew were rubbish.

On some level, there was a part of me that feared that as we both advanced in our vocations, there might be the risk that we would grow apart. So just as I acknowledged that there was definitely some intuition calling me to want to make a baby with Andy, I also realised that my rather off timing was probably anchored in an old pattern of thinking, one based in the self-limiting belief that once he found this fabulous new world, I might not be worth sticking around for. With a big exhalation I let that go and chalked it up to something we were both going to have to get used to if we were really up for honouring the big vision that we had created together.

I knew Andy well enough to know that he wasn't saying, 'I don't want to have babies.' But what he did mean was, 'Jesus Christ, Vashti, I've got like 20 bucks left in my pocket, I'm sleep deprived and I'm trying to do this thing here all by myself without you here, and you are talking about something that's not even possible given that I'm in a different hemisphere at the moment!'

When we spoke the next day, neither of us mentioned the 'B' word. Andy was too excited telling me about the audition he was doing for a part in the movie *I, Robot* with Will Smith. He was very anxious about this audition, had a huge script to memorise, so many words to learn and he had less than a day to do it. He was really quite terrified about it but the audition was a major breakthrough for him and a huge opportunity to get in front of some serious movie people.

He missed out on the role, but when we saw who *was* cast, he was flattered. They were major movie stars like Bridget Moynahan and James Cromwell, and Shia Labeouf got the role Andy auditioned for. This really boosted Andy's confidence and cemented that he was on to something because he was being put up for big roles alongside famous actors. It boosted his energy too, and the drive to really push this as far as he could go. It made all of this effort worthwhile.

*

Andy was in LA for about three and a half weeks, and he signed with an agent, which was what he'd hoped to achieve, so he ticked off a lot of boxes and learnt a huge amount that would help him down the track. When he arrived home, he was much more relaxed and seemed happy to pick up the conversation about starting a family. He'd given it a lot of thought after our somewhat tense first discussion.

We both thought that if we waited another five years we might miss the window to make babies, but we both still had reservations. We had a great lifestyle as we were, and caring and being responsible for someone other than ourselves would be a huge shift. Andy was very honest and said that he absolutely wanted to have a family one day, but wasn't sure about the timing. He knew he was on the cusp of landing a big role and had been exposed to this new world in LA that we were circling, whereas I was thinking about what was next for us to build on as a husband and wife, something more meaningful and purposeful – and that was having a family.

'You know, we could wait forever if we are waiting for things to happen,' he said. 'Why don't we weave it all in together, our careers, babies, everything and just do it.'

So we agreed to give it a go and see what happened. And give it a go we did! After almost a month apart we had a lot of catching up to do and we practised making babies at every opportunity.

To our surprise, I fell pregnant very quickly. It was really exciting and we grappled with a mixture of emotions, both shock and delight. My mind very quickly moved into strategic motherhood mode and began thinking about what all of this would mean for us. But six weeks later, while I was proudly announcing our pregnancy to everyone, I began to feel a slight ache in my lower abdomen and when I did another pregnancy test, it showed I was no longer pregnant.

We were both incredibly disappointed but we looked at it philosophically. It was the sign we needed that we really wanted a baby, but it wasn't meant to be right then and there. Andy knew I was a bit fragile, so he planned for us to go away for the weekend to Seal Rocks.

The three-hour trip gave us the chance to talk and catch up and commiserate with one another and celebrate all of the amazing things happening in our life, which was as therapeutic as it was reassuring. Everything in life does indeed happen when it is supposed to.

Seal Rocks is a beautiful beach and it was one of Andy's favourite surfing spots so, while he was out in the water, I lay on the sand soaking up some sun and reflecting on this baby we'd lost. I allowed myself a little cry, thinking about it all, and as the pent-up emotion began to dissolve down my face, I felt ready to let this little person go and was quite okay about it, knowing in my heart that this baby would return at the right time.

That night as we snuggled up in our camp bed, Andy wrapped his hands around my belly and whispered, 'Everything happens for a reason. Let's just trust that things will happen when they are supposed to.'

We didn't know then that almost a year later to the day, baby Jesse would arrive and Andy would land his first major movie role. The stars were beginning to align for us.

*

In September 2004, we found out I was pregnant again. We were very happy, but of course there was always that tiny worry niggling away in the back of my mind, the 'what if something goes wrong again' feeling. But each week that passed helped ease our minds that this baby was going to stick around.

We decided that we would find out the gender of our little bun in the oven, as we'd had an incredible experience with a dear friend, when she found out she was having a son. Naming the little boy growing in her belly heightened her whole pregnancy and made meeting him seem even more familiar when he popped out. Andy and I were both at the birth of our friend's bub, and it was extraordinary witnessing new life coming into the world, such a gift to cherish. I won't say it wasn't intense for Andy, but as the designated photographer, he said it changed his whole relationship with birth forever – in a good way, I might add. So our scan showed, along with the exact profile he still has, a little willy on the tiny being in my tummy.

We both began to sob – Andy with delight, and me, to everyone's surprise, because I was absolutely overwhelmed. I had been convinced it was a girl. I always wanted boys, so I don't know why this was such a shock!

'I don't know how to be a good parent to a little boy,' I sobbed.

Andy held my hand and rubbed my belly, still slippery from the ultrasound gel. 'Vashti,' he said, 'you've got this. There is no one more perfect to bring a little man into the world than you.'

Andy was working really hard while I was pregnant. He was doing as much engineering work as he could, while I tried to ease off work a little, mindful of having lost the previous pregnancy. Little acting parts were coming up now, and he had roles in television series like *Packed to the Rafters* and *McLeod's Daughters*, but nothing really substantial, so we were still very reliant on Andy's engineering income. Some modelling jobs would've been great financially, but we knew it wasn't in the best interests of his career long term.

My pregnancy was very smooth, and the baby was healthy and clearly very happy tucked up in my tummy because he didn't want to come out! At 40 weeks, he still hadn't arrived and that final week drove me a bit mad. I felt absolutely enormous and my boobs were like basketballs, but this sleepy little fellow was in no hurry.

One afternoon when I was a week overdue, Andy came home from work and got a far more enthusiastic welcome than he was expecting. I was standing in the kitchen, all bust and belly, and as he started to tell me about his day I grabbed his hands and shoved them on my breasts and told him to twist my nipples as hard as he could. He raised an eyebrow and gave me a funny look. I'm sure he thought I'd lost the plot, but he was in the middle of telling me about some boring concrete report he was writing.

I said to him, 'For goodness sake, Andy, just grab my nipples and give them a really tight turn!'

There was absolutely nothing sexual about it, but I'd read in a book that this was supposed to bring on labour. Apparently if you massage your nipples for about an hour at a time, three times a day, it releases the hormone oxytocin, which brings on contractions. I didn't have time to have my nipples massaged for hours. I wanted this baby out now! So I grabbed Andy's hand, looked him in the eyes and said very seriously, 'Just twist!'

Without missing a word of his concrete report, Andy kept talking while squeezing my nipples and telling me all about his day. It's hilarious when I think about it, but it actually worked, because my waters broke an hour or so later.

Having been born on the floor in a cottage in Wales and raised by two delightful earth-loving hippies, there was probably no question that I'd have as natural a birth as possible too. I didn't want any intervention if it could be avoided. I'd booked in at the birth centre at the Randwick Women's Hospital, which was a very relaxed, natural environment and much warmer surroundings than a hospital room. It was a very reassuring place for me to be because I had the support of a midwife, but if something went wrong, the labour ward was just down the hallway.

My contractions began very slowly after my waters broke. I'd been at the deliveries of a few friends' babies, so I knew how it would unfold. I'd decided to stay at home for as long as I could and deal with the contractions, which were fairly mild, until it was time to go. At one point Andy and I waddled down to the supermarket and grabbed a bag of food so he had something to take to the birth centre in case he was hungry, then we slowly walked home and he snoozed on the sofa, holding my hand, while I calmly worked my way through the early contractions.

They were mild for most of the night until around 6 a.m. when things started to get a bit more serious. I woke Andy up and said, 'It's time to go.'

At 11.55 a.m. on 18 May, our precious son Jesse Red arrived. He was born in the bath and Andy was there to lift him out and give him his first hug. It was such a special time for us, Andy was with me through every single minute, and it wasn't lost on either of us how different this was for him as a father in comparison to the experience of his own dad, who was relegated to the waiting room. Andy cherished being with this tiny little person who had already turned our lives upside down. He was absolutely smitten with Jesse.

Normally, you'd stay at the birth centre for a few days until the midwives were sure everything was okay. We stayed the night and Andy slept in the bed alongside me. It was lovely to have him with me on our first night as parents. He snuggled up with his little man and I could see from the moment Jesse was born that he and Andy had a beautiful, special connection. Andy was so proud of his tiny son, with his perfect ten toes and ten fragile little fingers that moved so slowly they were hypnotising.

My recovery was very good and Jesse was fine, so we were allowed to go home the next morning. There was no time to rest! We were straight into life with a new baby, fumbling our way through the first days of parenthood.

Jesse was a text book baby, everything was very straightforward – and I can say that with confidence because the inner control freak in me had read every baby book I could get my hands on to prepare for his arrival!

Having had this rather boundary-less, alternative, hippie kind of childhood, I was determined that everything would be the opposite for my baby. Nothing was going to be left to chance, so I was probably a bit more obsessive about it all than I should have been, but it worked. I did everything by the book, wrapping Jesse up, putting him to sleep at the same time every day. I was really diligent in honouring sleep times and feed times and he settled very well. He was a very calm, good little baby.

When Jesse came along all of our priorities changed, of course. No one can really prepare you for what it's like to have a child until you are actually holding that baby you created in your arms. The moment Jesse was born Andy snapped straight into the 'hunter-gatherer' mode of being the provider and carer and looking after us. He knew I wasn't going to be working for a while, so he was taking the load, and that meant doing more engineering and probably less acting.

He decided that there weren't many great acting roles on the horizon, so he'd focus on engineering for the time being and get back into acting when it suited us at some later stage. He was very manly about it all and there was clearly a greater sense of purpose for him with a wife and baby to take care of, but I could see he was torn, and I could see the underlying conflict for him. Andy had this huge pride and love for Jessie, and he was bursting with a raw sense of fatherhood, but he also had to trust that acting would come back into his life at some point.

That point came much sooner than we ever could've imagined, because about three weeks after Jesse was born Andy was called to audition for a role in a feature film. A feature film was a big deal, and *Gabriel* was a very dark sci-fi film that was being made in Sydney. Technically it was an independent film, but Sony were behind it, so it had strong backing and the potential for huge international distribution.

A few weeks after his first audition, Andy was called back to meet the producers again, which was a great sign. Jesse was about six weeks old by then and we were still acclimatising to being new parents. It's a whirlwind when you have a baby in the house. You really don't think straight and the sleepless nights can be gruelling, so how Andy managed to snap into acting mode, I'll never know, but he did.

About a month later he came home from work and said, 'So Vash, I've been offered the lead in this movie!'

I was ecstatic, I was like 'OH MY GOD that's incredible!'

I had visions of it being shown on big screens and an over-whelming feeling that this dream of ours was really happening.

Andy explained that the movie was fully funded by Sony, which was amazing. I was beside myself with excitement. Then his voice changed a little and he said, 'But the thing is, there's no pay, not until the film is sold, so it's a deferred payment. I will get paid, but I don't know when.'

There was a long silence. I didn't really know what to say or what he was thinking. The shoot would take about three months, so that would be three months without any income.

Andy had already made up his mind about whether to take it.

'It's just not possible for us to do that,' he said, 'so I'm going to say no. Something else will come along.'

We were sitting in the kitchen of our house in Paddington and I had Jesse cuddled up in my arms asleep. I looked at this perfect little baby and I said to Andy, 'What would you rather tell your son, that you took the safe option because we might not have any money, or that you seized an opportunity for the thing you were most passionate about and went for it?'

He didn't speak, just smiled, grabbed his phone, called his agent and said 'Yes'.

*

It was winter when they began filming and most of the shoots were at night. This was a very dark film, and the scenes were very black. They were filming in back alleys and awful dark lane ways and grungy, gritty places you would never normally go. The movie was about an archangel, Gabriel, played by Andy, who is sent on a mission to rescue the world, so it was sci-fi with a touch of horror and Armageddon all thrown in.

Samantha Noble, John's daughter, was Andy's co-star so there was a real sense of camaraderie and friendship about this film before he even began. The nights were long and freezing cold and the actors were often in the rain for hours on a set that was made to look like a no man's land between heaven and hell. By the time Andy got home in the morning he was almost hypothermic. Filming took a huge physical toll on him. He'd sleep during the day, so I was pretty much on my own with Jesse, but it was okay. Jesse and I had a good routine happening, and we did all that we could to support Andy through this job.

It was a really exciting time for us. He had this huge new project and I had a new baby to look after. We both felt like we were giving birth to wonderful new additions to our life. And because we were sharing the journey together, there was no frustration or resentment. We both did the best we could to support one another in building a legacy for the future.

The shoot lasted three months but the movie was in post-production for ages, so by the time the movie was ready to premiere, I'd given birth to baby number two, Indigo Sky!

Indi was three weeks old when *Gabriel* premiered at Fox Studios. It had taken two very long years after they finished filming before the movie hit the big screens. The night of the premiere was the very first time I'd left Indi's side; she was only a newborn and I was really anxious about leaving her.

I left her for two hours to quickly walk the red carpet with Andy, see the film then dash home to feed her. I was wearing a very long, white, flowing maxi dress trying to disguise the not-yet-gone baby bump, and I had the most gigantic knockers you've ever seen. I honestly looked like a pasty white version of Queen Latifah!

I was breast feeding Indi and my boobs were absolutely humungous and while everyone else was watching this movie, and I was trying hard to be present for Andy, all I could think about was my boobs, which were filling with milk and getting bigger and bigger by the minute! As soon as the credits began to roll, I dashed out of the cinema like Cinderella as the clock's about to strike midnight. My boobs were almost spilling out of my dress. It was awful. The milk and my boobs were all in free fall.

That whole period was a strange time in our life. The day after the filming of *Gabriel* ended, Andy had to go straight back to engineering work. There was no down time (or money!) to soak up feeling like a movie star. He'd gone from the excitement and creativity of being on a movie set, back to waking up at 6 a.m. and off to scale buildings for the day.

On set he could fulfil this wonderful creative side of himself, but when that ended he was back to work and our lives snapped back to what they were before.

*

I found out I was pregnant with Indi in early March 2007, about the same time as my gorgeous friend Kate had given birth to her second baby Scarlett. Kate and I had met when she hosted my surprise 30th birthday party at her Bondi café, Zucchini Flower. We instantly clicked and she soon became a business coaching client of mine. Our relationship developed into a close friendship; we were bonded by the fact we'd both had our first babies close together.

Kate had a wicked sense of humour and would light up any room she entered. She and her husband Marcus had their first child Eloise just before Jesse was born, and I'd learnt an enormous amount about motherhood and pregnancy from her. It was beautiful watching her when she was pregnant and she was an amazing mother to her girls. I later became godmother to her second daughter Scarlett, but always adored Eloise, Jesse's first true love, in equal amounts.

A short time after Scarlett's birth, Kate hadn't been feeling well, but she put it down to a combination of sleepless nights and the changes your body goes through after growing and birthing a gorgeous little baby. But on 14 May 2007, things took a turn for the worse and she was admitted to hospital suffering a haemorrhaging kidney. There was a huge tumour on Kate's kidney which was removed and diagnosed as malignant. Kate had a very aggressive form of cancer known as Ewing Sarcoma and by the time the doctors found the tumour, the cancer had already spread to her lungs. Despite several rounds of very aggressive chemo, it wouldn't budge and we knew the outcome wasn't going to be good.

It was an incredible privilege to be able to spend so much time with Kate through her treatment. The day before she was to begin her chemo – and this is *so* like Kate, by the way – she took herself off to the Toni & Guy hair salon and asked for the top stylist to give her a glamorous blow out. But the funny thing is that she had already planned to shave her hair off later that day, all ready for her chemo and, in Kate's very practical way, to avoid having to have her soon-to-be moulting hair all over her pillow. So in a matter of hours she went from having shiny, shaped locks to an all-over bristle from a number one buzz cut. She was brave, tenacious and larger than life.

Marcus called me up one day and told me Kate wanted to make a video for her girls, a keepsake so she could share all of the things she wanted to tell them when they were growing up, a way to say goodbye to them and hand on all those little snippets of motherly advice that she wouldn't get to give them in person. Marcus had organised a professional film crew to come, and I interviewed Kate about her life and the lessons she wanted to share with her girls, who at that stage were only very little and couldn't understand what was happening to their mummy.

It was such a moving time, and a real privilege to be with Kate and help her create a presence for her girls that would last a lifetime. But it was also heartbreaking and surreal to know that, as Kate's body was slowly dying away, I was growing a life inside mine. It was a profound experience. As we brought the interview to a close, we snuggled up on her luxurious sofa, my tummy huge with Indigo and Kate's beautiful head wrapped in an incredible burnt orange and black Hermes scarf.

She turned away from me and towards the camera and, looking straight down the barrel said, 'And you, my girls, you look after your daddy. Because he won't always get it right. And remember that I will always, always love you. Goodbye.'

No one spoke a word. The harsh agony of the moment was brought to a close by the camera man gently and softly calling out, 'Cut.'

As Kate's days were coming to an end, Marcus called me into the palliative care ward to come and say goodbye. That was the first time I'd ever been to the Sacred Heart Hospice; it was calm and filled with an air of kindness. It was nearly mid-October and I was due to give birth any day, so I was enormous. Kate was in and out of lucidity, but when I got there she sat up in bed and called me over.

I stood beside the bed and held her hand and she put her head on my belly, resting for a few moments, like she was listening. She seemed very serene and calm, and after a minute or so of this lovely embrace, she looked up at me and said, 'I've met Indi, she's going to be fine, she's on her way and she'll be here soon.'

And those were the last words she said to me.

It was the strangest experience and yet quite incredible. As she'd risen to embrace my tummy, her eyes were closed and it was as if she sensed Indi was in the room.

I left the hospice later that afternoon and Kate died the following day. The next morning I went into labour with Indi and 24 hours later my precious little girl was born.

It was my first real experience of the death of someone so young and close to me and I saw it, just as I saw birth, as something of incredible beauty and meaning. As much as it was an ending, it was also a beginning. It was as though I saw very clearly what I call the trap door of life. These two incredible forces passed one another along the way on the journey to wherever they were going. It gave me a belief system around life and death, a sense that both happen through the same place. As one departs, another arrives. I was giving birth to my legacy as Kate was leaving hers behind. It was quite overwhelming to have experienced the passing away of a dear girlfriend at the same time as I was welcoming a new little girl into the world, and Kate will always hold a special place in my heart.

Indigo's arrival was much like Jesse's – a very forceful, but wonderful experience, in the bath tub at the Royal Women's Hospital birth centre. But what I hadn't bargained on was just how much having a daughter would impact on me. I'd watched this with Andy and Jesse; they had this 'thing' going on between them, a father–son bond, which was very different to what I saw my role as.

When Indigo was born, it was a totally different experience becoming a mother to a little girl. Instead of the love and over-whelming responsibility I felt raising a happy, grounded little man, I felt this almost primal thing. The love for both was equal, but raising a little boy had seemed far more scary, although for the record, ironically it has been nothing but the complete opposite.

With Indi's arrival, our little family felt complete. Andy and I were totally content, if not a little frazzled. I felt the hugest sense of gratitude for our two healthy little cubs and the lives we were living. We were exhausted, overwhelmed and almost broke, but insanely happy, with an exciting plan on the horizon.

The excitement of Indigo's arrival came at the same time as the build-up for the launch of *Gabriel*. We were pinching ourselves that the day had finally come when this very long project would be born too. As I had given birth to Indi, Andy was giving birth to his cinema debut. It was a huge time for him and we were both really excited about it.

On the night of the premiere we did the red carpet walk and Andy squeezed my hand the whole way. I could tell he was really happy to be in this space. There was a huge buzz about the film and I must admit I was blown away by Andy's enormous presence on screen when the curtains peeled back. I was so proud of him. That he had found that place where he could be this character was pretty awesome, and I reflected on that time of filming with a new baby in the house and all of the craziness of our lives, and yet he pulled it off.

Andy put everything into that role, and I now realised what it had taken for him to do that and who he had become with the courage and balls to go for it while at the same time being a rock at home for us. I knew everything he went through to make this happen, and it reinforced my belief that anything's possible if you put in the work and have the dream.

It was all worthwhile. *Gabriel* was a massive turning point for us. Suddenly lots more offers began coming in and Andy was being asked to audition for roles he never would've been considered for previously. It also led to better representation in the US. The LA manager he'd signed with wasn't so great, but Sam Maydew came into our lives and took Andy on. With Sam's help, suddenly doors were opening without Andy having to knock them down. *Gabriel* was the game changer we'd hoped it would be.

After all of the anxiety of shooting *Gabriel* and not being paid, then waiting two very long years for the film to come out, it was suddenly like a massive energy shift had come upon us. One of the roles Andy was invited to audition for was the TV series *True Blood*, a hot new crime series filmed in the US. Andy got down to the final two, but it was another Australian actor, Ryan Kwanten, who landed the part. He was so close, it had to be his turn next.

During all of this we'd been renting apartments around Sydney, but my mum had come into an inheritance after my grandfather died and she very kindly split it up. So Andy and I were able to buy our first home. We could put our feet on the ground and be settled. It was the first home we owned, a beautiful apartment in Double Bay, overlooking the water.

Everything that we had worked for was falling into place, but little did we know, very soon a new man would enter our life and turn our world completely upside down. His name was Spartacus.

14

Roll the Camera

Life is simple. Everything happens for you, not to you.
— Byron Katie

March 2009

The arrival of Spartacus into our lives was immediate and massive. When Andy was asked to fly to Hollywood to audition, we both felt somewhere deep down in our souls that this role was his. There was absolutely no doubt in either of our minds. So when he rang me from Los Angeles to tell me he'd got the part, he simply said, 'Pack your bags, baby, we're leaving for Auckland in three weeks!'

There was the prospect of the shoot being in either Canada, LA or Auckland, and when you've worked your bum off for as long as we had getting to this point, we were gunning for either of the first two. So when we were told it was Auckland we were a little bit disappointed at first, but in hindsight it was wonderful and we both grew to love New Zealand.

Andy was already well into preparation mode by the time he landed back in Sydney. He was absolutely crystal clear about what he had to do, and I had begun to get the family logistical plan in place to support him and allow him the breathing space he needed to fully immerse himself in becoming Spartacus. We each knew our roles and we snapped into strategic mode to transition our lives straightaway.

The plan was that Andy would fly to New Zealand within days to begin training and rehearsing, while I shut down our life in Sydney. Then the cubs and I would follow when the house was packed up and we were ready to go.

Filming was scheduled to begin at the end of April, but there were weeks of preparation for Andy first. From the moment he arrived in Auckland, before he'd filmed a single scene, he had to hit the ground running. Already he was being treated like a Hollywood superstar. As the show's lead actor, he had an entourage of people at his disposal – a PA, a driver, a masseur and a personal trainer. His food was prepared for him; if he wanted a coffee he just had to snap his fingers and someone was on hand to get it for him. And he was surrounded by a group of sexy, young, energetic actors, all taking the ride of their lives together.

Suddenly he had found himself in a space where he just gets up every morning and doesn't have to worry about me, or the kids, or money. Everything is taken care of, he's made it. It's an intoxicating environment. All he has to focus on is training his butt off to build up the physique he needs for the role; he doesn't have to think about anything other than physically and mentally becoming Spartacus.

For the first three weeks, all of the actors were put through an intensive boot camp to build up their bodies and get them ready to film this very violent period TV show. The first series was titled *Spartacus: Blood and Sand* and it was set in 73 BC. The script focused on Spartacus' life before historical records began.

Spartacus was a Thracian warrior who'd been captured and enslaved by the Romans then placed in gladiator school where he battled to save his life, gain his freedom and be reunited with his wife Sura, who happened to be a breathtakingly beautiful sexy earthen goddess, played by Erin Cummings. All of the characters in the show are Roman or Thracian warriors, gladiatorial and carved to perfection. Spartacus is rippling with muscles, and although Andy was fit when he was cast in the role, he was quite lean and certainly didn't have the muscle bulk required. He trained hard every day to build himself up as quickly as he could; basically, he trained like an Olympic athlete.

The producers chose a very basic, traditional body builder's gym for the cast, an old-fashioned sweat pit with big weights and barbells. They had massive Maori body builders whipping the actors into shape. They were in the gym for hours every day and along with the weight lifting, they were doing crazy things like pulling along giant truck tyres. Then they were off to stunt school to learn how to fight one another, and learn the techniques of fighting on camera and the steps behind the choreographed fight scenes. Although Andy had his own stunt double, a gorgeous guy named Vinny, most of the actors were doing their own stunts, so they spent hours practising manoeuvres to ensure there was absolute authenticity on film. Allan Poppleton was the stunt coordinator and put absolutely 100% into having the fights, stunts and action scenes as true to life as possible. They practised sword battles with Grecian weaponry, and learned stunt combat and how to roll and dive with a metre-long knife in one hand and a cat o' nine tails in another.

It was intensely physical work and Andy was exhausted at the end of every day. But he was also deeply satisfied. For so long he'd been totally immersed in our world, focused on building our little family and doing this relatively mundane job to support us. Now he was surrounded by beefy young blokes and stunt guys and camera crews, all making his dream come true. His new mates are very macho, and yet also unbelievably creative. He's living this amazing life, and this new reality was our future. It was intoxicating because it was so far from the struggle we'd been living and so satisfying because we'd made it happen.

The cubs and I were still back in Sydney, so Andy had no responsibility to anyone other than himself and the producers. He just had to do his job and a huge sense of freedom came with that. For Andy, it was like winning lotto.

Andy made friends very quickly, he always did. He was charming and fun, and he invested time and effort getting to know the guys he was filming with. From the very beginning there was a real sense of camaraderie and friendships were forming that would last well beyond *Spartacus*. He immediately hit it off with a young Australian actor, Jai Courtney. Like Andy, Jai had been landing small parts in shows like *All Saints*, and this was his first Hollywood production too. Andy and Jai shared the same cheeky sense of humour and a kind of boyishness that

In Delhi with my parents and younger sister Lowri, in the late seventies on the hippie trail. We lived in Greece, Turkey, Pakistan, India, Nepal, Afghanistan and Iran before coming back to Wales.

In India with Pushpinder, my faux 'husband to-be'. He was the son of a local hotelier, and after I saw my first splendid Indian wedding on horseback, I wanted to get married. And so on his tricycle with some garden flowers we did! Not sure how pleased his dad was about his beautiful son marrying the hippie kid with white hair.

Me with my doll strapped on, and my lovely friend with her baby brother on her back, while her mother worked.

A little Andy aged three in the back garden at Anglesey.

Andy aged fifteen in 1986 at school in Amlwch, Anglesey.

Andy with his parents Pat and Rob at Bull Bay, Anglesey. We visited them in 1998 before our move to Australia.

With Andy on New Year's Eve seeing in the new millennium at Potts Point, Sydney in 2000.

A big kiss in a moment alone on our wedding day at Gertrude and Alice Bookstore, Bondi in 2001. We are wearing the outfits we bought in New York the day before we were going to marry in Vegas – the day before September 11 and the towers were hit.

At the premiere of *Gabriel* at Fox Studios in 2005, where I had to literally run out of the theatre and feed Indigo, who was born just three weeks earlier.

A beautiful portrait of Andy shot in May 2011, while he was having radiotherapy, and where, for a short while, he seemed remarkably better.

The role that saw the shy engineer transform into a provocative and inspiring actor. Andy as Spartacus, the role that changed his life.

Andy and Jesse Red.

With my cubs Jesse and Indi at our Auckland home while *Spartacus* was filming in 2008.

Despite all the media attention on the promo trail for *Spartacus*, nothing prepared us for seeing this gigantic billboard in Times Square, New York!

We loved everything about LA and imagined it to be a place we would soon be calling home. Andy was a hot but humble newcomer and was literally being pointed at on the street.

With the cubs in LA, where we still had to keep pinching ourselves that we had really made this whole new chapter.

The actor and Andy's best buddy, Jai Courtney (*third from left*), me, director Lilibet Foster (*second from right*), and the manager of Jai, and once Andy, Sam Maydew, on the *Good Morning America* show for an extended interview for the world premiere of the inspiring documentrary *Be Here Now: The Andy Whitfield Story*.

Back in the crazy, wonderful world of LA, taking some down time to photograph the colourful walls of Venice's streets.

Indi finds Andy at the front door, a couple of months after he passed away in 2011.

With my gorgeous cubs in 2016, on a tiny plane to Great Barrier Island, New Zealand.

belied their manly exteriors. Even though Jai was a lot younger than Andy, it was obvious he had a depth and worldliness about him. Both Andy and I believed Jai would go a long way, and since *Spartacus* he's been cast in some incredible productions like the movie *Jack Reacher* with Tom Cruise and *Suicide Squad* with Will Smith and Jared Leto.

Andy and Jai were inseparable on the set of *Spartacus*; they rehearsed together, trained together and did stunts together. At night they'd get together with other cast members and hang out and play Xbox. Seriously, it was hilarious, a 36-year-old playing Xbox, but Andy loved hanging out with these guys and it was a hell of a lot more fun for him than being at home changing nappies!

All of the male actors were on very strict diets. Normally on a movie set it's the female actors who are worried about every gram they eat. But in this case the guys were predominantly the lead roles and they were going to be dressed in little more than skimpy loin cloths every day with every inch of skin on show, so they had to follow a disciplined diet to carve their bodies up in the shortest amount of time. There was no room and no tolerance for the slightest slip-up – no sneaking into the mini-bar at the hotel, no craft services on set. Craft services were the caterers who did all of the food for the cast and crew, and they always had the yummiest food. But for these guys there would be no cakes or biscuits, not even a sneaky little scone for afternoon tea. They were consuming masses of protein bars and shakes and egg white omelettes and tonnes of lean chicken.

Andy would tell me how hungry he was all the time. After hours of really gruelling physical exertion, they'd get these tiny little boxes of food for dinner that had to sustain them, and it really wasn't enough. The meals would barely have fed Jesse, let alone a ravenous man. They ate lots of protein and very few carbs, and the portions were incredibly small for adult men who'd done hours of elite physical training. The dieting was particularly obsessive because the producers had a very clear idea of the look they wanted from the cast and it had to be consistent; they all had to look like these buffed, ripped warriors who'd just stepped out of an ancient Roman fighting ring. There's no doubt it worked; the incredible weight training and dieting got these guys into serious shape in a matter of weeks, but it was a pretty brutal regime.

It was a few weeks before we arrived in Auckland and when we saw Andy again the changes in his body were really noticeable. He had six pack abs and glutes popping out and muscles everywhere – a very obvious transformation. But I could also see that after a few weeks of this intense schedule, the novelty was definitely wearing off. Andy was starving and exhausted; the reality was that learning stunts, training for hours every day and preparing for the role was actually very tough. Nonetheless, he was having a ball, laughing his arse off with all his new mates and literally living the wet dream of a 37-year-old man, father and boy.

The set itself was not very glamorous at all. We were a long way from Hollywood! It wasn't like arriving at Universal Studios each morning. The whole show was being filmed in a series of big old empty industrial sheds on the outskirts of Auckland. The main shed was like a giant aircraft hangar that had been converted into multiple sets for different scenes.

Other sheds with different sets were scattered about this enormous property.

Andy told me that as he drove through the industrial estate on his first day, along a pretty crappy old dirt road towards what looked like a giant tin warehouse, he wondered what he'd led us into. But the magic was definitely within and nothing would dampen his excitement of seeing the *Spartacus* sets for the first time. When he arrived on set everything was still in the early stages of production. Trailers were arriving, big wooden backdrops were being trucked in, dozens of artists were painting props and bits and pieces, costumes were arriving and locations like the gladiators' arena were coming to life.

Sand had been trucked in, huge lights were swinging precariously from the scaffolding and the dolly rails were being laid out in readiness for the cameras. Enormous green screens were being erected for filming scenes that would later be digitally edited. With each progression Andy's excitement built. From the outside, all he'd been able to see were these ageing corrugated iron buildings and lots of huge old carparks. There was really no hint of the magic happening inside. But soon the sheds were transformed into a huge colosseum, a Roman bath house, a Roman battle arena, a prison and all sorts of ancient landmarks. From a freezing cold Auckland winter, Andy would literally step into the simmering heat of gladiatorial 73 BC!

While Andy was in rehearsal phase, I began setting up house in Auckland so when he actually began filming he had a home to come to, rather than the apartment he'd been living in for the past few weeks. Everything we did was geared around supporting Andy and making this transition as smooth as possible.

The final few days before filming were all about getting his look right. Andy had costume fittings. He had his own make-up artist, Georgia Lockhart, on hand to spray tan, trim his beard, fit wigs and get the body make-up right, because it wasn't just a case of rippling muscles, there were prosthetic bits, fake scars and wounds from sword fights. On this job, Georgia's canvas was actually Andy's whole body, not just his face.

Andy spent most of his days in what was basically an over-sized handkerchief! Filming began at 7.30 a.m. sharp every day, and the actors had to be on set ready to go. For Andy to be on set on time, he was up at 4.30 a.m. and he went straight into the make-up chair. From the minute he was up it was all go. It took Georgia about an hour and a half to get his make-up done, then he had to go to the costume department, then sometimes back to Georgia for any last minute touch-ups. Then he was Spartacus, ready to roll. Somewhere along the line he'd squeeze in breakfast as he was going over his lines in his head.

On the first morning Andy was terribly nervous. He'd been in flight or fight mode for days beforehand, and I walked around on eggshells, trying to keep everything calm and supportive at home so there was no added stress for him to deal with, which is a challenge with a three-year-old toddler and a baby. He spent the night before the first shoot going over the script in his mind and checking every detail of the scenes he was filming the next day. He was totally focused on the task and totally immersed in what he was doing, and he felt a great sense of responsibility to everyone on set to honour the opportunity he'd been given.

He was fairly subdued, not at all like 'wow, here we go', and I knew deep down he was very anxious about it all.

'Vash, can I really pull this off?' he asked me.

I could feel the weight on his shoulders. This was a multi-million dollar production with co-stars like John Hannah, who was in *Four Weddings and a Funeral*, and the amazing Lucy Lawless of *Xena: Warrior Princess* fame, and Andy didn't want to let anyone down. He felt that the success of the show rested on him because he was Spartacus and the self-doubt simmered away in the back of his mind even though I constantly re-assured him that he wouldn't have the role if they didn't think he could do it! He was not that little Welsh boy too frightened to step out of his comfort zone anymore; he'd already proven himself. Now he just had to let go of those doubting shackles and be who he knew he could be.

Andy had no need to worry. When he walked onto the set dressed as Spartacus on that first morning of filming, the whole cast and crew spontaneously burst into applause, clapping and cheering his arrival. It was a fantastic moment.

His first scene was a meeting of the Thracians and the Romans, set in a wooden room like a hall, lined with animal skins and lit by torches. Andy was the Thracian warrior rallying his men. He was wearing a long matted wig and looked like he'd been through a war. He circled the other warriors and delivered his first lines.

With desperation and heartbreak in his voice, he shouted, 'To what end? TO WHAT END? The Getae have raided our villages, in the past killed our children. Each time we have pushed them back, only to see them return.'

The director then shouted 'cut' and the first scene was done. Andy Whitfield and Spartacus had arrived.

Filming was intense and the days were very long, Andy left home long before dawn and didn't get home until around 9 p.m. They'd finish filming around 7 p.m., then he'd have to go back to the make-up department so Georgia could remove the layers of dirt, prosthetics and make-up. He was often covered in fake blood or mud, but the worst was the day he had to film a scene with Jai in a makeshift sewage pit. Their characters had been imprisoned by the Romans in a garbage pit so the make-up teams painted up their bodies in a foul, muddy-looking goo which was some sort of indescribable, inedible food concoction, then they had to immerse themselves chest deep in an enormous tank that was made to look like a cave with dead animals and sewage floating in it. It was all fake – except for the dozens of live cockroaches that were set free to crawl all over them. Andy said he could feel the grimy water seeping down through his butt crack!

The whole thing was very tribal and gladiatorial, and the sets were unbelievably realistic. The fight scenes were very graphic, the violence was heart stopping, and the actors could easily do ten or 20 or more takes before the directors would cut. There was blood and guts and gore everywhere. The sex scenes too were disturbingly real; in fact, I sometimes struggled to watch. Every actor left nothing on the table; they pushed themselves to create breathtaking images and it was a very fast paced show.

After I'd been on set the first time I knew I couldn't take the cubs to visit Daddy at work. There were actors walking around with fake limbs hanging off and ripped-up faces. One actor had lost his head in a scene, so he came off set with half a head hanging off!

It was not until a few weeks after they began filming that I got to go on set for the first time and I was totally blown away when I saw Andy in character. He was able to completely let go of himself to become this person. It was breathtaking watching him act and he sent my pulse racing, he was so amazing. It was like watching a child taking their very first steps or riding a bike for the first time, I was so proud of him.

Outside the hangar, it was misty grey Auckland with actors running around in dressing gowns and woolly Ugg boots and huge puffer jackets to keep warm. But inside was an incredible fantasy world that was completely mind blowing and transformative. And it was so much fun! Andy and Jai were kindred spirits. When the cameras weren't rolling they were like naughty little school boys, having the time of their lives with all the other guys. Whatever was happening in those actors' lives, when they stepped on set they became someone else and part of something amazing. There was a lot of mucking around, practical jokes and school boy humour, but they were a team.

When you stepped inside the hangar it was completely pitch black. There was sawdust all over the floor to buffer sound and if you poked your head around the corner of a set backboard, you could find yourself in the middle of a sword fight with body parts and fake blood flying everywhere, or in a hedonistic and extremely realistic Roman orgy with exotic dancers and way-too-lifelike sex scenes! Around every corner there'd be a crew member or assistant director with their fingers up to their lips to remind you to be silent because they were filming on the other side.

I could only get on set every few weeks when I was able to arrange for someone to look after Indi and Jesse. But when I could go I loved it. I'm most at home when I'm in unusual and wonderful places, so I immersed myself in the theatre of it, and soaked up the amazing atmosphere and the energy of the production while I could. To feel a part of that and to know that this was our life going forward was spine tingling.

Although Andy was working very long hours, along with filming he was still training to keep up the muscle bulk. He was doing at least five big gyms sessions a week, which meant there wasn't a huge amount of chit-chat by the time he got home each night. I'd be exhausted from chasing after two toddlers all day and Andy would be pretty wiped out too. And he often still had lines to learn, so he'd bring his tiny box of dinner home, eat a morsel, then collapse into bed ready to be up again when the car arrived at 4.30 a.m.

Every few nights Georgia would come around to our house to re-do Andy's spray tan. It was amusing watching him in a little black G-string getting all browned up. Georgia would always tell me funny things that were happening on set and keep me in the loop. We talked about how graphic and gory the show was, and one time she told me a hilarious story about how she'd pulled into a supermarket on her way home from work one night and couldn't work out why the girl behind the counter was looking at her so strangely. It wasn't until she got home and looked in the mirror that she realised she had dirt smeared all around her neck and fake blood splattered all over her face. She must've looked like she'd just murdered someone!

From the moment Andy met Georgia he raved about her. She was one of those gorgeous human beings who could always read a situation and either remain quietly in the background, or know when to jump in with a brilliant tale of one of the many great projects she had worked on. I absolutely loved her. She's an incredibly talented woman, but so warm and lovely and down to earth; she was one of the few real connections I had to the show because, with two little cubs, I couldn't be on set with Andy very often at all.

Andy and I were best friends, so if it'd just been the two of us, I would've gone in every day and watched him film and just hung out with him. But with two toddlers it was practically impossible, and as filming went on I began to feel quite removed from everything and that was difficult at times. It was a strange time. People from the set would always want to talk to me about how the kids were. It was a bit like when people talk to a tourist in the street and continue to speak in English but raise their voices slightly higher, thinking this might make what they're saying easier to understand.

Where had Vashti gone? I began to feel invisible. I was basically a single parent. I'd wave Andy off each morning and wouldn't get to speak with him or see him again until late at night, by which time he was absolutely wrecked and so was I.

Admittedly, on my very first set visit there was a lot of fuss made over me. I was ushered in by a team of assistants and introduced to everyone as 'Andy Whitfield's wife, Vashti'. It was so strange to have to be introduced; I'd never really been introduced before because everything we'd ever done we'd done together, Andy and Vashti as one. Now the kids and I were referred to as 'the family', and I struggled to cope with that; it implied we weren't part of this, it was them and us. Although this was Andy's and my big adventure, and we both had busted a gut to get here, the people on set saw only Andy.

That moment of introduction really cemented the feeling that Andy and I were living very different lives and that I couldn't be part of the journey. I was an outsider, a visitor, and I would never be part of the team. The invitation to this party was for one person only.

As the weeks went on and the kids and I barely saw Andy, it was clear that, although he was living with us, he was living a totally different life. He completely lived and breathed his role on and off set, effectively shutting everything else out. He shut out the rest of the world, and he became disconnected from the kids and me. He was so exhausted every day that when the adrenalin was switched on, it was for acting and there wasn't much left of him for us. The only glimmer of connection to us during the day was when he went back to his trailer and saw the cute drawing of a spider that Jesse had done for him stuck on the wall; the rest of the time he was completely immersed in the task he had to do: being Spartacus.

It was quite a strange period in my life, and to be truthful a very challenging time for me. I felt like an absolute outsider in

Andy's life and I'd never felt that before. He was expecting me to be the strong, resilient backbone of the family, taking care of the children. Which I was, but I was also in a new country with no friends or family around, struggling with two little children and stuck at home every day feeling completely unsupported.

The cubs hardly saw him, because they were asleep when he went to work and asleep when he came home. They missed their daddy terribly. It almost broke my heart when Jesse said to me one day, 'Can we go and visit Dad now that he doesn't live with us anymore?'

Jesse thought Andy's trailer was his home now.

A month or so into the shoot, there was a three-day break for the cast. I was so relieved that we would get to spend some time with Andy and have a few days away from all things *Spartacus*. So you can imagine the look on my face when Andy came home and said, 'I've been working so hard, do you mind if I go on a road trip with Jai and Erin?'

Now Erin happened to be the very gorgeous young buxom brunette who played Andy's wife on the show. She'd spent days on end with him, discussing the script, their roles and the parallel world that they were all living in. Like young Jai, she had no family of her own, so unlike many of the other actors who relished the thought of heading off to have time with their kids or partners, not for a moment did she think that her new best friend would do anything different than hang with their tight little trio.

Andy couldn't understand why I was so upset about this! I think it was the first time I'd ever really gone off at him, but he'd pushed me past boiling point. He had begun to become so disconnected that he hadn't even registered that his own little Jesse Red believed that his dad had left us and moved out.

All I could think was, 'Okay, this is going to be a big journey ahead!'

I had not only signed up for but also had helped create this adventure, so I told myself to buckle up and hold on to my hat. But my heart hurt.

15

Spartacus and Me

Life's deepest meaning is not found in
accomplishments but in relationships.
— Gary Chapman

The gloss of this glamorous, new, exciting life of ours had worn off pretty quickly once Andy was in the thick of filming. The lure and enchantment of being on a film set in a faraway place began to lose its charm once his gruelling routine was in place. There was always fun to be had on set, though, as the cast and crew shared a sense of humour and a strong feeling of camaraderie bound them together.

Andy's days continued to be long and exhausting. It was cold, wet and muddy in Auckland most days, and by the time he got home to us at night he was freezing, hungry and tired, with very little of anything left to give. He expected that I would and should understand. He had always known me as a strong, capable woman and couldn't understand why I didn't feel grateful to be able to stay at home with the kids. He didn't really see that I was also making big life adjustments.

The absence of Andy and his inability to see my vulnerability in this new life was incredibly challenging and hurtful. I was exhausted from adjusting to a new place and a new routine with the cubs, while at the same time trying to be there for him. Without the warmth and closeness of our friendship, I felt isolated and confused. Close friends seemed very far away, and the absence of Sydney's blue skies and the warm, healing powers of the Australian climate made living in Auckland feel akin to the long dark days growing up in Wales.

In my mind, Andy and I had begun to live separate lives. I could feel us drifting apart. He was totally immersed in *Spartacus* and the daily grind of training, dieting, rehearsing and filming. He was giving his all to everything that he believed in, and he believed he was doing it for us. And he was.

With both Jesse and Indi being so little, the friends I made were other mums from nearby play groups, or from chatting at a muddy park somewhere in Auckland. Some of the production team and crew also made a real effort to include us in social get-togethers, with family picnics and group visits to set.

But here I was, all of a sudden, missing my right hand man, emotionally and physically, and spending most of my time with two little ones. I missed the buzz and diversity that the extrovert in me needed to stay sane. I was very lonely and, as much as I adored Jesse and Indi, who are the light of my life, being stuck at home all day endlessly feeding, snuggling and trying to occupy them could at times be mind-numbing. The flame of creativity and drive that is intrinsically part of who I am was barely flickering.

I remember Andy buying me a new laptop for my birthday and suggesting that I start writing or doing something else creative to give me something apart from the kids to focus on. He had put great thought into it and meant it with love. But at that particular point I could only see his gift as yet another sign that he had no idea what was going on for me, or that what I most needed was him and the chance to connect with other people. I found this disconnection between Andy and me really challenging to deal with because we'd never been like this before. Andy and I had always worked as one; our lives were woven together and this strange feeling of being out of alignment was foreign to our relationship.

Andy was giving this his best shot and he was working so hard to make it all a success for us, but we needed to find a loving and committed way of supporting one another and realigning ourselves. This became blatantly clear one Saturday morning when Andy and I took a rare break together to get a coffee. The kids were with Shona, a nanny who helped us out sometimes, and as we crossed the street to our local café, I had what can best be described as a moment from *The Jerry Springer Show*. We had never yelled at each other before but Andy's exhaustion, which I misread for distance, triggered something in me.

'This is not what I signed up for,' I yelled. 'Losing my friend and the enthusiastic and present dad you were was not part of the deal. I will literally pack the kids and my bags and go tomorrow, if this is what it is going to be like.'

He was furious and couldn't understand what I was talking about initially, but the shock of my outburst and the intensity of the situation showed him how much I was struggling. As we sat across the table from one another, Andy said that he would leave it all behind if that's what it took for us to find our way back to Vashti and Andy.

This was not what either of us wanted, so we needed to find a way to navigate through these rather choppy waters. I was trying hard to understand the intense and ongoing challenge of being in a relationship with an actor. The reality was that sometimes Andy might not only be unavailable emotionally, but also might even be away in another country for months at a time.

It was one of the hardest and yet most inspiring moments in our relationship because I learnt that it was okay to have the occasional conflict in a relationship. But it also inspired Andy and me to seek support and guidance. Most important of all, it taught us that we had to learn how to adapt and grow, and to communicate, honestly, in order to keep our relationship passionately moving forward.

We started seeing a therapist called Suzanne Henderson. She was in her late fifties and from the outset felt like an old family friend. She was warm and sharp, and she got both Andy and me in a heartbeat. She gave us the space to share our feelings but didn't hold back when it came to her feedback. After only a few sessions, it felt like we'd hit the reset button. All of a sudden the huge wall of defence that I had put up around me dropped. Andy insisted that we get a nanny on board more often so that I could spend far more time on set with him and hang out with the crew, and the producers began to factor in time for Andy to bring the kids to the set. Jesse loved this more than anything, especially when he got to go to the stunt gym and practise *Spartacus* roles with the stunt trainers.

Once the kids and I went to watch the filming of a scene with both Andy and Jai in it. It was set in the baths, very dark and candle lit. They had placed three tall chairs for us to sit on. The director, who was also called Jesse, was sitting just in front of us so that he could look at the monitor that was capturing the scene. I had already explained to little Jesse Red that once filming began he must remain completely silent. But barely five minutes into the scene this little voice pipes up.

'Hi! Excuse me, Jesse. Could you please move out of the way because I can't see my dad!'

The whole set erupted into laughter and all of a sudden, as if by magic, we had become a family again.

16

We Asked for Extraordinary . . .

Andy was absolutely exhausted. He was totally depleted, physically and emotionally. His immune system was shot to pieces, which wasn't a surprise given the last few years of this crazy lifestyle of having babies, him being the breadwinner, and burning the candle at both ends trying to juggle acting and engineering. The added stress of going straight into a transformative dieting and physical training regime to get ready for *Spartacus* took its toll.

As filming progressed, Andy picked up a rattling cough that wouldn't go away and his body was becoming increasingly racked with niggling injuries. His back was particularly problematic and he needed physio sessions every week. We put it all down to the intense physicality of the battle scenes they were filming. He had an ache in his lower back that flared up every time he lifted a sword. It seemed like he'd pulled a muscle or injured himself somehow, and that probably wasn't going to go away until he had finished filming and was able to give his body a break. As it turned out, the cough wouldn't go away either and, about halfway through filming the first season, Andy was diagnosed with pneumonia.

It was July 2009 and Andy was ordered by his doctor to have complete bed rest. Much to everyone's relief, it seemed, the producers called a hiatus on production and everyone took a well-deserved break. Andy's doctor told him that he would not clear him to resume filming until he was completely recovered, which was a brilliant circuit breaker for us and proved to be something of a blessing in disguise.

Sensing our mutual exhaustion, the producers of *Spartacus* insisted we have a family break and flew us all to Fiji for a holiday. It was just what we needed and we were so utterly grateful. It honestly couldn't have come at a better time. It was the first time since we started *Spartacus* that we were treated as a whole unit, rather than it being Andy and 'the family'. I truly loathed that title we were lumped under.

The Starz producers very generously sent the four of us to a five-star resort in Fiji. It was magnificent. We were staying on a tiny island off the mainland, so when we arrived in Fiji, we then had to catch a helicopter across to the island. Our chopper was a really cool, old retro-looking machine, like something you'd see in a seventies cop show or *Magnum, P.I.* It was silver with a bright pink hibiscus flower on the side. Andy and I both loved flying in helicopters, and Jesse got to sit up the front near the pilot, so this was a huge adventure for us – which was what *Spartacus* was always supposed to be: an adventure for four, not one.

We landed on the most picturesque little island, it was stunning. We were separate from everyone else on the island, so it was very private, the perfect place for us to heal our hearts and Andy's frazzled body. The only other people on the island were the gorgeous and hilarious Scottish actor John Hannah, who everyone fell in love with in *Four Weddings and a Funeral* and *Sliding Doors*, and his brilliant wife Joanna Roth, who is also an actor. Andy really looked up to John during the filming. He and Joanna had their children Astrid and Gabriel with them, and they were so much fun to be around, it was wonderful and very therapeutic for us.

John and Joanna had been navigating this strange life of filming and being apart from one another for some time. They were old hands at coping with the separation and intensity off camera and the life juggle that this involves, so I felt a sense of connection to them, and their experience and wisdom was very healing for both Andy and me. They gave us a crash course in 'this is the shit you have to navigate'. It was good for Andy to hear it coming from someone else other than me, because I was living in it and I know Andy was so immersed in the role that he couldn't see beyond it. John had become a mentor for Andy; he was the lion giving the cub survival advice and it was so welcome.

It was the first time in ages that Andy and I had time to just be together. He could swim with the kids and muck around in the water. We could go walking up the mountains; we could see one another again and hang out and have fun without having all of this extra pressure in our face. Andy was still watching what he ate because he had to stay in shape, but John and Andy took the boys off for adventures like snorkelling, which was lovely and gave me time to just be and re-group. It took about 48 hours for Andy to shed the tension he was carrying around and relax. Without lines to learn or somewhere to be, he was coming back to being present with us. The old Andy was bubbling to the surface again.

We had this beautiful little cabana hut, and when the kids had an afternoon snooze we sat together and talked about what we were feeling and what we'd learned so far. It had been very easy to get lost in all of the frivolous Hollywood lifestyle happening around us, but we needed to be aligned about what this show was to us, why we were doing it and what it would bring us. The sunshine on our backs and the peace and serenity of Fiji was just what we needed to heal our fractured little hearts and re-set our focus.

Andy was infinitely better after a week in the tropical warmth, but he still wasn't 100% right when we returned to Auckland. The cough had almost gone, although traces of it lingered. But the break in Fiji was probably just the booster we needed to get us through to the end of the season. Then we could take a real break and allow ourselves time for love, laughter and complete renewal.

Andy was back on set filming again pretty much as soon as we arrived back in Auckland. The producers changed his shooting schedule around so it was a bit lighter for a week or so to give him as much rest as possible. He threw himself back into it, but in my heart I knew there was no way he was properly recovered.

Any normal human being with pneumonia would take a lower energy path, but Andy didn't. He went straight back into filming with as much energy as he could muster, straight back into mid-winter, cold, damp Auckland. His back wasn't getting any better and I started to become quite concerned about how often he was going to physio. It was bonkers. He had physio appointments at least twice a week and the sessions weren't alleviating his pain at all.

Andy had been seeing the physio since before he came down with pneumonia, but he still had this constant ache in his back, which was a text book filming injury. If you take a heavy sword and start throwing it around for hours every day, which is what he was doing, you are likely to be a bit sore. There was nothing that gave us any hint that anything was out of the ordinary, apart from the physicality of what he was doing every day, over and over again. His back ache was perfectly explainable. It was a no-brainer that it was just an injury from being on set; it was at the base of his back to the side, near the liver and kidneys, and we just assumed that's what it was. Later, of course, we would learn it was actually a giant tumour wrapped around his spine.

As the final episodes began filming, I could see Andy's spirit lift. There was light at the end of this very long tunnel and he was really looking forward to having a break. He was longing to spend more time with us and I could feel a sense of satisfaction settling on him that he'd achieved what he set out to do. Despite the hurdles along the way, we were going to make it, and we had learned a huge amount about ourselves on his journey that would shape our future.

All of Andy's initial anxiety about not being good enough and worrying about whether he could pull this off was gone; he'd done it and that moment to sit back, soak it up, savour it all and breathe was coming. There was a fairly low-key wrap party, but that's not to say that there weren't a good many drinks slurped. Many of the crew had other jobs to go to and families to reunite with, so as much as it was absolutely a time to celebrate, most people, including us, had their eye on the next exciting chapter. For us that meant Sydney, sunshine, friends, and the glitzy side of the entertainment industry that we had most definitely not yet experienced!

We arrived back in Sydney in early December with the intention of having a family Christmas and New Year, catching up with our friends in Sydney before heading off to Los Angeles in late January for the big red carpet Hollywood premiere of *Spartacus: Blood and Sand*. It was so exciting to be back in Sydney in summer, amid the familiar sounds and smells of home, and to relax in the soothing sense of just being us for a few weeks.

We'd come back to Sydney in such a different state of mind from how we'd left. We left feeling very nervous, anxious and slightly overwhelmed by the huge opportunity ahead of us, but also exhausted and almost broke from the years of struggle to get there. We came back with a TV show under our belts, we had money, and this incredible new platform of life which we'd worked so hard for had come to fruition; we were in a good place.

To have some predictability and continuity in our life was such a relief too. Andy was contracted to do the second series of *Spartacus*, so we knew where we were going and what we were doing for the next twelve months.

We were also about to indulge ourselves in the first bit of real luxury that came with *Spartacus*, a family trip to Los Angeles for the premiere. We were so excited about this big adventure. Andy would be dressed up, looking every bit the sexy, gorgeous young star he was, rather than slopping around in the mud all day. He would be treated like a star – and we would be too. To have that, after taking on such a challenge, made it all worthwhile.

So we had this wonderful time before we left for LA, hanging out in Bondi and going to Redleaf Beach, catching up with friends, popping in to Gertrude and Alice for a coffee, just being around with no pressure at all about where the next dollar was coming from, no struggle. I loved being back in our space with Andy, and the random hugs or little kisses on the cheek that signalled we were good. They were Andy's way of acknowledging me and us. But I noticed every now and then that Andy would go quiet. I'd see him doing a little side stretch or giving his back a rub. He'd be standing there without making a big deal about it but I'd say, 'Are you okay?' and he was like, 'Yeah, it's just that my back's killing me today.'

He did lots of yoga, and went to a sports physio for massages and treatment sessions at least twice a week. Everyone had a quick diagnosis. 'Oh, it's because of this or that,' they'd say. And the rationales always made sense. 'This is what happens when you fall.' Or, 'This is what happens when you stretch this way or that.' We put our faith in everyone because there was always a logical explanation for the pain. But bizarrely, no one was saying to Andy, 'Go and have a scan.' They were just saying, 'I need to see you in two or three days.'

And so that's what he did, with no sense of alarm or concern. At night time, though, Andy was in the worst pain. He'd be in and out of bed, trying to stretch his back, and when he had to lie down he really struggled, it was excruciating for him.

On New Year's Eve 2009, Andy was literally in so much pain he was on the floor doubled over, groaning like a woman in labour.

'Sweetheart,' I said, 'this isn't right. There is something terribly wrong here.'

But he wouldn't go to hospital because he thought with the craziness of New Year's Eve there would be too much of a wait and it would be too much hassle. Clearly he needed some pain relief, so we drove across town to an old friend I knew would have some pot. Andy smoked a joint, but by this time he was crying he was in so much pain, and the marijuana gave him no sense of relief at all.

He toughed it out through the night, despite me pleading with him to go to hospital. Bizarrely, the next day he seemed okay and didn't mention anything more of it. Maybe the joint was just what he'd needed after all and the pain relief was simply delayed. Or maybe deep down, with only one week to go before we flew out to LA for the press junket, he didn't want any diagnosis that would jeopardise the trip. I don't know.

But a week later we were boarding a flight to Los Angeles to begin the publicity campaign for *Spartacus*. The four of us were going, and we had business class seats, so we spread ourselves out across the plane and enjoyed the absolute luxury.

We were greeted at LAX by the driver of the most enormous black stretch limousine you could imagine. Jesse's eyes nearly popped out of his head when he saw our name on the little board he was holding up – this wasn't for George Clooney or the President of the United States, it was for us! The limo took us to our home for the next three weeks, which we lovingly came to know as the Porno Mansion. It was an enormous mansion in Beverly Hills, which was apparently where stars stayed when they were in town. No expense had been spared to look after us on this trip. Apparently a very famous actor, who shall remain nameless, had recently stayed there before us and had been very difficult to deal with. So our little family, who were gobsmacked and bemused by the ostentatiousness of it all, were quite easy and charming by comparison.

Everything about the house was extreme and overdone. It had a huge ballroom, a gigantic spiral staircase with overly detailed and ornate balustrades, and lots of gold and bronze as far as the eye could see. The huge black marble bath could fit eight to ten people, and it wasn't a stretch to imagine that eight to ten or more had been in it on more than the odd occasion. The house also came with its own butler, Nestor, who was there to help us with anything we needed.

The launch of the show was as huge as any mainstream US film release, with all of the red carpet premieres and A-list parties that you could imagine. After the relentless months on end of gruelling filming, training and dieting in rainy Auckland, the abundance of luxury, glamour and time to eat, play and be acknowledged in sunny LA was eagerly lapped up by all of us. And Andy relished the opportunity to step out of playing the tortured warrior that Spartacus was and swap his metal breast-plates and skimpy loin cloths for something a little more grown up and sophisticated.

We had a babysitter on hand, so I could accompany Andy to the big events. When he did television interviews like on *Chelsea Lately*, I was able to sit in the green room with him. It was fun to be able to share these moments and do these things together.

Andy's back appeared much better while we were away; it didn't seem to be bothering him like it had been. Whether the pain had lessened or he was just getting used to it, I'm not sure, but he didn't mention it at all. I often wonder whether the adrenalin and excitement of what was happening in LA meant he just wasn't conscious of it. He was living very much in the moment, and lapping up the huge amounts of affection and attention that were being gifted to him.

Andy did heaps of interviews. There were magazines and newspapers, radio and television. But nothing prepared us for the excitement of seeing his striking gladiatorial image on a gigantic billboard in Times Square. There he was, high above the rushing crowd below, on a billboard the size of a skyscraper.

Jai had also finished filming by now, so we said to him, 'Come out here!' We had plenty of room for him to stay. It was great having him around during the day. If Andy had any down time, they'd pull out their guitars and have these massive jam sessions together. They were inseparable and I loved their friendship; it was really wonderful. And the cubs and I had a great time hanging out with Jai too.

Before long though, I began to notice that Andy seemed very tired. One afternoon when we were upstairs in our bedroom,

I was sitting on the edge of the hideously ugly, kitsch four-poster bed and noticed Andy do this kind of twitch thing with his back. There was a slight grimace, so I said, 'Are you okay?'

'Yeah, yeah,' he answered. 'The pain hasn't been so bad this week.'

But his whole life force seemed really low. His eyes weren't sparkling in the way they normally did. He was fine and smiley and lovely, but there was a sense of fatigue shadowing him, and that's when I first felt something was different. I really didn't know if it was just exhaustion, because I could still tick off a lot of reasons why he would be feeling that way.

There was a media premiere of *Spartacus* where they showed the first episode at a theatre on Sunset Boulevard. We walked the red carpet and watched the show together. Andy chuckled the whole way through it and whispered to me, 'We did it, baby!'

He wasn't punching the air, it was more a subtle sense of fulfilment that we'd made our dream come true. The audience reaction was overwhelming. Everyone loved that first episode; it was violent and sexy. And the media loved Andy, not only because he was a fresh new face on the scene but also because he was incredibly humble.

Jai was with us the night *Spartacus* went to air on television in the United States. It was 22 January 2010 and the show was an instant hit – 'television's new guilty pleasure', as one critic described it. That was the moment everything really came to life. Within 24 hours of it airing, the show had been sold into Canada, the Netherlands, the UK, Poland, Hungary, Ireland, Brazil, Turkey, Italy, Pakistan and Slovenia. Over 1.5 million people watched the premiere episode and it averaged 1.3 million viewers for every episode afterwards. Suddenly, literally over-night, we had gone from obscurity to stardom. Andy was being recognised on the street, the paparazzi were following him (that was bizarre!) and he was the toast of the town.

A few days after the premiere, we were invited to a party hosted by Jay Z and the American rapper Ludacris at the famous restaurant, Mr Chow, in Beverly Hills. It was hilarious. We were the *only* white people there and it was the most booty-licious, sexy crowd I have ever seen. There was a huge white Bentley with gold trim parked out the front of the restaurant and you could smell the marijuana from across the street. We felt so out of our depth, but people were coming up to get Andy's autograph or have a picture taken with him. It was an amazing night.

We were devastated when the time came for us to leave Los Angeles. We hated leaving the mansion. We loved LA and could imagine ourselves living there. We'd spent some time looking around Santa Monica and Malibu, checking out different places to get a feel for what it would be like if we moved there after filming the next series of *Spartacus*. We were beginning to think about the next phase.

Our farewell to LA was with heavy hearts. We really didn't want to go, but we were hopeful we'd be back there again soon.

It was hardly tough coming back to beautiful Sydney, although we only had three weeks before Andy was due back in New Zealand to start filming Season 2. When we got home, both Andy and I noticed a different attitude around us. People were acknowledging what he had achieved. It was like, 'Wow, you did it!' and that was really nice, especially from our friends. Los Angeles is a very superficial town and you don't have to search too far to find someone willing to pat you on the back and tell you how great you are, but it really meant something when it came from the people we loved and respected.

Within a week of us coming home Andy's back pain began to resurface. He'd been going to a friend Aaron, who is a holistic personal trainer, and during one of their sessions to get Andy back in shape for *Spartacus*, he told Aaron about his back. Aaron said, 'Why don't you just go and get a scan and get it sorted out? What are you waiting for?'

So Andy was like, 'Oh, okay.' Simple as that. Andy felt a bit foolish that he hadn't done it much earlier, and Aaron was the first person who'd suggested it, but it made perfect sense after months of following the 'have a treatment and come back in two days' routine.

Andy went to a sports doctor on the North Shore. He'd had a scan and was sitting in the office with the doctor when he called me. I will never forget it. I was standing at the kitchen sink of the rental house, packing stuff away for New Zealand and thinking about all of the things that had to be done. Jesse was going to start school when we returned to Auckland and, while it was a really exciting time, there was a lot to organise. I saw Andy's number come up on the phone and in this strange sort of voice he said to me, 'Babe, I think I'm in trouble.'

I was a bit puzzled. 'What do you mean, darling?' I asked, thinking he'd done a disc in his back or something.

And he said, 'I think I've got cancer.'

Part Five

THE LONG GOODBYE

17

I've Got Cancer

Life is either a daring adventure or nothing.
— Helen Keller

11 February 2010

When Andy says, 'Babe, I think I'm in trouble', I am not thinking cancer, it just doesn't even come into my mind. Not one bit.

I'm thinking, 'Bugger, it's a ruptured disc or a fractured vertebra' – something that might require momentarily pressing pause on our lives, but not cancer. In the split second he told me, my brain just couldn't process what he was saying.

'What do you mean, Andy?' I asked.

And he said, 'I think I've got cancer.'

There it was, those same words again.

My brain did get it then. There was no mistaking what he'd said. I just froze. My mouth and body wouldn't move, and

I started to feel pins and needles in my head. All I could manage to say to him was, 'Stay there, I'm coming now.'

I ran over to Annie, our neighbour, sort of half dragging, half carrying Jesse and Indi with me. I knocked on the door and somehow through a flood of tears I managed to get out, 'Annie, I think Andy has cancer. I need to go.'

And I left the cubs with her, jumped into a taxi and belted across Sydney as fast as I could.

I ran up the pathway and burst into the clinic and there was Andy sitting in front of me, his face sickly white. It was a tiny little waiting room with a couple of wilting pot plants in one corner and a pile of dog-eared magazines on a coffee table. The door to the doctor's office was open and he ushered us in as soon as I arrived. On the wall was a very basic lightbox with the scan of Andy's spine lit up. I could clearly see the white outline of his skeleton and these shadowy black patches everywhere. Absolutely everywhere.

The doctor was a lovely man. He simply said, 'I think this needs more focus than I can give.'

He referred us to an oncologist at North Shore Private Hospital. As soon as we got home, we made an appointment. They sent Andy for an MRI the next day and we were to see the oncologist a day later. We were both in a state of shock; the only other time in my life I'd ever felt like that was when we were in New York during 9/11. In the hours after the towers were hit we went through a strange sort of frozen-in-time twilight period of not knowing what to do next or what was ahead – of wondering if it was all real or whether the situation was going to become something even worse.

Other than my beautiful friend Kate, we'd never had anyone we loved go through anything like this and we never thought anything like this *could* happen to us. So we were in a weird void, waiting until we could see the oncologist and get a handle on exactly where we were at. In the meantime we were momentarily helpless. There was nothing we could do, no plan we could make, we just had to wait.

The oncologist was also a lovely man, very distinguished with greying hair. He had a soft, calm voice, was very wise and articulate, and he didn't beat around the bush.

'I'm very sorry,' he said, 'this is a shocking situation because you have Stage IV non-Hodgkin lymphoma. It is extremely aggressive and advanced. The problem is you have a huge mass wrapped around your spine.'

With some positivity, he continued, 'However, if you're going to get cancer, then this is the one you want. You're young and fit, and it is absolutely treatable. But if you don't begin treatment straightaway the tumour will render you unable to walk within three weeks. The position of the tumour is such that it is crushing your spine and it will do irreparable damage. It's already pressing on your spinal column, which is why you are in agony – it is squashing the centre of your nerves.

'It's damaging you now,' he continued, 'but if it presses anymore you could lose the ability to walk.'

That was the most horrific thing we could hear. The thought of being in a wheelchair for the rest of his life was terrifying for Andy. We hadn't even factored in the obviously worse scenario.

The doctor recommended that we get on with our lives and get treatment booked in as soon as possible. But in my state of shock and anxiety I blurted out, 'But he is supposed to start filming in New Zealand in a few weeks!'

We also had Jesse booked in to start school in Auckland.

After a couple of calls, the doctor put us in touch with an oncologist in Auckland. He agreed that if we had a home set up there and Andy was comfortable and happy, there was no reason why he couldn't have the treatment over there.

Although Sydney was home and Andy could've had treatment in Australia, it seemed nonsensical not to return to New Zealand. With Jesse ready and excited to start school, and our house all set up, everything was organised and familiar. It also, and perhaps most importantly, meant that Andy could stay connected to his adopted NZ family that the huge cast and crew of *Spartacus* had become, which would prove to be an important morale booster for him. New Zealand is a very nurturing place and the Kiwis are such wonderful people. During filming the year before, we'd found them to be very respectful and supportive, and it seemed like the right place for us to be.

The doctor then very wisely repeated his instruction for us to get on with our lives.

'This treatment is straightforward. Let your son go to school, and forge on with your lives around the cancer. Commence the treatment and continue on as if this is going to be the best case scenario. I can't guarantee the outcome,' he said, 'but you are in the percentage that has every chance of beating this. But don't stop living.'

It was the best advice we could have received, so with those words, 'Go on living your life, but factor this in', we did just that.

In the car on the way home, I said to Andy, 'Baby, we asked for extraordinary and this is what we got! Clearly, making it to Hollywood wasn't enough. Life has decided to throw something far more spiritual and challenging and uncontrollable at you to see what you can do with it.'

At home we tried to be as normal as you can be when you've been told you have cancer. For the rest of that day, Andy just wanted to be with the kids and hang out. He was glued to my side, so we stuck close and lived in the moment. We were both very calm, if not a little quiet, but there were no histrionics even though neither of us slept that night and I know Andy must have had so much going through his mind.

He never verbalised the words out loud, but I know he was thinking, 'Why didn't I get a scan before? Could I have prevented being in this place now? Why is this happening to me?'

Whereas my mind was racing with the logistics of what needed to be done. I was lying next to him in the same fight or flight place thinking, 'Am I packing up the house? Am I flying with Andy or going later? How can we get there as quickly as possible?'

Not at any stage did we think, 'Oh my gosh, is Andy going to make this?' That never came into my mind, nor Andy's. We never, ever questioned that the treatment wasn't going to work. It was more about putting the first foot forward, then charting a path to dive straight into the centre of this new situation. It was about embracing this chapter we didn't predict and moving with it as best we could.

The next day we rang the oncologist in New Zealand and started the process. Andy needed to get over there as quickly as possible. He got on the phone and rang family and friends and his agent Sam Maydew to let him know what was going on. Then we got on with business. The amazing thing was that we realised we just had to let people know because they would step in and help us, and we felt supported right from day one. Sam immediately took control of the *Spartacus* end of things. He got a press release ready, let the producers know, and sorted out that side of our lives so I could concentrate on Andy and the cubs.

In the first few days, I noticed that Andy needed me to make decisions for him. He wasn't wanting to dwell on any of the very important, but in the scheme of things quite small issues; he just wanted to hang out with the kids and know that things were under control. It wasn't about me being all stoic; it was more about the practicalities of getting a plan locked in place for Andy, me and the kids, so he could relax, trusting that everything would be alright.

So within two weeks of diagnosis, we'd moved back to Auckland and were ready to confront cancer head on. Dr Richard Doocey was the oncologist we'd been referred to in Auckland. We were both a bit shocked when we first saw him because he looked younger than us! He was in his early forties and had very kind eyes; he was very warm and personable, and immediately struck us as someone very genuine. He didn't look like a stiff, starchy type of doctor who was just going to give us a mouthful of meaningless statistics. At our first appointment, he pretty much laid out where we were at.

'Your cancer looks like it hasn't been there that long, but the tumour has spread extraordinarily fast,' he explained. 'But you're 37 and you're fit. There's no reason why you shouldn't be one of the 65% who survive this type of cancer and go on to live a healthy, happy, normal life.'

'NORMAL!' we both laughed.

'We don't do normal,' I said. 'We've only ever asked for extraordinary, so clearly we are getting extraordinary!'

Of course we would never know for sure, but I believed the cancer started to present itself around the time Andy had pneumonia, which was also when the pain in his back began. Non-Hodgkin lymphoma can be difficult to diagnose because the symptoms can be attributed to other things like weight loss and fatigue, both of which Andy experienced. So to be honest it's a waste of time even trying to guess about these things, but in my heart I felt the cancer had been there since before we went to Fiji.

As the shock dissipated, we collectively rolled up our sleeves and said, 'Okay, let's do this', both of us knowing that somehow the lessons we were to learn from this unexpected new chapter in our lives would unveil themselves at the right time. We left Dr Doocey's rooms feeling hopeful, with a plan in place. Doctors never make false promises and I think he genuinely believed that we would come out of this on top. We had a sense that we were heading in the right direction; we had to embrace it (we had no choice!) and deal with it as best we could.

Behind the scenes, the *Spartacus* crew were working out how to reschedule filming. They decided to call a temporary hiatus on production so they could write a new script for a prequel to the first series, which could be filmed while Andy was having treatment. This meant the crew could keep working and there would be a new show to tide the hungry *Spartacus* audience over until the filming of Season 2 could take place. Some scenes Andy had already shot for Season 1 could be used to give him some presence in the prequel too.

For Andy, there was a lovely reassurance knowing that he had *Spartacus* waiting for him when he was ready to come back. He knew he had the whole cast and crew behind him. He just had to relax, rest and go through treatment before picking life back up again. So instead of feeling hugely anxious about returning to New Zealand, we were back to what we knew. The familiarity of Auckland, the friendships we'd made there, and the quiet camaraderie of knowing that the *Spartacus* cast and crew just down the road were keeping everything rolling, were just what Andy needed.

That said, cancer did throw up some surprises. The first of which was deciding what we should do with Spartacus' sperm! We hadn't contemplated having any more children, but Dr Doocey warned us that Andy's chemo would likely render him infertile. He suggested storing some of Andy's sperm as a precaution, in case we decided to have more children some day.

Okay then, we thought, that can't hurt. So off Andy and I went to a nearby fertility clinic. Now, I must admit that when Dr Doocey suggested we go along to a fertility clinic to make a deposit, if you know what I mean, I really had no concept of what this would entail. All I could think of, in my childish, pathetic, probably slightly delirious frame of mind, was something straight from a Benny Hill sketch. You know, the crazy music, a nurse with gigantic knockers and a cheeky G-string under her uniform kind of thing. I'm thinking it's all very nudge-nudge wink-wink stuff – very immature, I know, but hey, we had cancer . . . a girl's got to find a laugh somewhere.

I'd been teasing and goading Andy about it all morning, lovingly of course. But when we arrived at the clinic, it was all very serious and super new and glossy and nice, and I was kind of surprised. Andy was being very calm and sweet and slightly apprehensive about it all because he'd never had to go into a room and, frankly, knock one out into a cup! And he was a little bit nervous too, and there I was cracking jokes and carrying on like a naughty school boy.

But we get into the lift to go up to the fourth floor and we're sharing the lift with two other couples who are obviously trying very hard to get pregnant. They're very well dressed and looking lovely, and you can feel the weight in the air of these people going on a massive journey to start a family. So my silly, Benny Hill/ *Carry On* movie, smutty double entendre smirking is brought to a grinding halt until the lift stops. They get out and go to the left, and we are ushered to the right down a very long corridor towards a wooden door. As we're walking along I start to get the giggles again. I can feel my body shaking with laughter and I'm losing it, to the point of inappropriateness. Andy is saying to me, rather curtly, 'Pull yourself together, Vashti. Stop it!' and giving me a dead elbow. And then he starts to giggle. I don't know what was going on with me, but the more I tried to stop laughing the more I laughed.

We got to the end of the corridor and there was a little counter with a glass window, which we slid open. And there before us was not the big, curvaceous, sexy, red lipped G-string wearing Benny Hill nurse that I'd imagined. Instead, we were greeted by a short, very old, spotty faced and rather effeminate gay nurse in blue surgical scrubs. And that was when I lost it completely. I was laughing so hard Andy was kicking me under the bench.

The nurse, who was in fact a very sweet man, gave Andy a plastic jar and took us into a little room. He asked me if I wanted to stay. The thought of me hand shuffling Andy into action was too hilarious. There was no chance! So he explained to Andy that there were some magazines, and unfortunately the video wasn't working but if he needed any more support to just let him know.

The thought of Andy coming out to ask for help completely broke me up. I was laughing so hard that Andy said, 'Vashti, you need to leave the building. I'll meet you in the car.'

So I'm kicked out of the sperm bank! I wait in the car and I'm thinking, 'What is taking him so long?' I don't want to put too much of a fine point on it, but I know my husband intimately and I know how long 'it' takes, and this is taking three times as long as it should.

When Andy eventually arrived back at the car I was like, 'What took you so long?'

'Vashti, it was so horrible,' he said. 'When I opened the drawer, there were three magazines for me to use. One was a gay men's porn mag, one was S&M with people dressed doing things with things I could never imagine doing, and the pages of the last magazine were stuck together and I couldn't open it to where there was anything sexy!' Then he added, 'And all I could think about was you laughing at me!'

I was in hysterics, I honestly don't think I have ever laughed so hard. But it was mission accomplished. Spartacus had banked his sperm.

Our next task to tick off – beginning chemo – would be a lot less fun. This was our entree into the strange things chemo would bring into our life, but I think Andy realised that there was no way I was going to walk around sombre and sad through all of this. No matter how strange the situation, we would find humour in it and deal with it in our own way.

Andy started treatment in April. Dr Doocey put him on a fairly gentle chemo treatment plan to begin with. Every fortnight we went to Auckland City Hospital and we'd spend half a day tucked away in a little room at the back of the hospital, this miracle chemical cocktail dripping through Andy's system. We were both very nervous about the first treatment and held hands walking through the hospital corridor. But as much as we were both anxious, we were also a bit excited. It felt like we were doing something about the cancer; we were taking control of the situation and doing something positive to get rid of the tumour. It was a bit like a long haul flight; every session would get us a bit closer to the end.

We were in a state of ignorant bliss, I think, happy to have this underway and not fearing what was to come because we didn't know. For Andy, the prospect of his back pain going away was a relief too. He had the same oncology nurse each time he went for treatment; she was a slim girl with short spiky hair and an almost Scottish accent even though she was a Kiwi. She was a real live wire and absolutely hilarious, and we had some very funny conversations about how much she liked to drink whisky.

Andy would lie down on the bed and the nurse would plug him into the chemo machine. There was a little bookshelf alongside, with books like Lance Armstrong's *It's Not About the Bike*, and a few by other cancer survivors. I sat next to Andy and kept him company. We talked about a lot of things over those few hours, then we'd go home and Andy would rest and I'd snap straight back into 'Mummy' role.

Because his chemo was very mild, Andy was okay at the beginning. He'd get tired and nauseous for a few days, then he would pick up and be able to do gym workouts. We'd go for walks and he could play with the kids. He slept more and we were careful about his weight. Usually about three days after the chemo he'd be at his worst, then he'd lift right up again. By the time he was back to his normal self, he was in for chemo again.

I'd braced myself for something far worse because I remembered my friend Kate lying in my lap and crying, 'I don't think I can do this' while she was going through chemo. But Kate's treatment was far worse than what Andy was going through.

In many ways it was a really special time for us. *Spartacus* was doing its own thing, so Andy didn't need to worry about that, which freed up headspace for him to just be. He spent a lot of time with the kids and me. This was when he really got to know Indi; they firmly bonded because he was present for her, which was lovely. He took her to the park and pushed her on the swing, and he'd sit on the floor and read to her or play with her.

Andy had his own plan in place for how to handle this. He was keeping fit and utilising the time to tick off some things he'd been wanting to do. He did a writing course, and he wanted to do a photography course too. I encouraged him to keep himself busy as much as possible and we looked at this time through a prism of absolute positivity. Here was a great chance for Andy to do some things to nurture himself.

Andy's treatment started in April, and in May Jesse started school. In New Zealand you start school when you turn five, no matter what time of year it is, so after celebrating his birthday Jesse was off to school. We were all so excited! He was enrolled at Bayview Primary, literally across the road from our house in Herne Bay, which is a really lovely part of Auckland. We were renting a very nice Edwardian house with a beautiful cottage garden, up on the hill above Cox's Reserve and the gorgeous little beach on Cox's Bay.

Jesse's teachers were well aware of what was happening at home. We'd briefed them before he began so they could help us make starting school as smooth as possible for him. But we didn't need to worry. He settled in easily and they were wonderfully supportive of him. We both walked Jesse across the road to school for his first day. He absolutely loved it and seemed quite happy to wave us off!

Andy had undergone two rounds of chemo by then and his hair was gone. I'd cut his hair short before the first treatment, but the impact of chemo is cumulative, so after the second round his hair had completely fallen out. We didn't tell the kids he had cancer; we told them that Daddy had something wrong with his blood and was going to see a special doctor to have special treatment for the next few months. We reassured them that Daddy's hair falling out was a normal part of what was happening.

They didn't know any different. Indi was nearly three years old, and Jesse had only just turned five; their little minds couldn't understand the disease, they were just excited that Daddy was going to be around during the day for them to play with. Which he was. All of a sudden we had Andy around all the time, and he was very gentle and very patient. He soaked up every minute with the kids that he could, and he and I got to hang out as

Andy and Vashti, which we hadn't done for a long time. It was so nice, and we were able to plan what we would do together in the future. There was zero thought that the treatment wouldn't work; the cancer was just a blip on a very big radar.

Andy kept having chemo every fortnight and, as the treatment went on, so too the effect on him was gradually building. He had twelve sessions lined up and by the middle of them he was very tired and really feeling the full effects of it. He'd lost the ripped muscle look he'd built up from the *Spartacus* training, and he'd also lost a fair bit of weight, because chemo really drains you. His hair had gone but he still had his eyebrows, and although he was thinner, his face still looked quite chiselled. Towards the end of the treatment I started to notice that little crow's feet began to appear on his face and the colour of his skin was yellowing. I could see that he'd slightly aged too, but he was still ridiculously handsome.

The first three or four days after each chemo treatment were the most intense. Andy would sleep for most of it. He often felt queasy and it was really hard to get him to eat; he had that metallic taste in his mouth that a lot of chemo patients get, and nothing tasted good or right. I made broths and simple things he could eat, and I was really diligent with juices for him; we were right into the juicing thing. His sense of taste was really heightened; he could pick up the slightest hint of salt and foods he normally ate now were too rich, so it was back to very plain, basic food. He couldn't eat anywhere near the amount he once did, but he never looked emaciated.

The most extraordinary thing though was that almost immediately after the first treatment Andy's back pain started to subside. By the second treatment it was virtually gone.

The tumour around his spine was shrinking, which was totally liberating for him. To take the pain out of the equation gave Andy freedom to function without holding him back. We both noticed how much better he could walk and move, and his spirits lifted too because we knew if the tumour was shrinking, the treatment was working. He had been very stoic about it all, but I can't imagine how much pain he'd been enduring every day for almost twelve months with this wretched tumour strangling his spine. When I think about it now, I am in awe of how he was able to film all of those action scenes when the pain must have been so excruciating and clearly far worse than any of us had thought.

Every couple of weeks a batch of fan mail would arrive from Andy's agent, which really gave him a boost. People would send cards and letters, or we'd get a random parcel of hats that someone had knitted, or photos from complete strangers who would share their very personal stories of cancer. At times it was overwhelming because the compassion and care people had shown was quite breathtaking, but equally it was lovely knowing that so many people cared. The nicest thing was the acknowledgement that Andy had touched people's lives. He'd worked so hard to build this role in *Spartacus* and it was a tangible sign that the work he'd done was valued by others. It also meant that he hadn't just disappeared; people were in awe of this great warrior having to fight a different battle and that was so powerful. It lifted Andy's spirits no end and although he never said as much, I suspect it reaffirmed his resolve to knock this cancer out and get back to doing what he loved as soon as possible.

For me, one of the toughest things to cope with was the competing demands on my attention and love, and the juggle of trying to be all things to everyone. I'd always struggled giving the children to anyone else to look after when they were little. When Jesse was a baby he barely left my side and I was there for him constantly, which I expected to do for Indi too. However, I needed to put her into day care when Andy was having chemo, so I could take him and be with him. She loved it, mind you, and always looked forward to those few hours every couple of weeks. But I felt this intense anxiety about leaving her, and as we'd head into the last half hour or so of Andy's treatment I could feel the tension building within me and a desperate need to get to her as quickly as possible. I was torn between needing to get Andy home to rest and nurture him, and to be there for my babies.

It was an emotional and physical balancing act. Giving everything I had caring for the children and Andy, sometimes I felt like I was split down the middle. I would go through deep feelings of being very present and in the moment with Andy and the children playing on the living room floor, or visiting the botanical gardens or the beach. At other times the overwhelming knowledge of Andy having cancer and all that entailed would hit me. The moments when we were both really present were some of the best moments we shared as a family, but equally there were days of great anxiety, with me feeling like I was completely stretched trying to be all things to everyone; it was frustration and helplessness at the same time. I was juggling being a wife, mother, carer, nurse, nanny, nurturer, cook, cleaner, driver, chief morale booster, best friend, lover and listener, and I was exhausted. But in hindsight, this was a breeze by comparison to what was to come.

*

One Saturday morning I had to take Jesse to a little friend's birthday party and I told Andy that I'd do the grocery shopping while Jesse was at the party. So I dropped Jesse off and on my way back to the supermarket I spotted a tattoo parlour. This particular day I had been feeling like the world was closing in on me, and the relentless daily grind had caught up with me. Andy had endured a bad week and he was feeling exhausted and fragile. And, for the first time, I was beginning to feel very afraid.

I walked into the tattoo parlour and I got the word 'breath' inked under my arm, because I thought if I don't remember to take a breath, I'm not going to make it through this. The tattoo pen didn't hurt at all scratching into my skin, and it didn't detract at all from what was churning me up inside. Afterwards it did remind me to pause and breathe, and that was poignant for me because in that moment I could disconnect.

When I got home, Andy could see the sterile plastic on my arm and with a very cheeky grin he asked, 'What's that, Vashti?'

Very nonchalantly I said, 'Oh, it's just a little thing I needed to mark this moment and to remind myself that whether it's the beginning, the middle or the end of this journey, all we need to do is breathe. It's the first thing we do when we come into the world and the last thing we do when we go out; it's the key to all wellbeing.'

Andy burst out laughing. 'Vashti, you are the only person I know that went to a kids' party and came home with a tattoo.'

He thought it was absolutely hilarious but, for me, it was just what I needed to remind myself every now and then not to fall into a place of feeling overwhelmed. We were in this together,

I was side by side with my gorgeous best friend, and it would all be okay.

Not long after that I got myself a personal trainer and did kickboxing sessions. I literally kicked the shit out of him for 90 minutes a couple of times a week. If the truth be known, I went berserk, because I was letting go of all of the stress and anxiety that had been building up in me over the past months. I trained so hard when I was in the gym people would come up to me and ask, 'What are you getting ready to compete in?'

I felt powerful when I was in the gym, I felt like I had control, whereas life beyond the gym was very much out of my control. I tried to focus on all of the things we should be grateful for, and despite the grey cloud of cancer there was a lot to be thankful for. We were lucky that we didn't have to go out and work during the day. I can't imagine what it would be like if you had to work full time to support your sick partner and family, as well as being the carer who supports everyone at home. It would just be horrendous.

We were also very lucky that we were taking this journey together, step by step, supporting one another as best we could. During one of Andy's chemo sessions, I could overhear a doctor having a conversation with the man in the cubicle next to us. He was a big strapping Maori fellow; we'd seen him come and go sometimes and he was always on his own. I heard the doctor ask him, 'Have you told your family yet?' and he replied, 'No, I haven't.'

'But you do realise you may only have about six weeks left?' the doctor said.

The man replied, 'I know.'

The doctor was insisting that he tell his family and he said, 'I know, I know' in a very unconvincing tone. My heart was in my mouth, I felt such gratitude that we weren't in that place. I felt so sad that he was so alone and that for whatever reason he couldn't tell the people he loved the most. I watched him walk away down the corridor that day and it was like slow motion time lapse; he was there one minute and gone the next. I watched until he was gone and it was the first time I allowed my mind to think, 'What if that was Andy?' It was ridiculous and impossible, of course. I realised how grateful we were that we weren't in his shoes, we were surrounded by love and support. But still it struck me how lonely this journey can be for some people, and how awful it would have been for that man's family that they didn't know what he was going through.

Andy was having regular scans to see whether the treatment was working or not, and after his sixth session, about halfway through, the scan showed the cancer had gone down by 75%. The cancer was Stage IV at diagnosis. Now, after six chemo sessions, the mass that was in Andy's abdomen had almost disappeared. This really correlated with how Andy was feeling, because he was feeling quite well and the pain in his back had gone away. This was such incredible news. It gave us both a serious energy and adrenalin boost to keep going through the final rounds of chemo. It validated what we were doing, and gave us the strength and resolve we needed to carry Andy through the rest of the treatment.

Quietly I'd been hatching a little plan to surprise Andy and take his mind off what was ahead. I'd organised for Jai to come and stay with us for a few days. Jai's character in *Spartacus* was killed off at the end of the first season, so he wasn't in

New Zealand filming, but I knew that a visit from him would be just the thing.

When the doorbell rang and Andy opened up to see Jai standing there, he was ecstatic. They hugged and cried and there was complete joy on both of their faces. That was the first time I really noticed the impact of the chemo on Andy physically. He didn't look any different but his life force was that much less. Jai was so full of life that he felt like an enormous presence by comparison to Andy, who was understandably very fatigued and fragile by then.

Andy and Jai had a few days together and it was a really beautiful time. They were kindred spirits and just having Jai around lifted Andy. The playful boyishness between them was a lot of fun, and I think it gave Andy a sense of normality. A few days of laughter was just what we all needed.

During Jai's stay, Andy asked Jai if he would be Indi's godfather. We were all down at Cox's Reserve one afternoon, mucking around at the pebble beach, when Andy said, 'I need another big strong man in my daughter's life. Will you be her godparent?'

Jai said yes without hesitation, and then added, 'But I'll be taking Jesse under my wing too.'

Andy and Jai had a beautiful relationship and I was really thrilled that Andy had asked him to do this. Jai was young and fit and determined to make the most of his life. He represented everything Andy wanted in his future and in the children's future; he was a great role model. But maybe somewhere in the back of his mind, Andy was beginning to have doubts about his own future. I've often wondered since whether this was his way of putting things in place to make sure a father figure would be around if he wasn't.

18

The Warrior Returns

*I believe in opportunity and the power
of reason to seize upon it.*
— Andy Whitfield as Spartacus in *Spartacus: Blood & Sand*

July 2009

In early July Andy had his last chemo infusion for the first round of treatment. The end of the treatment meant that he felt better and better with every day because the chemo was moving out of his system. Physically and psychologically, he was beginning to feel good again and, although he was still vulnerable, every day was a giant leap forward and he felt stronger and more alive.

A month after his last treatment, Andy went back in for a full MRI to see where things were at. We were both incredibly nervous, but when we sat in Dr Doocey's rooms the day after the scan, he said, 'Congratulations, Andy, the scan is clear.'

There was no sign of the cancer. It was amazing. We were ecstatic, I could see little tears welling in the corner of Andy's eyes and he kept wiping them away with his big hands; he was very serene but the sense of relief was washing over him. We laughed and cried. Even Dr Doocey had a tear in his eye.

That mixture of relief and joy was so momentous and intoxicating it was overwhelming. It was an incredible moment. We'd kicked cancer in the guts. We'd had it, we'd experienced it, and we'd beat it. Dr Doocey was like, 'Okay, you can get on with the rest of your life now.' And so we did.

We were given back this amazing gift of Andy's wellbeing and with that came such gratitude, the sense of which we'd never known before. And the cream on top was knowing that he had the role to go back to. He was the star of a Hollywood television series and hero to millions, and he was going back to that in September. Spartacus was back.

Hearing Andy pick up the phone to our families and the producers and say, 'I no longer have cancer, I am all clear' was a huge, remarkable thing; it was almost unbelievable. As the days ticked over, Andy's recovery was amazing but he'd still been knocked for six, so he was doing anything he could to rebuild his body. He was going for acupuncture, doing light workouts. He was starting to connect with people again, talking with the producers, going in to see *Spartacus* people. Life as we knew it before diagnosis was resuming.

When Andy rang his agent Sam Maydew and told him the good news, they began to put in place a plan for Andy's return. The first thing to do was a press release announcing the news that Andy had beaten cancer. Then Sam suggested Andy go to

Comic-Con with the *Spartacus* team. Comic Con was a huge international festival held in San Diego every year where fans and stars of TV shows and movies that are super hero, sci-fi or action based get together for a massive convention. The *Spartacus* team were going and Andy really wanted to be a part of it. Sam thought it was a great way of announcing that Andy was back and that the second season would soon go into production. It also would give fans of *Spartacus* the chance to meet him and say hello. So it was agreed. Andy would go.

Comic-Con is amazing. Over 100,000 people turn up to the San Diego Convention Center, many of them dressed up as their favourite characters. They line up for hours to meet the stars and get autographs and take selfies, or buy memorabilia, or watch sneak previews of shows. It was a massive thing and Andy was really looking forward to it. Lucy Lawless and John Hannah were both going and it would be an opportunity for Andy to reconnect with the crew and fly off all fancy pants in business class! He was back from being the guy on the chemo ward to having this rock star lifestyle again.

This was just the pick-up Andy needed to get back into 'normal' life, without chemo and cancer being the centre of every waking minute. He was a little nervous to be heading off without us, but I was delighted that Andy could be going anywhere without needing my care; it was an incredible acknowledgement of how far we'd come and I was really relieved we'd reached this point.

Comic-Con was everything Andy expected. When they arrived there was a massive press conference to introduce the *Spartacus* stars. Hundreds of fans had gathered and when Andy was introduced there was a massive standing ovation that went for about three minutes. People were cheering and whistling and yelling out, 'Good on you, Andy.'

When I saw the footage of it later, I could see that Andy was genuinely moved by the reaction. He absolutely loved it, but he was so touched, and I could hear his voice almost breaking up when he took the microphone to thank everyone for their good wishes and emails and all of the letters and things he'd received. When the crowd stopped clapping, Andy said, 'It was so profound to get that connection, so thank you. It truly gave me a lift when I needed it most.'

When I looked at the vision of that press conference, I could see Andy's face was leaner, but anyone who didn't know him wouldn't know. I could see indents in his temples and his normally thick eyebrows were thinner. Being his wife, I could see the shadow of what chemo had done. To the untrained eye he looked great, he looked amazing, but I could see how and where the storm had weathered him. I could see the mild fatigue still about him. There was a sense of someone who had a scar that would never quite heal. Although he was feeling really well, he wasn't exactly getting out of bed and running a marathon every day. But he was good and his spirits were soaring.

For anyone who has been through cancer, not having to go to hospital anymore is such a joy; not having to beat that path backwards and forwards for blood tests is really wonderful. It gave us a sense of freedom. And for Andy, it was fantastic to not have things shoved in his back and his bones, and not be poked and prodded. It was liberating and such a relief for us to know that we didn't have to do that hospital drive again. Now we could plan a few weeks ahead or say, 'Next weekend we are going to go to blah (insert your fantasy destination here).' We had freedom again to think about our future rather than just taking each minute step by step.

Andy returned from Comic-Con with a renewed sense of energy and excitement about getting back to work. He was back at the gym getting fit again and feeling really good about his preparation to resume filming. He was feeling well enough to help out at Jesse's school, which he loved doing. He'd do reading group or classroom helping, and Jesse loved having him around. And he did a lot with Indi. He'd pick her up from day care and take her to the park for a push on the swing, or he'd lie on the floor and play with her. She had just started to speak and they had lots of cuddle time, which was so beautiful.

We savoured all of these moments, those very humble day-to-day things that were precious to us, like going out for dinner for a yummy meal together, or sneaking off for a ride around the block on Andy's motorbike – which under his contract he was not allowed to do! To some, these are probably mundane daily tasks, but for us, it was a great privilege just to be here to do these things. This was what life was all about. When you think those ordinary things might be taken away from you, you appreciate the simplicity. Being forced to stand out of the show and face his mortality gave Andy a remarkable chance to bond with his children in a way he otherwise may not have had.

Normally if you've gone into remission you don't go back for a check-up for three months, but Andy had to undergo medical tests before that. He had to be 100% right for the insurance company to give the green light for the resumed production of *Spartacus*. As soon as they got the thumbs up, they could hit pre-production in full swing. The cast and crew would be called back in, rehearsals would begin, scripts written, costumes fitted, all of the fun stuff.

So Andy had to have blood tests and a scan. There was apprehension, of course. We thought everything would be fine, but ultimately so much was riding on this. If he was given the all clear, life resumed; if he wasn't, *Spartacus* would be over and the prospect of that was too daunting to contemplate. These tests would determine our future path.

The tests showed that a lymph node in Andy's abdomen was inflamed. In a normal person, this is probably fairly insignificant and might be the sign that they've got a common cold. But for Andy, there was the potential that this could be something more sinister, so further tests were called for. Andy's doctors took a sample of the lymph node early in the week and we had to wait until the Friday to get the results.

The night before the results were due back, we went for dinner at our favourite restaurant, Prego, in Ponsonby Road. It was a gorgeous little Italian place that had become very special to us during our time in New Zealand. We had a beautiful dinner of fish and our favourite Caprese salad. We chatted happily, neither of us daring to take the first step into the 'What if?' conversation. But I could see Andy was anxious; when he held my hand I could feel a slight shake in his grip.

'This is it baby,' he said. 'This is when we go back into the crazy world of *Spartacus* that we created. How do you feel about that?'

'Andy, I can't wait!' I told him. 'I feel so different about it now. We've worked through all of our crap so that's not going to come up again, and we know how to play this game now. We know the machine and how to get out there and be our best. We've beaten cancer, we can do anything, so let's take it on and go for it.'

For the first time, a new tone came into Andy's voice. 'But what if we haven't beaten cancer, what if I'm not okay?'

I knew that he'd been thinking about this because my mind had wandered to that dark place a little bit too. 'Andy, if it's back, it's back. We just deal with it.'

A girlfriend had given me the book *Be Here Now* by Ram Dass for my birthday a few months earlier and while it wasn't front of mind I had been thinking about having the words 'be here now' tattooed, because all you can have is the presence of the moment. Ultimately that's where I was with it, and that's what I'd learned from the experience we'd been through. If it was back, we would deal with it one day at a time, but to worry about it today doesn't serve what may or may not be in front of us tomorrow.

'I've been thinking about getting a new tattoo,' I said to Andy. 'I've been thinking about the words "be here now" because that's all we've got, baby. All we have is what we've got today.'

Andy looked at me with those lovely eyes and put on this silly voice that he sometimes did. 'I love you, Vashti, that's why we're together.'

As it turned out, he'd been thinking about getting a tattoo as well, but it was never the right time. He wasn't allowed to get one while he was filming and he couldn't while he had chemo, but right across the road from the restaurant there was a really upmarket tattoo studio, very LA chic, not biker grungy at all. It was perfect, so in that moment we wandered across the road and ordered ourselves matching tattoos. The young guy behind the counter recognised Andy, and greeted him with 'Yo, Spartacus bro' as we arrived, which made us both giggle.

We chose the font, then got our matching tattoos – Andy's on his forearm, mine on my bicep. It's not what everyone does for dessert when they go out for dinner, but for us it was about marking that precise moment in time; it was a declaration that we were in control of our bodies and that everything was going to be okay. The next day we would get the test results. Neither of us slept very well because the apprehension about what might be ahead of us was enormous. It was make or break time, and we both tossed and turned until eventually exhaustion got the better of us.

Dr Doocey was due to ring around 11 a.m., so we were huddled on the sofa with the phone between us waiting for the call. Andy pressed speaker when the call came so we could both listen to what Richard was telling us. The news was devastating.

Dr Doocey said, 'I'm very sorry, Andy, the test results are in and we have found cancer in a lymph node in your abdomen. It's a very aggressive form of non-Hodgkin lymphoma. We are treating this as if you were never in remission.'

The cancer was back. Well, it probably had never gone away. And it was such an intensely aggressive cancer that if at all treatable, it would require a whole new level of chemotherapy.

We were both in shock. We were being told that Andy could die. It was catastrophic. I felt like someone had thrown me in a pool of icy water and when I was just at the point of drowning they reached in and lifted me out; that feeling of gasping for and sucking up air and being unable to breathe washed over me.

Dr Doocey explained that if Andy didn't have treatment he had at best three to six months to live. We made an appointment to see him the next day to discuss the options.

About an hour later, Andy said, 'I have to do something with this. For whatever reason, this has come back and I have to do something with it.'

He called Sam Maydew and then he called Chloe Smith, who was one of the producers of *Spartacus*. 'We're going to make a story about this,' he told them. 'I don't know what's going to happen or how it's going to play out, but I want you to follow me with a camera everywhere I go from this point forward.'

I think in that moment the cancer gave Andy some purpose, a place to focus his mind on something positive, rather than dwell on what we'd just been told. It gave him a sense of control over his future.

Again, we sort of rallied ourselves and said, 'Well okay, we're going to go through another round of treatment. It's not what we'd planned, but we'll just go through it and knock this cancer on the head.'

We both believed we'd stay in New Zealand and just press repeat and do the same thing again. But when we went in to see

Richard Doocey the next day, it was clear that this wasn't what we were dealing with at all. Richard was lovely, but again there was no beating around the bush.

'Andy, you've got three to six months maximum without treatment because it's come back already,' he reiterated.

I could see that Richard was as shocked as us. He felt awful because he too thought Andy would be the good luck story.

'We now have to treat this as a non-responsive, highly aggressive cancer,' he said. 'What this means is that after all that treatment, effectively the tumour hasn't responded. So as soon as you stop having treatment the cancer is instantly back. This is very serious. You are one of the percentage that doesn't respond to treatment. I strongly recommend you go home to Sydney and explore what other options there are to deal with this, but you need to let go of the fact that you are going to do *Spartacus* again, because it won't happen.'

That was the tidal wave. Having to accept that we needed to go down a totally different path was terrible. We had to let *Spartacus* go and suddenly the future was nothing like what we thought it would be. It was the first time we'd acknowledged that Andy might not make it. Everything that we'd held onto that had kept us going through the first treatment was wiped away. Letting go of *Spartacus* and the future we'd worked so hard for was devastating, but that was nothing compared to the prospect that Andy might die.

I held Andy's hand and we both cried. We were speechless. I think we were in shock. Then Andy suddenly lifted himself and said, 'This has to be happening for a reason.'

We had always shared the philosophical standpoint that life keeps sending you the same lessons until you get the message worked out. So we had kind of gotten to this emotional place where Andy said, 'Well, obviously I didn't get the message I was supposed to get the first time around, so this time, we need to look further.'

And this was where the thought of not going down the obvious treatment route came up for him. He wanted to make a film about this new journey. He wanted to understand what he could learn from this, what he could share from it and what we're here on this earth for. That's when making the film and following a totally different healing path became our focus.

Andy was a very pragmatic person. 'It just doesn't add up to me why I have this and how I got it,' he said. 'When I asked the oncologist what caused this cancer, he had no idea. How can you fix something if you don't know what causes it?'

He was already really interested in things like Ayuverdic medicine, meditation, acupuncture and vitamin C injections. Now he was looking at a whole gamut of holistic and alternative treatments to heal his body, and he was very determined to take control of his cancer and explore every possible option.

'I'm going to poke around in every corner of the world if I have to, to understand this,' he said. 'And if I'm going to do this, I need to share it.'

These discussions on the first day were good because it felt like there was positivity in what we were doing. Andy had the passion and drive to beat this, and he had a focus for his energy moving forward.

Later that night he rang his parents in Wales, and then we rang my mum and dad in the south of France. Andy told them, 'It's back and we need to get clear about what we are going to do.'

Like us, they all thought we'd just continue on with treatment and everything would be okay; no one knew how challenging things were going to become.

The idea of going back to Sydney was a bit strange, even though it was home. Physically saying goodbye to New Zealand and all that it meant for us was going to be tough, but Dr Doocey was right; Sydney was our home. We were paying rent in Auckland and still paying the mortgage in Sydney.

We needed to simplify our life, let go of *Spartacus* and get back home where we could regroup and focus our energy in a new direction. So while I started to get my head around the logistics of that, Andy was busily researching all sorts of unusual treatments. Soon we'd have a film crew capturing it all. In fact, within about two days of getting this devastating diagnosis, we were filming. It was just the beginning of a very long journey that tested every part of our resolve.

19

East Meets West

Turn your face toward the sun and the
shadows will fall behind you.
— Maori proverb

September 2010

The immediate few days after the diagnosis were a time of real emotional challenge for us. Both Andy and I were searching for answers to impossible questions. He wasn't prepared to just go straight back into chemo again without exploring every option available to him, and he couldn't accept that chemo was the only answer. In his heart he felt there must be something more. To Andy's mind, he'd done chemo already and it hadn't worked. He wanted to find a treatment that would take away the underlying conditions that caused the cancer in the first place, not just hit the symptoms.

For him, this presented an opportunity to look for answers beyond what we were being told was the norm and what was presented as perhaps the only hope. As we snuggled on the sofa one afternoon, Andy, with that beautiful deep voice that had a European sort of lilt and just a touch of northern lingering said, 'Vashti, in my heart I am convinced this is what this is all about. This is what is supposed to be right here and right now.'

And so it was.

I think Andy had an underlying fear that he'd already done chemo and even though it hadn't been a particularly hard core treatment for him, it was remarkably overwhelming, so it was logical to wonder whether there was another path to follow. Maybe the lesson we were supposed to get from all of this was to search beyond what we knew, maybe there were other answers out there somewhere. Andy believed that the cancer was back for him to discover something more meaningful in his life. And so the search began for what other treatments were available, with a particular focus on Eastern healing.

There was never a question in my mind that this wasn't a good idea, because it took us out of the rut we felt stuck in immediately after his diagnosis, and it took us beyond the day-to-day coming to terms with living with cancer again. But Andy and I did have a few conflicting moments about all of this.

I was allowing my fear of what might happen to heavily influence the decision I needed to make now. It was almost as if I was watching myself react and respond to something without any control over it, and yet in my heart all I wanted to do was support every aspect of Andy's journey and the choices that he wanted to make when it came to his path of treatment. My emotional reaction was almost knee-jerk. I was frightened of what was coming although, if I stopped and really thought about it, the last thing I wanted was for him to overpower his already fragile body with more chemo. Right then and there, though, I just wanted him to start having treatment again as soon as possible because that would mean that we were doing something towards changing the possibility of him not being here to see his children grow up.

Andy was torn because he knew that both his family and I wanted him to take what we thought was the quickest, easiest route to getting him better. But only someone who hasn't experienced the intensity of chemo on their own body could ever see that treatment as the 'best' option. The divide between Andy and me, who had always been inseparable in our choices, hurt like hell. I felt like I was torn in two, but the fierce lioness inside me would momentarily put my love aside to do anything to ensure that my babies didn't lose their dad.

It was such a confusing time and I'm almost ashamed to say I put my feelings for the safety of our children over the needs of my beautiful husband. And of course this was all amplified by having a camera crew right over my shoulder, capturing these emotional conversations. But we talked and worked through it. I was able to express my fear and Andy spoke from the heart about how important it was, this time round, to explore this whole experience with a more purposeful focus.

We had always believed that the same life lessons would keep coming to you until you got the learning being offered. If we went about this in the same old way, more than likely we would end up in the same place. This way, not only did we have a chance for it to be different, but in pursuing something else in terms of treatment we might learn and experience something completely unexpected.

'We are here for a reason,' Andy said again, 'so let's ride this wave together, even if we don't know how it will turn out.'

The irony of Andy being the one who had to talk the manifestation coach, his 'anything is possible if you put your mind to it' number one fan, back to a place of calm was almost poetry in motion. Somehow cancer, for all the darkness it brought, began to show the light shining through.

Andy went to see Dr Richard Moat, a world renowned health practitioner in New Zealand. Richard did a lot of work around the direct link between emotions and physical ailments. He believed that if you were thinking and feeling great things on an emotional level, then great things would happen on a physical level. In his mind, negativity, fear and unacknowledged emotions could breed illness, but with the right frame of mind you could turn the state of your health around.

This really resonated for Andy, because it was very much in tune with what we both believed: that how you think manifests what you become. We're also both big meditators and have a strong interest in Panchakarma, which is an ancient Indian method of healing. In India Panchakarma is famous and very highly regarded for its healing powers, even for people with cancer. Panchakarma is all about rebooting the digestive and nervous systems, and Andy was keen to explore this. The belief is that if you reboot your system of functioning then you have a much higher chance of working through any illness, so Andy was researching a wide range of different medicine streams and healing beliefs and wondering if this was the right path to follow.

He had been told about an amazing Ayuverdic healing centre in Rajasthan, where practitioners focused on rebuilding the mind, body and spirit through lots of massage, oil treatments, colonics, diet, mindfulness and wonderful concoctions of ancient herbs to cleanse the body. There was an emphasis on meditation and yoga, and they worked on healing your centre, calming the soul and rebalancing the body. As soon as Andy heard about it, he wanted to go there. At this stage, he only had a tiny showing of the cancer coming back in his lymph nodes and there was no sign of him being in pain or any of the stuff he'd had previously. To look at him you'd never know he had cancer, so if he was going to go, it had to be now.

The doctors meanwhile were warning us that if there was any chance of beating this, he would need a very different type of chemo than he'd had previously and it would be horrendous. This terrified Andy, but to be honest, to me the more gruesome it sounded, the better I felt because I thought it might do something; it felt like 'They're rolling in the big guns now'. It was a strange sort of reassurance that we were leaving nothing to chance; the bigger the chemo, the better his chance of survival.

Andy was feeling the opposite. He argued, 'It's a big call to put all of your faith in one camp (Western medicine). What if they're wrong?'

I just wanted him to get well again as soon as he could. And I worried that if he went to India, it might slow down his recovery. I was nervous about anything that might prolong the cancer, or allow it to grow so much that any form of treatment would be futile. It wasn't about not supporting Andy, and if it was me in his shoes, I would've done the same thing and chosen to go the alternative route, one which might include our whole family embarking on a journey into the unknown. The fear of losing Andy overwhelmed my rational thoughts.

There was a really challenging time when Andy felt conflicted about what treatment path to go down. He was longing to find something other than chemo and as each day went by I was actually starting to imagine he might die. Some days I'd get into the shower and have these awful images flash in my mind of Andy's funeral. And when I put my head on the pillow at night, I was having nightmares of us arguing and me screaming at Andy, 'But it's too late, you've left the chemo too late.'

Each of us had a huge weight on our shoulders. We were sitting around the breakfast table one morning, talking about it all. Jesse and Indi were buzzing around in the background and Andy said simply, 'Vashti, I just need you to support me.'

As he said it, Indi came bouncing up asking for something. In that moment what I'd been grappling with became crystal clear: I was juggling trying to support Andy while being the chief caregiver to these two little beings who ultimately might lose their dad if we didn't do something quickly.

Andy on the other hand just wanted to escape, go off and explore a little before he decided what to do. He argued that we had time because he was well, and we didn't have to be back in Sydney to confront whatever we were confronting for a few weeks.

The next morning he woke up and said, 'I'm going to do this, I'm going to India. This will help rebalance my system before I go back to Sydney. And if chemo is the answer, I will be in the strongest possible condition before I begin. Because if I go back and I am at all vulnerable it's going to hit me hard.'

I think that he needed this psychologically as much as physically. It wasn't just about rebalancing his body, it was about him feeling like he had a choice over his future. Andy was at the mercy of the oncologists and their diagnosis, and one thing we learned very early on in this cancer journey was to accept the diagnosis, but don't accept the prognosis. For Andy this was very real now. It became 'accept the diagnosis, but absolutely do not listen to the prognosis'. If we did, Andy could be dead within three months.

As soon as you take on a prognosis as your future, it is what you will become; it is like signing your own death certificate because you believe that this date on the calendar is when you are going to die. For Andy it was a case of, 'I accept that I have cancer but I do not accept what you tell me'. All I could do was support him and keep my fingers crossed that everything would be okay.

Rather than battling the disease initially, Andy was battling the norm. He challenged the belief that Western medicine was the only answer, which wasn't his view. His attitude was 'Whatever the outcome, please let me be the master of my destiny'. 'If I chose this path and it's still my time at least I've done it on my terms; it's been my choice, I've not been pushed into something,' he said.

Andy wanted all of us to go to India with him, but I was very anxious about taking the kids to a place that I didn't know. I had no idea how Andy would be when he was there. Even though he was incredibly well at this point, we didn't know what was ahead, and the thought of being so far away in India with two little children and no support if something went wrong didn't sit well. We also had to pack up the house in Auckland, so Andy's gorgeous dad Rob offered to fly to India and meet him there, which was wonderful. It allowed precious time for the two of them and it gave me huge peace of mind that he had someone with him to look after him.

So the idea was that he'd go off to India and get as well as he could. I would pack up the house, shut down our life in New Zealand and re-establish ourselves back in Sydney, so that when Andy arrived back we were ready to confront everything head on. We'd been given a deadline for chemo by the oncologists and we were honouring that; we knew that this cancer was advancing very quickly and Andy needed to begin treatment within a few weeks if he was going to accept chemotherapy. It wasn't like we had months of spare time up our sleeves; the clock was ticking.

One of the toughest things Andy had to do was say goodbye to New Zealand and all of the hopes and dreams that had been built there. He had to submit a formal resignation to the Starz Network who produced *Spartacus* and that was tough. Andy gave them full permission to let him go and replace him in the lead role, and that was a really big thing for him. He literally had to put into words that he understood and accepted he was being replaced. Pressing send on that email was pretty devastating. *Spartacus* was now formally over for us; it was a hard thing for both of us to accept. And it was sad too. I felt so sad for Andy that the dream he had focused on and that had helped get him through his previous treatment had come to an end.

Starz were incredibly supportive of Andy; all the way through from the first diagnosis, they were amazing. When the cancer came back, they helped us with the filming of the documentary and made sure Andy wasn't forgotten. They invited him on set and acknowledged his contribution in making *Spartacus* such a success; we were both very grateful for that.

Young Australian actor Liam McIntyre was chosen to replace Andy and he visited the set one day to meet him and wish him well. Starz President Chris Albrecht issued a beautiful press release that read:

> Since no one can really replace Andy, we realized that we should instead find an actor who can truly lead *Spartacus* forward. It was important to us to have Andy endorse the idea of recasting this part, which he did in the same heroic manner that he's dealt with his whole ordeal. And that, coupled with our fortune in finding a young actor with the gladiator credentials and the acting ability of Liam, makes it easier for us to keep this hit franchise going.

The cast were initially concerned about the impact replacing Andy would have on the show, and the psychology of it all because Andy's presence was everywhere around the set. His pictures were up around the gym where they trained, he was in every scene, so it was a big deal to actually say goodbye and allow someone else into that role, but Liam fitted in really well. We were both letting go of something we loved, but we knew it was in everyone's best interests. Although it was hard, we had to surrender to what life was throwing at us now.

I waited until Andy flew out to India before I began packing up the house, because I thought it would be too confronting for him to see it all being boxed away. The morning he flew out, he honestly looked amazing. He was wearing a beautiful blue and burnt orange checked shirt – I know that sounds kind of hideous but trust me, it wasn't. With his G-Star jeans, a gorgeous scarf wrapped around his neck and his aviator sunglasses resting on his head, he looked like a superstar. Incomprehensible to think this Adonis of a man who looked so fit and well, and incredibly handsome, had this bloody disease eating away at him inside.

When the taxi arrived, we stood outside the house hugging and crying. All I wanted was to grab hold of him and not let him go, but he was happy and looking forward to this big adventure, so I put on a brave face and wished him well. One of the biggest challenges for me was that when he decided to go down the Ayuverdic path, I explored moving us all to Bali where they did the sort of Panchakarma healing that Andy wanted. We could've enrolled the cubs at a local Balinese school and set up our life there, but Andy really wanted to go to India, and so it was. He had to face things he never wanted to do on his own and I didn't want him to do this on his own, but for the best interests of everyone, we had to separate our energy.

The taxi drove off with a cameraman following. A new cameraman was waiting for him to arrive in India. Every moment of this trip was being captured.

The whole concept of Andy's dad going was incredible. Rob is an incredibly intelligent man who is very open to learning, but he's also very traditional, particularly in relation to medicine and healing. Rob was adamant that he wanted to help Andy in any way he could, and that in itself was incredibly inspiring for us and wonderfully supportive. He flew out from Wales and met Andy at the Ayurveda Bhavan Treatment Centre in Rishikesh. To know that Rob was by Andy's side was the gentle reassurance that we all needed, so I waved Andy off and began the task of packing up the house.

All of our stuff was being shipped back to Sydney. It would take a month to arrive, so we had way too many things stuffed in way too many suitcases, all of the things we thought we'd need in the meantime. I was a machine at packing and unpacking, and I had the job done very quickly. I had a mission to get back to Australia, get our things out of storage and set up our house again, ready for Andy to come home. So there I was at Auckland airport with a ridiculous number of suitcases piled up around me, a pram and two kids under my arm, ready to set off on our next adventure.

Three hours later we were back in Sydney. We were home. It's hard to describe how I felt at this stage, because I had to get used to living in a state of not knowing. I know that probably doesn't make a lot of sense, but I was now in a space where answers weren't clear and we couldn't at all predict our future sometimes from one day to the next. Until we were face to face with the next doctor or practitioner who was going to guide us, we were in the wilderness a bit and had to accept that was how life would be.

Even at that stage, I wasn't factoring in that Andy might die. That didn't seem real at all, it just seemed like we were embarking on another crazy chapter in the life of the wandering Whitfields. I was a little overcome with emotion when I was unpacking our things back into our Sydney apartment, knowing that the last time we were there I was packing up to go off to *Spartacus*. That hit home: what's past is past.

Andy was going to be in India for three weeks, so while he was away I got referrals for every doctor and oncologist I could get my hands on. I spoke with all of them and checked out hospitals and treatment centres to see who Andy would best fit with. I'd started to speak with Dr John Gibson at RPA and he seemed really positive. To be honest, he was one of the few that were, so I made appointments so that when Andy got back we had someone to go to. Oncologist ticked off.

Meanwhile, Andy and Rob were each greeted by their own personal Vaidya – an Ayurvedic practitioner – when they arrived in Rishikesh to help them get the best out of their stay. Rishikesh was a picturesque little pilgrim village nestled at the foothills of the Himalayas. The majestic Ganges River runs alongside the village. Andy described it as 'magical, beautiful, colourful chaos'. It was a beautiful location with stunning mountains on one side and fields of flowers on the other. I could see why Andy would want to go there.

Andy called at the same time each afternoon to tell me what he'd been doing. He was having amazing treatments, like the wonderful ritual of oil poured on his head, which is incredibly relaxing and spiritually cleansing. There were also deep massages, colonics and highly nutritious food prepared by their own chef. It was a very warm, nurturing environment.

Some other Australians were there too, so Andy got to meet a group of very high powered executives who also followed Panchakarma and lived a very Ayurvedic-inspired lifestyle. It was fantastic for Andy and Rob to meet these guys who were a little older, about the same age as Andy's dad, who'd been meditating for many years. They were very successful businessmen who had found balance in their lives and lived according to these beliefs. It was very supportive for Andy to see the long term benefits of this type of treatment and to know that it really can be incorporated into a successful life.

In between treatments, Andy and Rob went motorbike riding and shopping at the local markets. They took a boat ride down the Ganges. It was such a time of togetherness for them as two adults, not just father and son but friends, and I know Andy treasured that time with his dad.

One afternoon when Andy rang, he told me he'd been to see an Indian astrologer who'd read his charts and predicted his future.

'It was incredible,' he said, and started to tell me all of the positive things.

The reading had picked up on the fact he had a very strong wife and his children would be fine. But then the astrologer said, 'You have three children.'

When Andy said 'no', the astrologer said, 'Oh, but you lost one. There are three children here, and he's still around in your lives.' Then he went on to say, 'You are going to be very successful and have a great career.'

Andy paused momentarily and then said to me, 'And then all of a sudden, Vashti, he stops when he gets to my health.'

In the documentary, keeping in mind a camera was following this whole journey, the astrologer says to Andy, 'You are not well. In the health department you have challenges but if you make it through this year until 2012 everything will be okay.'

But when I spoke to Andy on the phone he'd changed the dates and told me the astrologer had said to him, 'If you just make it through the next few months everything will be okay.'

Andy didn't want to alarm me that this was going to be a long battle.

The astrologer also said, 'Your blood is weak, this is a difficult time for you. You may have a short life. In my opinion, you will overcome it. There is a lot of support for you in the planets. I think you need to do a bit of Western healing and go back and do some chemotherapy.'

Well, that was a gigantic kick in the guts for Andy and he struggled to accept it. Everyone around him, even the Eastern practitioners in whom he had placed such faith, were saying that he needed to return to Australia for chemo. The message coming in from all sides was loud and clear.

In the moment when the astrologer said, 'You're not well', the first cracks in Andy's armour began to appear and he questioned whether he would survive. He thought, 'If this Eastern route doesn't even believe I'm going to make it, then what hope have I got?' I could hear the change in his confidence over the phone; he was feeling very vulnerable. For me, that's when Andy's light started to go out. The belief system that he so passionately followed was questioning his future. At that point I think Andy knew he had no choice but to come home. His cantankerous determination that this alternative treatment would be the answer had been challenged; the candle that was his hope had melted away and he was terrified about the future. So he packed his bags and returned to Sydney, reluctantly accepting that chemo had to be done.

Ironically, he was radiant when he arrived home, he really looked well. It was impossible to imagine this glowing, strapping human being was so sick. The meditation had given him a great sense of peacefulness and his attitude was very much 'what will be will be, let's get on with it'. He was feeling energetic and he'd enjoyed the time he spent with his dad. He was in a really good place, but from then on I don't think he was ever further than a foot away from me.

Rob loved that trip to India too. He learned to meditate. Afterwards he said that, although he came for Andy, he got more out of it than Andy did. That was an incredible time and neither of us had any regrets about it. It was the best possible thing Andy could've done and to be honest, if the kids and I had been there with him, he probably would've stayed longer because he was so calm and peaceful and happy.

Once Andy got home, he was resolute about what had to be done and why. He would do anything to be around for his kids, so whatever treatment was available and whatever it took to be there for Jesse and Indi, he'd do it. I think that was tough for Andy. In fact, I think it's tough for a lot of people going through cancer. No one wants to have to go through chemo. And it's hard for carers too, because our tendency is to push our loved ones into doing anything that might keep them alive, when sometimes that's not necessarily what they want.

Within a week we were at the Royal Prince Alfred Hospital seeing Dr Gibson. We sat in his tiny little fluoro-lit office to hear what our options were. He was a very kind man with a very dry sense of humour and he made a few jokes which put us at ease. He looked at Andy's notes and reaffirmed what we'd been told. This news wasn't good. Andy had to do another round of chemo, but Dr Gibson gave us a choice. He said that because Andy was so young and fit, he could potentially have a bone marrow transplant.

Dr Gibson explained that this was a very tough and intense treatment. He gave us all of the details, which were horrific. They basically kill off the bone marrow, which is the soft fatty tissue inside bones, and when it's almost gone they pump it full of healthy stem cells so all of the bad stuff is gone. He said it was very risky and awful to go through, and Andy would be very sick, but it was an effective treatment. Andy would be really unwell through the treatment, but there was a good chance that if it succeeded he would live a long and happy life.

So Andy had to have probably four chemo infusions through October and November to get rid of the mass in his stomach, then a scan. If the scan showed he was good, they could harvest stem cells. The plan was we'd then have a break over Christmas and enjoy a beautiful warm Sydney summer while Andy rebuilt his strength. Then in February he would go in for the transplant.

I burst into tears when Dr Gibson outlined this, because at last we had hope. We were so relieved that there was a positive option. We were back in the game and it was all going to be okay. We would go through this profound and horrific experience, but it was a chance at life and we felt we could do it. We left Dr Gibson's office with a renewed sense of positivity for the future; we'd been given a road map and we knew what was ahead. It was pretty scary but we'd already learned not to fear what we didn't know. And regardless, it was clear this was our only chance.

20

Welcome Back to Chemo

One often meets his destiny on the road he takes to avoid it.
— Jean de le Fontaine (with credit to the Whitfields'
favourite movie, *Kung Fu Panda*)

This was the beginning of a very different cancer journey for us. The first step for Andy was to undergo a round of chemo to get the lymphoma count as low as possible so that his cells were in a good place. Then stem cells could be extracted and frozen to be reinfused through a bone marrow transplant after Christmas. We were very positive about this; we knew it would be pretty heavy going but we were really confident this was a good path forward. We had such a clear purpose about what this would achieve and Andy approached it with absolute gusto.

The chemo would be administered over a few days, so Andy would be admitted to hospital for this treatment, because it would knock him around and he needed to be monitored. We were also warned that with this particular concoction of chemotherapy drugs, there was a one in a million chance he may have a bad reaction. But that couldn't happen to us, right?

Georgia Lockhart, Andy's make-up artist in *Spartacus*, was in Sydney at the time, and she often came to visit us when she was in town. On the weekend before Andy was due to go into hospital, Georgia turned up with her big hairdressing bag and shaved off Andy's hair. We told the kids that Daddy had to have more medicine to fix his blood and help his sore back, and his hair would fall out. So then Andy said to them, 'Why don't we all cut it off?'

We made it fun. We got the kids involved and they helped shave his head. Then they took his hair and made pretend moustaches with it. We all laughed a lot that day and it was great to have Georgia around, she lit up the room.

The next morning we were off to the Royal Prince Alfred Hospital. The moment we pulled up at RPA, the contrast with what we had in Auckland was very clear. The hospital was a big, old, imposing building and we were greeted by people who were clearly unwell with hospital gowns on and their bums hanging out the back, chugging away on cigarettes outside the front entrance! I still can't grasp the irony of that image. We both found it so bizarre that these people were obviously here for healing and yet they're fagging away as if their lives depended on it, while across the road there's a methadone clinic for drug addicts, with people queuing up to get their drugs. Not quite the green juice and meditation mindset we shared.

I wouldn't say RPA is an ugly building, but it is rather bland to look at. However, the environment on the outside, with these clashing ideals and rather unfriendly and unwelcoming habits greeting you, is in complete contrast to what happens once you step through the door. Once inside, RPA is an amazing place with little miracles happening behind every door. The hospital buzzes with life and energy and is a very welcoming place.

When Andy was settled in, I hung out with him for a while and then raced home to pick up Indi from kinder and Jesse from school and get everything calm at home again. We were living in a beautiful but reasonably far away apartment in Double Bay, and our apartment was at the top of an enormous flight of stairs with no lift access. Once you got to the top it was magic and our views of the harbour made it well worth the effort, but it was a bit of a job to get there in the first place. You couldn't just drop around to our place. It was tricky to find parking and we were tucked away, and then you had to conquer the stairs. It wasn't the 'drop by' place which our house in New Zealand had been.

So that day, as the stairs loomed in front of me, and I was trying to get the little people back home with school bags and shopping and stuff, I became very aware that I was soon going to be looking after someone who needed serious help in a fairly unfriendly environment. This was not going to be easy. I could see we faced a test of endurance on many levels.

After three days in hospital, the treatment was over and Andy was ready to be picked up. As we drove home, Andy showed me his arms, which were like pin cushions. He looked more like he should've been queueing for the methadone clinic than the rippling warrior who once graced our screen. I jokingly told him it was high time he returned home to fulfil his husbandly duties, and mockingly threatened that I would otherwise have to get a lover. He laughed and suggested a lover was a good idea because he would be too busy maintaining a strict new regime of popping pills and taking meds each day. It felt good to be able to laugh with one another and find humour in a rather humourless situation; we were always able to bring a lightness back to the situation.

Andy was quite stiff and sore and was walking like an old man. As we went to mount the staircase at home he pretended he had a walking stick and put on this hilarious old man's voice and said, 'I am Spartacus' as if he was 100 years old. We both giggled and I took his arm and helped him up the stairs, with Andy leaning on one side of me and his bags on my other shoulder to balance me. We got him in and settled and he seemed okay, albeit a bit fragile. The cubs were ecstatic Daddy was home and they all snuggled up on our bed and watched *Kung Fu Panda*. It was good to be reminded of the wisdom that children's animation sometimes offered.

After his treatment, Andy usually had 'chemo' brain, as he described it. He was present but he wasn't really thinking very clearly; he was a bit jumbled and it was tricky to focus on things like reading a book or watching a film. He was just feeling a bit foggy and sore all over. It was like having the flu and a monster hangover at the same time, so he just rested on the bed.

The days that followed were when the chemo began to wage its war on the cancer, and in the process strip away much of Andy's insides. One of my roles was to inject drugs into his stomach each day, which wasn't fun, I can assure you, but we got through it okay. When he took off his shirt, I could see that the nurses had placed a cannula in his arm but unfortunately they'd struggled to find the right place for it so he had holes everywhere and he was very battered and bruised.

Andy slept on the sofa and seemed to be comfortable, so when he was sound asleep I went to bed too. But one night he had a massive reaction to the cocktail of drugs they'd given him. He was among the 'one in a million' the doctors warned us about – well, we asked for extraordinary!

While I was sleeping, oblivious to what was going on in the lounge room, Andy was in a psychological battle with a very dark side of himself that had emerged from the drugs, and was wanting to throw himself out the window. He was caught in a terrifying nightmare, except he was awake through all of it. He was convinced that throwing himself out our huge double glass windows that looked out onto water would be the right thing to do, and it wouldn't have been that hard for him to do. All night long, he had to talk himself down off the ledge in his own mind, battling to silence the voices goading him to jump. He had no control over his thoughts, but luckily he somehow found the strength to listen to the intuitive voice that told him not to put his darkest thoughts into action.

When I went in to him in the morning he was already awake and saying very strange things, as if he was hallucinating. I had my running gear and a cap on, because I lived in my sports gear at that time, and he said, 'You need to take that cap off because it's evil and it's bringing bad luck into this house.'

'Andy, what are you talking about?' I said.

It was quite frightening, because he was staring at me like he didn't know me. He's a big guy and although he wasn't violent he was quite aggressive and angry – and he was obsessed by my 'evil' cap. He was completely on another planet.

I settled the kids into my bedroom and put on a movie while I called a friend to come over. Meanwhile, Andy was present one minute and then gone the next. It was like being with a schizophrenic so I said, 'Andy, I don't think you're very well. I'm calling the doctor.'

They told us to come into the hospital straightaway. Andy's brain had responded really badly to the drugs and they had to try to flush the chemo out of him. He stayed in hospital for another three days.

As he began to come around, he was telling me what had been going on for him, and honestly it was terrifying. He was describing some very dark places he'd gone to in his mind; he said everything felt grey and dark and the same thought – 'I'm going to die' – was on loop in his mind. He couldn't make any sense of it. He said he felt like he was in a Stephen King film, and he had to talk himself off the ledge several times.

That was our first round of this new treatment. Welcome back to chemo.

This was going to be a huge journey for us. It wasn't drifting back from chemo and me nurturing Andy with peppermint tea like it had been in New Zealand. This was a very different experience and it was multiplied by where we were living. As much as we loved our apartment, it was totally impractical and exacerbated the immense effort everything now seemed to involve.

That first experience was horrible for Andy. He felt that he wasn't in control and was worried about his capacity to make decisions when he was on the chemo drugs. He was confused about who to listen to and what to do, which is why the role of caregiver is so important. You have to facilitate the best possible decision making, and include the loved one, but ultimately make the best choice on your own. Andy and I had conversations about this and he trusted me to make the right calls for him if he couldn't.

I wouldn't say I was feeling alone, but at this point I was very aware that my role as a caregiver had jumped up a notch. I was now the decision maker and the voice for Andy, and I had a responsibility to honour what he needed and wanted, and what was in his best interests. And if that meant pulling the pin on the treatment, then so be it. I shifted my mindset to 'We are not going to do anything that impacts his wellbeing, especially his mental health, even if that means making choices that go against what the doctors say'. Andy wanted quality of life, not life at any cost.

So the oncologist reduced the chemo dose and Andy coped okay, but it was still very intense and after the second round the impact was very obvious. He started to lose weight and was getting very tired but the scans were showing that things were looking good. He wasn't in any pain and the mass had shrunk by about 60%, so everything was positive and we were full steam ahead to have the bone marrow transplant.

As each treatment finished, the stinging tail of chemo came around to hit Andy again and again. He always stayed in hospital for about three days when he had the treatment, then by the time I got him home he just wanted to sleep. He couldn't handle any visitors for the first week afterwards, he felt so awful, so it was important that we kept things very low key. We had to be really careful with the kids; as soon as he was home they wanted to jump on him and cuddle him but his body was too fragile. We also had to make sure they didn't have any sniffles or colds, and they had to take a very gentle approach with their daddy.

Andy was very depleted. He had developed painful cold sores on the inside of his nose and his mouth was covered in ulcers. His stomach felt like it was burning and his skin was hot all the time. It was like he'd been in a nuclear blast, and as the treatment went on, the sicker he would become.

He had tests regularly to see how he was going. Most were routine scans or blood tests but he also had to have a bone marrow test, which really tested my resolve. The doctors gave Andy an anaesthetic, including a blocker, a special drug that blocks memory, so he has no memory of this experience, which gives you an indication of how intense the procedure is. As my big strong man lay on his side, with his cute and still very firm, white bum poking out of his hospital gown, the doctors took what looked like an old corkscrew and began to screw into Andy's spine. They were drilling into his backbone to take a sample of the bone marrow to check if the cancer had spread to a place that would limit his chances of receiving the transplant.

The doctor doing the procedure was a young and very petite woman. She wasn't strong enough to get the screw into his back, so as she buzzed for support, I watched in horror as two people used their full body weight to penetrate my husband's spine. It was surreal, horrendous and at the same time remarkable what they were able to do. It was one of those moments where I had to pinch myself to realise that this was all real, this was our life right now. I was standing right beside them as they were boring into my husband's spine and it was just horrific. If I thought too much about what they were doing, it would've sent me loopy. I had to keep repeating in my mind, 'This is for the best', but deep down in my heart I wanted to scream at them and wrap Andy up and run away with him. All I could think about was when I might wake up from the crazy nightmare that I was having.

Seeing him in the place where I'd seen my friend Kate during her cancer battle was really challenging but I had to keep in my mind, 'This is what we signed up for, this is what happens during this treatment path, we knew it would be bad'. It didn't make it any easier, though, watching what was going on. I had to remember that what looked like it might kill him, might just in fact save him. We'd got away lightly with the impact of Andy's chemo the first time around. Sometimes I wondered whether that's why the cancer came back, and if we should've gone harder the first time. We had to trust our instincts that this was going to be worthwhile. We had a huge carrot dangling at the end of this round of chemo: Andy could have the bone marrow transplant and the cancer would be gone. I just had to trust the process, step back and let it happen.

For Andy, there was massive bright, shining, warm light at the end of this dark tunnel. If he got through this there was a big break at the end, and it was sunshine and summer and beach before a life-saving bone marrow transplant that would help us live happily ever after. Christmas was coming and we would get to spend a few weeks soaking up life in Sydney, without hospitals and without chemo. As simplistic as it sounds, that's what it came down to. That was the dream we clung onto with an iron grip. Santa was going to bring us the best gift ever: time with Andy.

21

The Long Goodbye

We cannot direct the wind, but we can adjust the sails.
— Unknown

The warm Australian festive season was always a welcome delight for the Welsh Whitfields and even after so long in Sydney, the novelty of a sunny hot Christmas Day never wore off. Somewhere in our distant memories, Christmas was embedded as wet and cold, so the idea of sunshine and barbecues was still totally bonkers to us! We were so incredibly excited about this Christmas coming that even if it had snowed, it wouldn't have dampened our spirits because the arrival of Christmas and the New Year heralded a new chapter for us.

Andy couldn't really sit in the sun because his skin was paper thin from the chemo and very susceptible to burning. But even to be able to sit in the shade, filling his lungs with warm air, was a gift we didn't take for granted.

That summer, we spent a lot of time at our friend's house down on the water at Double Bay. It's a beautiful home with a pool so we could swim and lie around, and luxuriate in the space we didn't have in our apartment; it was such a sense of abundance. We often looked after our friends' dog Rosie. The kids adored her and loved being with her too, so everyone was in a very happy place. We didn't have to battle our way up the stairs at our apartment and we were away from anything associated with what the past few months had been. It was like a luxurious holiday but just down the road from home.

Because we didn't have any hospital visits and Andy was feeling so much better without the chemo, we were able to do very normal but beautiful things with our family. Andy wasn't in any pain, so we could all take a slow walk together to the beach and have a swim, go out and eat together, hang out by the pool, catch up with friends we hadn't seen in a long time and go to a movie – which for Andy and me was like a religion. We got to just *be* for a while.

Andy's mum Pat was with us from Wales, and my parents flew over from France, so I organised a big Christmas dinner together, which was very special because normally we are all apart. It was a wonderful day, but also bittersweet; there were a lot of emotions going on for everyone. Although no one dared to say it, I'm sure that deep down we were all wondering if this would be Andy's last Christmas and silently praying it wasn't. Rob was back in Wales by now, so he and Pat were apart. My parents had arrived in the middle of our chemo storm when my focus was on making every minute with Andy count, which meant I couldn't be as attentive to them as I would've liked.

So we were all feeling a bit fragile and tender and we didn't make a huge fuss out of the day, just quietly savoured it in a very low key but special way.

As each day passed since chemo, Andy got better and better and was able to do things he hadn't done for months – simple things like pushing Indi on a swing or lifting her up into a tree. Just waking up with Dad there and being able to go and give him a cuddle made the kids and Andy all so happy. The fact that he could walk to the corner store and buy the newspaper, or get up and make breakfast was wonderful, because he hadn't been able to do those things for so long. For the first time I really under-stood what being present meant, and we enjoyed every moment. Those 'normal' (and I really do dislike that word!) things that people often take for granted were very significant to us and we were so grateful to experience our old version of 'normal' again.

In the lead up to Christmas I had been feeling quite stressed, and as the thought of the transplant and all that it entailed began to drift more regularly into my thoughts, layer by layer, all that had been going on in our lives was beginning to weigh me down. I was exhausted, and the effort of trying to keep a smile on my face while being the carer, wife, mother, nurse, driver, cook and cleaner, and watching my best friend go through this horrible and confusing time, was actually bloody hard.

I was also beginning to fear that Andy might not make it through this. Some days I'd get in the shower, turn the taps on and cry. I'd been having these awful visions of Andy's funeral. I'd see it playing out in my head and I'd think, 'How's it going to be for Jesse at school without a dad? Will I go back to full time work?' So many scenarios momentarily flooded into my mind.

I knew it was wrong of me to even think about Andy dying, and that in itself would make me cry, but there I'd be, sobbing my heart out while the water washed over me. As soon as I heard the squeak of the taps turning off, I'd snap straight back into the present. The shower was the only place I could escape to. We were living in a small apartment, and with all of these people around me I was trying to maintain an air of strength and positivity for everyone else. The shower was the only place I could let it all go.

On one particular evening just after Christmas, Andy was home and feeling okay, and a few of my girlfriends were going out for a drink. He really encouraged me to go and have a few margaritas with my friends and enjoy myself. He felt fine, he told me; he wanted a quiet night watching the soccer, and he wanted me to have a break.

So I did. We went to this very cool bar, the Lotus Bar in Potts Point, where a young, hip and very funny Italian barman started bantering with us. It was brilliant to spend a few hours laughing and catching up on other people's lives and to listen to their troubles. By comparison to mine they seemed like nothing, but still gave me pleasure to engage in.

The barman and I had a brilliant rapport. He'd been paying a lot of attention to us all night, and when one of my friends left and the other went off on a long phone call, he came over and sat down with me. We had this funny, vibrant conversation about Europe, life, his future and many other things, except anything to do with my life. After a few drinks, our chat turned to a bit of fun flirtation. I realised that if I wanted to, I could turn this innocent banter into a night of a lot more, forgetting about my life as it was right then.

The alcohol had momentarily blurred my perspective and an old side of myself, who once searched for love in the arms of complete strangers, stirred within me. But here I was now, a mother of two, the wife of the actor formerly known as Spartacus, and the best friend of the man I loved more than anyone in the world, and absolutely terrified I was going to lose him. As quickly as the scenario of what could happen played out in my mind, I paid up, jumped into a taxi and raced home to Andy.

I walked through the door, threw off my shoes, snuggled into Andy's shoulder and began to cry.

'What's wrong, darling?' he gently asked.

'I just miss you,' I sobbed as he wrapped me in his arms. I couldn't bear the thought of life without him.

The next day, as I thought about why that old side of me had momentarily re-emerged, it hit me like a tonne of bricks. It wasn't that I was trying to escape the situation at home, but that I was behaving as if Andy had already gone. I was playing out being alone but forgetting all that I had learned from my life with Andy. And that's when I realised I wasn't coping as well as I had thought.

Feeling guilty for even allowing myself to think these things, I started researching loss and grieving and discovered there is a stage of grief called early grieving, or 'the long goodbye', as it's sometimes called. It's about the knot that sits in your heart, the dull ache you feel at the overwhelming prospect that this person you love might not be around. It's perfectly natural and quite common.

And I was doing my early grieving in the shower, the silent corner where I could let out whatever was lurking in my mind. Whatever was troubling me went down the plug hole and didn't come out of the shower with me. One of the most important things I've learned about the grief following the loss of something or someone you love is to honour the grief and let it come up, because as soon as you do that and acknowledge it, you can let it go.

Andy was grieving too at what might be. He worked through his grief by filming video diaries for the documentary. He went to a quiet place, turned on the camera and poured his heart out. That's where the process of making the documentary became so important for us, because it forced us both independently to confront our emotions and what we were frightened of; we were able to pour out what we were feeling right then and there and let it go.

On New Year's Eve we all went to a friend's apartment across the road and watched the fireworks over Sydney Harbour. My mum and dad and Grandma Pat, Andy's mum, came along, and we sipped French champagne. At 9.00 p.m. the most exhilarating display of vividly shaped and coloured fireworks exploded above the harbour and we happily bid farewell to the past year. Andy and I snuggled on the sofa. He had his arm around me and as the clock struck twelve, he became quite reflective about the year behind us.

'In some ways, this has been the best year of my life,' he said.

*

In mid-January Andy had to go for a scan to see how he was going. If the results were good, the bone marrow transplant would get the green light. He was feeling really good, he wasn't in pain and he'd recovered well from the chemo before Christmas. We were ready to take on this transplant and it felt like we might just be able to pull off a miracle.

But it wasn't to be; 2011 was off to a very different start to the year we had asked for. The scan showed the cancer had come back with gusto in a very short space of time. The tone of Dr Gibson's voice had changed dramatically when he gave us this news.

'What we are dealing with is an absolutely aggressive and non-responsive cancer,' he said, 'and unfortunately a bone marrow transplant is totally out of the question.'

We were shattered, absolutely devastated. The doctors decided to put Andy onto what they call 'the big guns of chemo', but it was a last resort. If he didn't respond to this, nothing would work. This was incredibly confronting. There'd always been another way, another option. This was the first time anyone had said there are no other options. Andy's death became a very real possibility, one we hadn't previously entertained.

Our minds now turned to alternative treatments again. We reconsidered whether we should go to Bali for Panchakarma. Suddenly we were open to absolutely anything that might give us a chance. We wondered if we needed to pack up and move to another country, maybe go back to Rishikesh. We were desperately searching for any answer, any skerrick of hope, because hope was fading fast.

Andy started the new chemo straightaway, and doctors were right about the impact it would have. It was the nuclear bomb of chemo. Almost instantly a rash broke out all over Andy's body. It didn't subside. His skin felt like it was on fire, his bum was bleeding, his mouth was full of ulcers, he had cold sores on the inside of his nose and he was very weak. It was like he'd emerged from Chernobyl. He was also in pain again, which meant the mass in his stomach was growing very quickly. Everything seemed to be speeding up and the truly awful thing is that this was exactly how the doctors had told us it would be. In our minds, we had to find another way.

We called a doctor in India who Andy had met when he went to Rishikesh. He was so desperate for someone to give him some hope, but when the doctor heard how weak Andy's voice was, he said very simply, 'I'm sorry, Andy, but I don't think you can come to India. You need to stay and do the chemo.'

That was a big smack in the chops for us both.

Lilibet Foster, the director of the documentary, had been working hard to secure a spot for Andy in an American hospital where they wholly embraced both Western and Eastern treatments and where the environment was nurturing and positive. But we were now getting to a point where he'd need to get permission to travel and documentation from his doctors due to the amount of medicines and painkillers he was on, and none of them believed Andy was fit to travel.

After a few rounds of chemo, Andy was admitted back to hospital because he picked up an infection. This was the really tricky stage where he had to be very careful about who he was around; his immune system had no resistance and one severe virus could kill him. I was the only one allowed to go in and see him, and I had to wear a mask. I stayed with him at the hospital as much as I could.

One day Jesse was doing a little performance at school. I hadn't been to any of his school things for ages and desperately wanted to go, but the doctor still hadn't been in to see Andy, so we waited and waited. We waited all day, then got to the stage where I had to go. So I raced off to be there for Jesse, then raced back to the hospital. On my way back to RPA, I got a call from Andy. He was crying, he was in so much pain.

A doctor had come in to see him with a group of medical students in tow. Andy described how, as he lay there with all of these strangers around his bed, the doctor, who didn't acknowledge Andy at all, started talking about him to the students, as if he wasn't even there. Then the doctor, who Andy didn't know, turned to Andy and very flippantly said, 'Well, mate, your chances are not looking good. This is the toughest chemo you can have. If it doesn't respond to this, it won't respond to anything, so then it's just a matter of time.'

Then they all walked off.

For Andy, that moment was devastating. He felt like an exhibit in a museum, not a man fighting for his life. It was cold, callous and totally inconsiderate, and he was gutted. I was absolutely furious. I'd stipulated that no one was to see Andy without me being there, for this very reason. He was fragile and needed to be spoken to in a way that gave him hope, support and understanding. I was so upset that a very basic request had been ignored.

Andy was holding on by a thread; he was very weak and vulnerable. I took him home, and a day or so later his doctor rang.

'There's no point doing any more chemo,' he said, 'it's just not working.'

Andy's pain was increasing significantly and the mass in his stomach was so big it was pressing on the nerves in his spine. He was prescribed OxyContin, which is like medical grade heroin, to ease the pain. It was serious stuff, but it did help a little and he was able to sleep.

As had happened in the past, when he came off the chemo he began to feel better and better. Even though I knew he was barely hanging in there, for him the pain was the major problem and even with the OxyContin it wasn't going away. The thing that had changed for me by now was the realisation that he might not make it. We'd been delivered the blunt news and with the 'big guns' of chemo not working, time was running out. Unwittingly, I suddenly stopped worrying about things. The shower break-downs stopped, and I became very calm and present. I wanted to be with Andy and not be scared anymore.

Andy was coming to terms with it too. In one of his video diary entries he said he'd been facing his own mortality and wondering what it would be like to die: 'It's liberating to say, well I might only have three months, this might be my journey and I've made peace with it.'

Andy's oncologist, Dr Gibson, thought we might as well give radiation a go. We had nothing to lose. It might shrink the tumour and take some of the pain away. So he referred us to a radiation specialist, Dr Angela Hong, who was lovely, a very beautiful, softly spoken oncologist. In her calm way, she clearly told us this would not be a long-term cure; it would not be anything other than buying us time.

All of a sudden we'd gone from 'You're going to get well', to 'You're going to get a bit more time'. In the flick of a switch, the conversation had gone from survival to quality of life, and I became like a lioness. I understood what they were saying but that was not necessarily what was going to happen. I felt we just needed to get Andy well enough to make choices again. If he was out of pain, he could make decisions about what would happen going forward, and if we could just get him well enough maybe we would all fly off to Bali and let him have treatment he wanted.

There was one lovely highlight among all of this grim news. A week or so after the chemo finished Andy woke up one morning with a giant boner. One of the many side effects of chemo is that it makes you impotent; it strips away everything, even your capacity to make love. The chemo made it difficult even for the kids to cuddle him because he was so sensitive and sore all over, so the idea of sex and making love was far out of the picture for us both. For months we hadn't been able to have sex, but we still had intimacy and that's what mattered. Andy and I had always had a very strong physical relation-ship, but while he was going through treatment our relationship transitioned to being more about love and caring. The lack of sex was never an issue though, because it was so far from our minds anyway.

That Andy woke up with a big old woody was, to us, abso-lutely hilarious. He limped to the bedroom and hopped into bed with me and we had this lovely snuggle and made love. It was very soft and gentle. I'm a bit of a tiger normally, but this was intimate, slow love making.

Afterwards, Andy rested his head on my chest and said, 'Darling, thank you for the sympathy shag!'

I burst out laughing. 'Andy, it wasn't a sympathy shag! It was gorgeous.'

'I know I was rubbish . . .' he started.

But he wasn't at all. It was about us connecting in a way we hadn't been able to and it was lovely.

We laughed, and it was good to laugh. It was a very funny, lovely moment but that's how our relationship was. We had an insane love and friendship, and we could always find laughter at the most inappropriate time!

Andy felt his manliness and virility had been stripped away by the chemo, but for me it was the opposite. Even though we couldn't make love as we once did, I saw him as more manly than ever because of what he was enduring, and the incredible strength and courage he showed, and his determination to fight for his family. He was unbelievably masculine and chivalrous.

We agreed with Dr Hong that Andy would have a course of radiation and we'd see if it made any difference. The first treatment was very painful, because he had to lie on his back and go through the big radiation machine, which can be quite claustrophobic. He had to lie as still as he could while the lasers lined up the point of treatment. The problem was that lying on his back was virtually impossible because the mass in his abdomen would press on the nerves against his spine, which was excruciating. The only way he could lie on his back was to curl his knees up against his tummy. But he couldn't do that in this machine; he had to lie straight, and he was sobbing and groaning it hurt so much.

Radiation is not dissimilar to having an X-ray so I couldn't stay in the room with him, but the radiographers let me come into their cubicle and talk to Andy through the microphone. He could hear me so with a very gentle voice, I talked him through some basic meditation and relaxation to try to keep him calm and take his mind off the pain. We worked on breathing and I encouraged him to focus his mind on good things as we counted down the seconds until he had finished.

The pain at this stage was tremendous and totally debilitating, and I needed to take Andy in a wheelchair most places now. The tumour in his stomach was so big it pressed on the nerves going into his legs, and he struggled to walk. But then miraculously, after the second round of radiation treatment his pain began to disappear. Something was working and he began to recover really well. Yet again, Andy as we knew him was back.

He could walk, he could move, he could sleep, and all of this had come after just two sessions of radiation treatment. We'd had our fingers and toes crossed for a miracle; maybe our little prayers had actually been answered. It gave us such a boost; all of a sudden Andy had a twinkle in his eye again. He was putting on weight and he felt so much better. The very dark fog that had shrouded our lives was actually lifting and we questioned the deathly prognosis we'd been given. Maybe the doctors weren't right, after all? Maybe Andy would beat this.

Andy was feeling so good, he dusted off his precious Moto Guzzi motorbike, which was his absolute pride and joy, and took it for a spin. He hadn't been able to ride the bike at all since we returned to Australia because he didn't have the strength. Before cancer came along, going for a long bike ride was one of his favourite things to do, and mine. I loved taking a ride on it too.

So on a beautiful sunny Sydney afternoon, he dusted off the bike, dug his leathers out of a storage box somewhere, and went for a ride. The tears streamed down my face, and the cameraman's too, as we watched him ride off. It was wonderful to have such a significant moment caught on camera. Of course, I was a little worried about him falling off, but more than anything I was so happy to see him take off with such freedom and a sense of *joie de vivre* that I hadn't seen in him for a long time. He felt totally liberated and, for a moment, so did I.

We allowed ourselves the luxury of planning a weekend away with the kids, and arranged to go away with some friends to Kangaroo Valley on the south coast of New South Wales, in the Shoalhaven region. We rented a beautiful house that looked out onto rolling hills and had a gorgeous view from every window. The house was massive, with more than enough space for two families to stay together, and we soaked up the serenity around us. There was a huge polished concrete bathroom with a floor-to-ceiling window that looked out onto the hills and a beautiful old claw foot bath you could soak in while taking in the view. One evening we were all in the bath together – Indi, Jesse, Andy and me – in our swimmers and having bubble fights. I remember thinking in that moment that Andy looked so well and happy you would never have known we'd been on this horrific cancer journey. My husband was absolutely full of life. He actually felt so well he called his agent and talked about going back to work. They lined up an audition for him in the television series *Paradise Lost*, so when we returned to Sydney he had that waiting for him.

That weekend was so special. Andy took his guitar and the boys had jamming sessions, we ate beautiful food and we relaxed as a family for the first time in ages. We even dared ourselves to talk about the future, because suddenly everything was looking really positive. Six weeks beforehand we'd thought Andy would soon be dead. It made us realise how destructive the chemotherapy was.

Those days away totally reframed our mindset. We still knew that Andy had cancer, but maybe he would survive.

'I'm not going to let cancer rule our lives,' Andy said. 'It was worse when they diagnosed it last year. I could go on for years.'

It became all about 'how to live with cancer' as opposed to 'how to die with cancer'.

22

Learning to Let Go

*You never know how strong you are until being
strong is the only choice you have.*
— Cayla Mills

June 2011

Andy continued on with the radiation and he was doing
really well. He searched for inspiration through other
cancer survivors by speaking with them, going to
support groups and reading positive survival stories, but found
that simply going about his own life, factoring in a slower pace
but pursuing things that made him happy, was the best way to
navigate life with lymphoma.

He went to auditions, albeit occasionally a little slurred in
his speech, depending on the level of pain medication he had
to take. He began teaching the odd acting master class, which
always left him inspired – all those young actors, hungry to get
their break. I opened up my coaching practice to a few select

clients and was loving being immersed again in the insight and wisdom that comes from facilitating the lives of others.

In early June we organised drinks with friends to celebrate both my 38th birthday and Andy just being there. It really was a miracle, after all we'd been told and after seeing how sick he was during chemotherapy. Now every day was a blessing and we felt like we'd been granted a second chance. I actually began to believe that maybe, just maybe, we were influencing his ability to keep the cancer from progressing. Andy stayed through the evening and chatted with friends. He wasn't drinking, but just him being present and a part of it was the best birthday present ever.

But then in the middle of June the pain began to creep back into his system. We were obviously worried, so he went for a scan, and the tests results were terrible. Although the main tumour had shrunk, it was growing back voraciously and new cancers had emerged. It was now in his lungs. In the doctors' opinion, there was no point in continuing with the radiation treatment. We realised the medicos were done with us. In their minds, it was now only a matter of time.

On every occasion that Andy had had treatment, whether it was chemo or radiation, initially something seemed to work and the tumours shrunk. Then, it was as if the cancer somehow re-rallied itself for battle and came back with a bigger army, more wretched little cancer cell troops, weapons up and stronger than before.

From that point onward, Andy was suffering incredible pain and he went downhill very quickly. He was getting colds and his system was totally worn out, and so we were introduced to palliative care. We had two lovely nurses from Sacred Heart palliative care come to visit us at home. It was time to change gear and welcome their support.

They were so wonderful and quickly the level of care we had changed dramatically. In Latin, 'palliative' means 'to cloak', to wrap a cloak around you from your pain, from your challenge, from your fear and, for so many, from the grief at letting go. The nurses were able to have a conversation with us about what was happening, how we were feeling and how to deal with Andy's pain. It felt wonderfully supportive and nurturing, and to be honest if we'd had that sort of care all the way along, this experience would've been so much better for the both of us.

These women were equipped to give us not just the science behind what was happening in Andy's body but all of a sudden the conversation changed and words like 'battle' and descriptions like 'beat this' were replaced with questions like, 'How are you feeling about what I've just told you?' and 'What support can we give you to focus less on your pain?' They reassured us this didn't mean it was the end; instead, they were there to help us learn how to live with Andy's pain and manage each day so that there was quality of life for however long that might be. I couldn't understand why all health care professionals, especially those who might get to throw out a prediction of when you might die, would not be trained to facilitate and talk with such grace, kindness and clarity.

We were still living in the apartment, which posed a problem functioning day to day because Andy could barely walk and the stairs were incredibly difficult to manage. My friend Kiki came around one morning and we decided to take Andy out to his favourite café for a cup of tea. There were three flights of stairs from the apartment to ground level and as I turned to close the apartment door behind me, all I could hear was a dreadful thumping sound. Andy had fallen down the stairs. He took the first step, then his leg gave way from under him and he had no feeling at all in his left leg. Soon Andy would no longer be able to walk.

Kiki and I bundled him up and carried him to the bottom of the stairs, which was no mean feat because he was still a big man, and I called the palliative care unit. I told them what had happened and the nurse said, 'It's nerve damage. Don't panic, this is not the end. Bring him in straightaway and he can stay for a few days and we will teach him how to walk again with a leg brace.'

It was wonderful to have that support. I could call them anytime and it was always a lovely, calm voice that greeted us and gave us the answers we needed. They were amazing.

So Kiki and I helped Andy to the car, as he did his best to keep his cool and not panic that his leg no longer worked. Then I raced back upstairs and grabbed a bag of his things and we drove straight to the hospice in Darlinghurst.

Andy was really welcoming of this. Day-to-day life had become such a struggle that the thought of being able to have a rest was a relief. He just wanted someone to look after him now; he just wanted to be taken care of and not have to struggle anymore. I also could have a little break while we worked out what to do next. I knew he was in good hands.

*

There were four men in Andy's room, all significantly older as you'd expect in palliative care. Among them was one very old man who was completely jaundiced. His eyes were almost rolling back into his head and his leg was hanging out over the mattress; he looked like he should've been dead already.

He stood out to me because he had old tattoos all over his body, as if he was once a merchant sailor or something. They were like a treasure map and I remember wondering what his story was. As he lay in the bed opposite my beautiful, young husband it reaffirmed to me that no matter how long or short your life journey is, you need to make it a story. I thought about the tattoos Andy and I had back in New Zealand nearly a year earlier and the relevance of what the words BE HERE NOW really meant.

There were two very funny cats that were the hospice pets, named utterly inappropriately but hilariously after chemotherapy drugs. The cats were wonderfully healing and the patients loved them, especially the older ones. These cats had an amazing sixth sense; they'd mooch around to whoever was next to die. I was so relieved they never came near Andy. It wasn't his time yet.

We both knew by now that the apartment was no longer an option; it had become dangerous and absolutely impractical for Andy. That was a big moment in our lives. Our gorgeous sun-filled apartment was our home and letting go of it was like letting go of *Spartacus*; we were letting go of another part of our life together.

Andy never went back to that apartment again. As soon as he was settled into the hospice, I raced home and jumped on the phone to try to find us somewhere new to live. We had to have a place that was easily accessible and didn't have stairs.

I wanted to live in Paddington again, near our favourite café and just around the corner from Jesse's school. I was driving down a street in Paddington when I saw a For Lease sign on the front of a house. I rang the real estate agent, explained the urgency of what was happening and asked if they could meet me there so I could take a look. It was lovely little semi nestled between two magnificent five-storey Paddington mansions, with a Japanese maple out the front. It was perfect. I put in an application that afternoon and bizarrely got a call first thing the next morning from the real estate agent.

'You're in luck,' she said. 'Your application has been approved, but the owner needs you to know that she knows who you are.'

And I thought, 'Oh god, is it some crazy *Spartacus* fan?'

But it turned out the owner of the property was Dr Angela Hong, Andy's radiation oncologist. This woman knew Andy was close to dying, but she still let us rent her property, even knowing I was about to become a single mum and a widow. I was totally touched by her generosity and, as I write this book, I am sitting looking out at the same little maple tree that warmly invited me in.

In the meantime, Andy was learning to walk again in palliative care. He had a leg brace and crutches, and he could get himself up and about, which was great. He was allowed to come out for a few hours to see the new house, even though there was no furniture or anything in it at that stage. His mum Pat had flown back over to help us, so Pat and I took Andy through the new place and we started to visualise how it would all come together. Andy hobbled around on his crutches and as we walked through it I very enthusiastically said, 'We'll put the dining table here, and the sofa here, and it will be wonderful, because the kids can run around out the back and you can sit on the deck in the sun.'

I was trying to be very positive about it all, but it was tough for Andy. He put on a brave face, but he had to leave the home we loved and that was a kick in the guts. He struggled to make it down the three tiny steps to the back deck of the new house, and as the main bedroom was upstairs, he knew he was going to be sleeping on the sofa. I was trying to paint a picture of our future life there and thinking of the house from the perspective of being a carer: there was a bathroom right next to the living room, so Andy could sleep downstairs and be near the toilet, and he could shuffle outside and sit in the sun if he wanted to. But deep down we both knew that I had found a place that would facilitate Andy only in the short term; ultimately it would be the safe little sanctuary that would transition us from being a family of four to one of three. I was showing him the space we'd be living in, but he was never really going to be part of it all. I can't imagine what that must've been like for him.

While Andy was in palliative care, we worked like sherpas to move out of the apartment and into the new home. Pat helped me get settled in and within a week Andy was home. He was starting to look very thin. He was on a constant stream of different drugs throughout the day, having laxatives to stop extreme constipation and taking pain killers so he could function, which he was barely doing. Pat was a godsend but curiously Andy didn't want his dad to come out. I think on some level he knew that if his dad was flying out from Wales, he was accepting that this time he was dying and I don't think he was ready to emotionally go there yet.

But on some level, despite his not wanting to go 'there', as if by speaking the words it might break all that he had left to give, Andy agreed that we should complete our wills. It was a bit surreal, sitting together and signing our names as to what would happen if neither of us were here for the kids. Andy joked about the crap inheritance of Ikea furniture that the kids might receive, and I was not to forget that his sperm was still on ice in New Zealand, so if I needed to make some extra cash later on to pay the school fees, I could sell him off for breeding!

'We made it this far together,' Andy said, as he squeezed my hand.

We'd heard about this amazing acupuncturist in Auckland, just off Ponsonby Road, near where we used to live. This guy apparently specifically treated people with terminal cancer to help them with their blood flow and to get their energy up. We couldn't find anyone in Sydney doing anything quite like it, and Andy was really keen to go and have some treatment with him. We weren't under any false pretences that this would be a cure, far from it. But we thought it might give Andy more energy or increase his quality of life. We were thinking about how we could boost his system to give him the best possible quality of life, however long he had left.

The stars for New Zealand suddenly began to align for us. Our friend Chloe Smith, who'd worked on *Spartacus* and was helping us with the documentary, was in Australia and had to go back to New Zealand. And we'd been invited to attend the wedding in Auckland of one of the *Spartacus* producers.

I couldn't go; there was no way I could take the kids and Andy and care for them all. But Chloe offered to fly back with Andy and Pat. They could stay with her and attend the wedding while Andy also had treatment. Pat would be on hand to care for him.

It all seemed quite logical and Andy was really buoyed by the chance to go to New Zealand again and catch up with his old *Spartacus* buddies. It gave him something to look forward to and even though I knew he was weak, it gave me a moment's pause to re-group. By now I was nursing him around the clock, bathing and dressing him, and taking him to the toilet. It was exhausting, so I could hardly say no. Besides, he needed some time to reboot and find his way again, which he'd done so many times before. And maybe the acupuncture would give us a few more good months. It was worth a go.

Chloe organised business class flights and paid for everything, which was incredibly generous. She arranged for a driver to meet them at the airport and be at Andy's disposal. Over the next 24 hours Andy had two treatments with the acupuncturist, who also gently manipulated his body to try to create better blood flow to his now redundant legs. Then some friends visited and, with his little entourage, they all went off to the wedding. Although Andy was in a wheelchair he somehow managed to muster some energy because he had his suit on. He went around to speak with everyone he wanted to see and, by all reports, he was funny and witty and very present.

I suspect all this was very confronting for his *Spartacus* buddies. So many people had only ever seen him as a legend on set, this big muscular hulk of a man, sparkly and alive. And yet here he was – thin, frail and in a wheelchair, his muscles gone but his smile as big as ever. The warrior they had known was now a man on the brink of a very different journey. But I still don't think anyone believed he wouldn't pull through.

A day after the wedding, I got a call from Chloe.

'Vashti, you need to get here and you need to get here really soon. I don't think Pat wants to say anything, but we are losing Andy.'

This was so tough for Pat, she was absolutely torn. She was adamant that she would do whatever Andy wanted to support him, and didn't in any way want to be the one who was disagreeing. I think she thought that if she was the one to call me she might be betraying him.

I wasn't sad, I wasn't happy, I just swung straight into crisis mode. I got the kids organised to stay with some friends, booked a flight and was there the next morning. When I arrived at Georgia's beautiful apartment, Andy was sitting there, very peaceful in an Eames lounge chair, wrapped in a blanket and looking out the window. He was comfortable but he was staring, smiling, sort of chattering to himself like an old man.

In my very clear, bossy Vashti voice, I said, 'Andy, Andy it's me.'

I was really the only one he would respond to. He'd have a little chatter and then he'd stare off into space again. I described it as Andy 'going off to the other room', because it was like he was somewhere else. He wasn't sad or scared, he just wasn't present. Every now and again he'd kind of snap out of it and be with us. Then his mind would drift off again.

That evening Pat was about to go out to get us all some takeaway dinner. Andy, who was sitting on the chair, said, 'I need to go to the bathroom.'

'Okay, hold on,' I said.

But before I could get up he said, 'Oh, I'm so sorry.'

In that moment his bodily functions had gone. The clock was ticking down very fast.

Pat rushed out to the shops to buy what none of us ever imagined having to purchase for her incredible son, and came back shortly afterwards with a packet of incontinence pads. Chloe was with me and she was so wonderful, very gently reassuring Andy that it was okay, there was nothing to be embarrassed about and it would take nothing to clean up.

Then the two of us with all of our might lifted him into the wheelchair so I could wheel him into the bathroom. There was a mess everywhere and I had to try to lift him and get him to the bathroom to clean him up. It took every ounce of effort he could muster to stand up and when he sat back down in the bathroom, he stopped breathing, it had taken that much out of him.

Suddenly from nowhere, in a huge raspy breath, he said, 'I can't do this anymore, Vashti. I need to go, please let me go.'

I remember feeling a wave of panic. A red hot rage surged through my body and I shouted at him, 'There is no way you get to die here. Andy, do you hear me? If you die here, your children will never get to say goodbye to their father. You do not die now, do you understand?'

And out of the blue he took this big breath and said, 'Okay, okay, help me up.'

At that moment he wanted to go and I have no doubt that if I'd let him he would've died right there and then.

I still had our very first oncologist Dr Richard Doocey's number in my phone, and I needed some guidance as to what to do. He very kindly took my call.

'Vashti,' he said, 'get him home as soon as you can. Get on the next flight and get home.'

If Andy had died in New Zealand, it could have been weeks before his body was returned to Sydney. And he wouldn't have been able to see the kids, which for me was such an important part of their journey in letting their daddy go.

So with that, it was game on. We all rallied around to get Andy home as quickly as we could. Chloe rang the airlines, while Pat packed up, and with a bit of wheeling and dealing Chloe got us on the next available flight, so we basically called the car and bolted to the airport. Soon, we were in the business class lounge. Andy was sitting in the wheelchair barely breathing and I was holding his head up because he couldn't even do that. It was like a bad scene from a Peter Sellers film, a complete comedy of errors, with two women trying to wrangle an obviously very unwell man aboard a flight. The male flight attendant seemed to sense what was going on and was incredibly helpful. He helped lift Andy into his seat, then gave me the space to attend to him without getting in my way.

Andy's body was shutting down, bit by bit. I virtually had to mould his legs into the seat, because the blood flow had stopped and they'd become like jelly. It was bizarre, but I felt completely unemotional. It was as though every aspect of my senses was heightened. I had to get Andy home alive and I would do whatever it took to make that happen.

My seat was just across the aisle from Andy's, on a slight angle. I couldn't clearly see his face, so I spent the next three hours saying 'Andy' very gently. He'd respond 'Yes', and I'd know he was still alive.

*

We left Auckland at 10 p.m. and arrived back in Sydney just after 1 a.m. I called the hospice from the car, but the nurse said, 'Look, there's no point bringing him in, it's only night staff. Take him home tonight and bring him in first thing in the morning.'

'But what if he dies?' I asked.

And she said, 'Then just be with him.'

So we got Andy settled on the sofa. Pat was with me every step of the way and she was amazing. This was her son and my husband, and we were doing things like changing his nappy. It was heartbreaking and terribly confronting for us both in different ways, but we were doing this together. The two women in his life, the one who gave birth to him and the one who gave birth to his children, going through this extraordinary experience together.

We probably would never have had that relationship if Andy hadn't been sick. Pat's courage was incredible. She stepped up to the plate at an immensely difficult time and was so supportive for me and Andy. She never questioned what was going on, she just guided Andy through and was there right beside him in whatever he wanted to do. She was there for every single minute of her son's final months; she brought him into the world and she was there to see him out. And we did it together.

It was an extraordinary process to facilitate someone letting go of their life. I lay next to Andy all night and stroked his face. Early the next morning the ambulance arrived and took him to the hospice. Pat called Rob and told him to come as fast as he could and bring Andy's sister Laura with him. I didn't ask my parents to come; it was all happening so fast that I just needed to focus on getting Rob and Laura here for Andy. We crossed our fingers he would hold on until they arrived.

The hospice was incredible, so nurturing and serene and incredibly peaceful, which was ironic given that it was in the middle of crazy, brash Darlinghurst. It was a very lovely, calm little oasis where you could let your soul go.

Very few people were invited to come and see Andy; we just needed quiet. I asked his dear friend Marty to come; she'd done acting classes with him and they became great friends. Marty came and sat with him and talked to him. He was in and out of consciousness. Some moments he'd be with us and others he'd be off 'in the other room', as we called it. The nurses would come in and ask how he was and I'd say, 'He's spending a lot of time in the other room today!'

He'd have these moments where he'd be away somewhere then all of a sudden he'd start speaking French! Not good French, mind you, but rather like Del Boy from the English television series *Only Fools and Horses*, more like someone speaking Franglais. Pat sat very patiently beside him saying, 'Okay, darling' and 'Yes, dear.' We didn't know whether he was hallucinating or remembering something from another time in his life. It was a very beautiful, peaceful and sometimes quite funny time.

The most challenging hurdle for me to face was getting Andy and the children ready to say goodbye to one another. There was a family room at the hospice, so we brought the children in and took them there first. There was a whiteboard and I had drawn pictures of Andy asleep next to a cloud, with a smiling pussycat in the sunshine and the sun and the stars above him. I explained that Daddy's body was broken and that we could no longer fix it. I said that soon he would need to go to sleep, and that once he went to sleep it would be so deep that he would never wake up, and this was called dying.

Jesse began to cry. 'But I don't want Daddy to go,' he protested.

'I know, darling, and nor do I,' I said, while giving him a gentle hug.

Indi was more interested in one of the cats that had managed to interrupt the conversation long enough for Jesse to stop crying. They both ran over and took to a cat each, so I left them for a minute and went in to Andy. In my loud bossy voice, which was the only voice he seemed to respond to, I said, 'Andy, Jesse and Indi are coming to say goodbye. It's time to wake up.'

And he did. We took Jesse and Indi into the room, and they climbed up onto the bed with him. Andy looked quite sweet, not at all scary. He'd lost a lot of weight and his bones were very angular, but his hair had grown back and he was very peaceful. When he heard the kids, he sat up and rallied himself. He hugged them both and in a very gentle, reassuring voice he said, 'I am going to go to heaven soon. I have to go to heaven because my body is really broken. It's like a butterfly when one of its wings is broken, it can't fly anymore. But don't worry, because I'm going to go up into the sky and every time you look up you'll see me.'

It was a very beautiful moment and I was in awe of how he was able to muster the strength one last time for those two precious cubs so they could say goodbye to their daddy.

On the morning of 11 September, Rob arrived. He came straight to the hospice from the airport. I had warned him that he needed to prepare himself a little because the Andy he had last seen wasn't who he'd be seeing today. I'd told Rob that this was it, and Andy might only have a matter of days left, we didn't know how long.

But Rob was adamant. 'There must be something we can do, there must be some treatment he can have.'

But it was way past that stage and Rob realised that when he saw Andy. The last time he'd seen Andy he was so well and healthy. It was almost unimaginable for him to see his son as he was now.

Then Laura arrived and she came straight to see Andy too; she made it just in the nick of time. Andy's breathing had become very intense over these past few days. His body was breaking down and he was taking very deep long breaths, a bit like Darth Vader, a kind of a haunting rattling sound. He was almost gone.

Once Laura and Rob were with Andy, I knew I could step away for a moment. I hadn't eaten for days, so I left the hospice and walked down the street to get a muffin and a cup of coffee. As I walked along this lovely leafy street in Darlinghurst, I felt a real sense of peace because I knew it was close. All the people who needed to say their goodbyes had arrived and that was a massive relief. Whatever would be, now could be.

I remember holding a coffee in one hand and a berry muffin in the other, and I can recall the way they looked and smelt and tasted, like it was yesterday. There was sunlight coming through the trees and my senses were totally heightened to everything around me. I was totally aware of the warmth of the spring sunshine on my back and I savoured this otherwise ordinary muffin as if it was the most delicious thing I'd ever eaten, because in that moment it was.

As I walked back to the hospice, I almost had a smile on my face. I was saying hello to everyone who walked past me. I was lost in the moment. There was no life or death or anything, it was all about right now. For me, somehow Andy had already gone. From the moment I'd arrived in New Zealand and seen him happily staring out the window, from moulding his misshapen legs into the leather seats on the plane, to listening to my best friend, the father of my children, say goodbye to his babies, with every little stage I had begun to let him go.

When I got back the hospice, Laura and Rob were coming out of Andy's room, very upset because of course they'd just said goodbye to their brother and son. I walked in and took a good look around. I saw a collage of family photos that went with Andy on every hospital stay. The kids' drawings were stuck on the wall. There was the blanket that the *Spartacus* crew had sent him when he was first diagnosed. And the body of my frail husband wearing a Triumph motorcycle t-shirt that was half cut off because the doctors had to get to him to administer painkillers.

I lay down on the bed next to Andy. Coincidentally, the double bed he was in had been bought for the hospice by our friend Mark Boysen when he lost his wife Kate. When Kate was sick, one of the most challenging things for them was that they couldn't lie down next to one another in her final days. So Mark raised money and donated this bed in memory of Kate, which we were able to share.

I laid my hand on Andy's chest. It was moving up and down, but he smelt different, and his breath was different. It wasn't him anymore. It was really peaceful and suddenly it was very quiet and I leant in to his ear and said, 'You can go now, Andy, it's okay.'

There was no more reason for him to be here. Laura had been to see him, his father had made it to say goodbye, and Pat had been there every step of the way. I snuggled into his lovely bony neck, which had always been my favourite place to rest, and I said, 'You don't have to be here anymore. You can go, Andy.'

It was strange, because literally there was nothing left in him, but all of a sudden he made a noise and out of the blue somehow he managed to mumble a sound that was like 'love you'. And then he exhaled a long breath and he was gone.

I just stayed there. I sobbed into his chest, but it felt like I was releasing him too. It was like catching a little bird and then letting it go. His body no longer resembled Andy; it wasn't my husband, my husband had gone. This shell of a body was there, but Andy was gone. He'd literally gone. Just like a beautiful butterfly that lands on a leaf in front of you one minute, in the blink of an eye, Andy was completely gone.

I got up off the bed, packed the bags, got all of our stuff together, left the room and didn't look at his body ever again. I walked out and embraced everyone. We were all sobbing and hugging, and then I left. I went home to Paddington and that was the last time I saw Andy, my gorgeous, precious Andy.

I'd lost my best friend, my lover, my husband and the person who taught me about life, death and everything in between. But here I was, ready to take on life once again.

23

Learning to Fly

*Just when the caterpillar thought the world was
over it became a butterfly.*
— Proverb

September 2011

As I left the hospital, my senses felt bizarrely sharpened. It was almost as if I could tune out from the buzz of the city and hear the tiniest sounds around me. I could make out every colour popping in the blossoms, as if all of a sudden I could once again see. For the last eighteen months I had virtually turned my back on everything external and given everything I had to Andy, Jesse and Indi.

I left everyone at the hospital, climbed into my car and dialled the US cell number of Andy's American manager, Sam Maydew, who was now also a close family friend. It was 11 September in the USA, a day when for so many, exactly a decade earlier, their own world had been turned upside down. Andy and I had narrowly escaped. Unlike so many others, we had been given another ten years together, able to experience births, deaths and marriages and so much else in between. All I could feel in that moment was enormous gratitude for the time I had with Andy.

As I told Sam about Andy's passing, I felt a little tear roll down my cheek. Somehow saying it out loud for the first time made it suddenly real. We would need to release a statement for the press, so I said goodbye to Sam after he let me know that he would fly over shortly for the funeral. Then I sat on the side of the road and typed out the press release on my Blackberry. It read:

On a beautiful sunny Sydney spring morning, surrounded by his family, in the arms of his loving wife, our beautiful young warrior Andy Whitfield lost his battle with lymphoma cancer. He passed away peacefully surrounded by love. Thank you to all of his fans whose love and support has helped carry him to this point. He will be remembered as the inspiring, courageous, gentle man, father and husband he was.

It was the last official thing I had to do before I could surrender to being cared for by others.

My dearest friend Lou Lou arrived from London and gently took me under her wing. My beautiful friend Kiki offered to look after the logistics of the funeral; she was a project planner extraordinaire and I knew she would help me to create something wonderful to pay tribute to Andy. So I just did what I was told for a few days, guided by these two incredible women who swept in to take care of me when I needed them most. All I had to do was say yes or no to things I most wanted to honour Andy and all those who loved him. His family graciously let me manage it all, trusting that I would choose a way that would be true to him.

Those first few days were very strange. I'd been so close to the illness and so immersed in caring for Andy that I was sort of floating around, not knowing quite what to do with myself and yet feeling like there where a million things to do. It was like I had been living in a huge house but only ever using the one room. I knew exactly how to function in that room, and then all of a sudden the whole house was opened up and I didn't know which room to explore first.

I wasn't in a hospital, I wasn't injecting Andy with drugs, I wasn't wondering if I was going to get home from the hospital to have dinner with the kids because I'd missed dinner with them for the last five nights and I wasn't missing Andy as I knew him. I was letting go of the sick broken Andy whose body I left in the Sacred Heart hospice.

I was beginning to remember the real Andy, the one before *Spartacus* and before his illness, the Andy I married. It was very strange allowing myself to feel relieved at letting my husband go, but what I hadn't yet realised was that I hadn't even begun to let my Andy go. This was grief as I came to know it, a state of perpetual haze for a few days. My true grief was delayed and didn't come until much later. At the beginning I was merely on auto-pilot, ticking off things that had to be done.

There was to be a funeral, just for the immediate family and a small number of close friends, then a memorial service later on for everyone else. We needed to have the funeral fairly quickly because some people needed to get back overseas; others needed time to get here for a memorial.

Having Lou Lou around helped me transcend all of the greyness of Andy's illness and death. She lifted me above the grief of the others around me and allowed to begin to remember Andy's and my life together when we first met in London. After all, she had literally been the one who brought us together back in 1998, so it was only natural that she was with me to help guide us apart.

The day after Andy's death I had to go to the funeral parlour with Kiki. The funeral director was a lovely guy, but we were ushered into this bland, colourless room with nothing on the walls, no pictures, no flowers, nothing emotive or decorative at all, just a desk, a chair or so, and some plastic folders on the desk, an array of coffin shopping catalogues. I guess the lack of ambience was deliberate because it didn't encourage any emotion. My task was to choose a coffin. How do you pick a coffin for a cremation anyway? The words that would be spoken mattered, the coffin did not.

That morning, with glamorous Lou Lou at my side, I had dressed into something other than the bog standard gym gear that I'd lived in over the last year and put on some make-up. I was putting on a false, but brave face. As Kiki and I were sitting in this very dull room at the funeral home, I realised that we were in fact the colour. Life is the colour in the world; it's not the things around us that create the music, it's the people singing a song.

There were many very funny and touching moments in the midst of getting ready for Andy's send off. Lou Lou and I had to choose the clothing for Andy to be dressed in for his cremation.

So here we were in my bedroom with his sharp grey Hugo Boss blazer, which always made him look like James Bond, his Deus motorcycle t-shirt, his blue Nudie jeans and his grey Converse sneakers, all spread out on the bed like a flat pack set of clothes. I decided to keep his dog tags, which had Jesse's and Indi's birth dates inscribed on them; later these would find their way to around their godfather Jai Courtney's neck.

But something was missing. In a fit of giggles, I realised that Andy's outfit was missing undies. Andy always wore undies, he hated going commando. So the two of us decided that to make his outfit perfect we would include his lucky red underwear. The hysterical laughter was so needed. How else could I cope with the fact that I was choosing the clothes to wrap around the shell of my husband's body that would shortly be turned to flame and then ash? It was all so surreal. I could imagine Andy laughing his head off at the two of us actually discussing whether or not he should be wearing underpants.

We had a small funeral service a few days after Andy passed away, then on 18 September, a week after Andy died, we all gathered together again for the memorial service at St Mark's in Darling Point. Although none of us are particularly religious we were so grateful for the opportunity to use this beautiful church, with its elaborate blue ceiling, with huge golden stars painted all over it. It was a work of art, a place where people came together collectively to celebrate life and death. It was the perfect place to honour Andy and all those who wanted to celebrate him and his life and our love for him.

People flew in from around the world, the church was literally overflowing with people who had been a part of Andy's life in one way or another. There was security outside to make sure that the press kept a safe distance, and I was surrounded by a small entourage of friends in a side room, so I could prepare myself for all the people who would soon come together right in front of me to remember the life that Andy and I had shared.

It was an extraordinary feeling to look out over a sea of heads and know that Andy had meant something to all of these people; it was very special. Jai had organised for his friend, a beautiful jazz and blues artist, to sing 'Amazing Grace', which instantly brought everyone to tears. Then the church was blasted with Oh Laura's 'Release Me', one of Andy's and my favourite songs. Chloe Smith, the New Zealand producer and now an incredible friend, spoke about Andy in terms of blood and sand, which was the sub-title for the first season of *Spartacus*, and talked of his warrior-like being.

We also screened the haka, the Maori ceremony that the crew had performed to honour Andy and bid him farewell. Their warrior cries and gut wrenching momentum made my hair stand on end. Sam Maydew read a prayer and talked about who Andy was at his essence. Beautiful Marty, with her soft eyes and long elegant body, read the Sam McBratney children's book *Guess How Much I Love You*, Andy's favourite book to read to the cubs. That now famous line 'I love you right up to the moon . . . and back' summed up what Andy had been.

When it was my turn to speak, it really felt like the most incredible honour to be able to stand up and talk about the man who was Andy. While I had thought about what I wanted to say and revisited the specific stories that I wanted to give reference to, when I looked out into all those blazing eyes staring so intensely at me, I could really do nothing else but speak from my heart. There was no stumbling or staggering over my words, it was as though the words just poured out intuitively and effortlessly.

I shared the story that Andy told the children about being a butterfly when he died, and I said that Andy had fluttered into everyone's life and touched them in some way with his humble beauty. I asked the congregation of people we held dear not to see it as a sad thing that Andy had flown out of our lives, but to see it as a beautiful opportunity to celebrate life and the influence he had and will have on us, both dead and alive.

I read an African poem, 'Singing Your Song', which Andy read at Jesse Red's naming ceremony. It's an ancient tribal poem about uniquely identifying who you are, 'your song', and using this on your journey through life to always remind you of who you are and where you come from. That was what Andy and I were for each other. We were there to remind each other of who we really were. With Andy now not being here, his absence would forever more remind me of what it really means to be true to myself, and to do the same for all those who came into my life.

After the hype and intensity of the funeral and memorial, we were left with a supposed calm, but it still felt far from that, inside my head anyway. We still had all of our family here, and some friends, and the thought of spending time with Andy's and my family all of a sudden seemed overwhelming. I felt like I needed space, some distance to begin the grieving process.

It was a time when suddenly the thing that had brought us all together felt very much like it had come to end. It was a strange but special time, because we were all grieving in different ways.

It was a little claustrophobic too. My tolerance, patience and sensitivity were off the charts in terms of who I wanted around me. I'd reached the stage where I just wanted everyone else who was grieving the loss of Andy to go away to give me the time and space to work out what was going on in my life. Having everyone else's grief swirling around me had become oppressive.

I distinctly remember watching Andy's father having a *Star Wars*, mini lightsaber battle with Indi and Jesse, and then seeing him quietly disappear into the bathroom, the sadness having taken over so powerfully that he just had to walk away. His loss was so raw that I badly wanted to hold him and pat him lovingly. But just as I wanted him to be able to grieve the death of his beautiful son, I also wanted the space for myself to be able to look forward without pain.

I know that all my mum and dad wanted was for me to collapse into their arms and ask them to stay, but their need to be needed was stifling. We were all very fragile, all dealing with our emotions in our own way, with no right or wrong. But the tension was building within me.

One afternoon we were sitting around my dining table. There were huge bunches and bouquets of flowers everywhere, and hundreds of cards. I would beg any friend that popped around to take a bunch of flowers with them, because it looked like a funeral home and it was becoming depressing.

Mum, in her very gentle sweet way, said, 'Oh no, darling. They're such beautiful flowers, you must keep them.'

It pushed me over the edge. I reared up like a cobra and growled at her, 'Do you really think I want all of these fucking flowers around to remind me that my husband is dead?'

My father jumped up out of his chair very dramatically and said, 'How dare you speak to Mum like that.'

I knew things were about to turn ugly if I didn't walk away. But it was my house, my home, and I knew in that moment I needed everyone to go. It was time for me to get on with my life. Was I being selfish? Probably. But the truth is, all I cared about – and all I was capable of at that point – was just being with my little cubs. I just wanted to take a walk down by the beach, breathe in the spring air of a new day, and explore the strange and bizarre emptiness and freedom of what tomorrow might feel like, with no cancer, no pain and no caring to be given.

About a week later, everyone left. Pat and Rob went home to Wales. Pat had been in Sydney for a long time helping us and she was a rock. We were sad to see her and everyone else go, but it was time. Then everything went quiet, but in a positive, calm way that allowed us to re-group.

I didn't go to Bondi running or do any of the normal things I did anywhere I could bump into people who might not know Andy had died, because I didn't want to have to talk about it or explain what happened. We just hunkered down and stayed very much between school and home, nurturing ourselves in our little Paddington community. I could walk to the corner café and they'd usher me in and give me breakfast without asking for money, then send me home with lasagna for dinner. The community was just wonderful and wrapped us up with love. School parents got together and made a roster to cook for us. We'd come home and there'd be a little delivery of home-cooked meals on the doorstep, for which we were so grateful. Really, those gestures were unbelievably kind and helped us feel incredibly supported within our neighbourhood. It was such a protective, nurturing environment for us to begin finding our feet again.

For the first little while, my real focus was on Jesse and Indi and getting them settled into life again. It had been a strange time for them. Their dad was gone, but they really hadn't spent much time with him in the month before he died, because he was in and out of the hospice.

In the days immediately after Andy's death, there were lots of people around. Their grandparents were here, there was always someone to kick a soccer ball around with them, and every time someone came to the house or we picked up the mail, they were given gifts. They got toys and Toys "R" Us vouchers, and people were lavishing attention on them, so it kind of seemed like a bit of a fun time, which presented a confusing set of emotions for them to deal with, given their dad had just died. But they'd said their goodbye to him and they knew he was gone; their acceptance was largely due to how Andy handled his farewell to them.

I'd been really diligent in trying to educate myself and understand the process of grief, specifically for the kids' sakes. I had this blueprint of 'you're going to feel this or that', so I knew what to expect, but straight after Andy died I just felt enormous relief. Not because I wanted him to die, but I'd been caring for him and looking after him for eighteen months. We'd been going through this journey together and being several different people for so long had really stretched me.

So in the first few months it was all about embracing life again, and embracing my grief and honouring it. I decided to sell our apartment to enable me to be at home with the kids and not have to rush straight back to work. I didn't want to have to worry about how we were going to survive, and I'm grateful I had the luxury of being able to sit back and reflect on the experience Andy and I'd shared. I came to a place of accepting what had happened and was able to look at the situation to see what it had given us and what it had taken away.

But there were moments of real grief that would come in unexpected waves. Indi's birthday was looming in mid-October and Andy's 40th birthday would've been a couple of days later. It felt gut wrenching to be thinking about Andy's birthday so close to having let him go at only 39 years of age, but the kids and I made that time a celebration of his legacies to us. Only a month after his death, he was already teaching me to re-frame everything to be an opportunity to celebrate life.

Nonetheless, as the dust began to settle an unexpected tsunami of grief began to creep in. At first I started questioning myself. What if I'd gone to India with him? Would it have made a difference? Would we have stayed there? I began to wonder what would have happened if I'd been a more supportive partner and not made him go through so much of it alone. If I'd supported him not wanting to chemo, would he still be alive? Could I have changed the outcome?

I started to entertain the thought that perhaps it was my fault that he had become so ill, so quickly. I was fine through-out the day, but when the night came, the cavernous space in my empty bed in the bedroom that Andy didn't get to sleep one night in, began to push me into the lonely corner of my mind and grief would take over. I missed him so much. But then the sun would rise and the little cubs' voices would fill the house, and those dark thoughts would be gone, because there was life to be lived.

A few weeks later I started taking myself off to the cinema during the evenings, after the kids had gone to bed and if I could get a sitter to watch them. While not being someone very much into snowy climates in real life, I found myself drawn to movies that were set in icy, remote parts of Scandinavia and faraway lands. The more remote and isolated, the more I felt drawn to them. And there, sitting alone in the Palace Verona cinema, having 'Andy time' as I called it, I would fantasise about being able to just disappear, like the characters in the film. To walk off into the barren mountains, to have the space to be free.

I'd sometimes go for long rides around the city on my bike late at night and would often find myself thinking that if Jesse and Indi weren't here then I could ride straight into a wall and it would all be over. I could be with Andy. I'd lived an incredible life, I didn't need anymore. But I didn't actually want to harm myself, and I had no intention whatsoever of leaving my two beautiful babies. They were all just thoughts led by the process of grieving that in some ways was text book, but regardless, it was still overwhelming. That part of me that didn't want to live without Andy, and the feeling that it made no sense to remain here, like all bad dreams, would only exist in my mind for a short time.

I began to read up about grief and neuroscience and about how loss manifests in different ways. I was able to identify what was going on for me and the stages I was going through, which not only reassured me about the normality of my thinking but also gave me a system of working through them. It wasn't that I wanted to speed track my grief, which is of course impossible, or that I wanted to deprive myself of feeling the gaping hole that was left without Andy's presence. I just wanted to understand it so that I could appreciate it for the necessary part of my life that it was. It was also very important for me to be able to healthily raise my cubs in a way that would absorb the bumps and challenges coming their way in the years ahead.

My life had been about Andy and creating a world with him. When I met Andy, I knew there was a reason in life and we were a force, we were meant to be together as one. When I revisited places we'd been together, restaurants or book stores or the beach, I'd look for him thinking, 'He might be over there.' That's when it hit me and I realised I was grieving. And I decided I was simply going to honour that. There were no right or wrong thoughts, I was grieving. What I'd had was just a thought and I understood where it was coming from, and having done that I could let it go. The pivotal point for me in dealing with my grief was just allowing things to come up and dealing with them – by talking about them with the kids if I wanted, by acknowledging how things impacted us. By the next day I'd have let it go.

*

A few months after Andy died, as I watered the jasmine plants on the deck one day, I saw Indi running frantically towards me.

'Look Mummy, look!' she squealed. She lifted up her little hands towards me and there, cupped between her two palms, she held a huge black and white butterfly the size of a man's hand. 'Daddy's here,' she said. 'He's come to see us and he even has a broken wing.'

It took my breath away.

Jesse and Indi had opened the front door to grab the mail from the mail box and there the butterfly was, perfectly laid out across the doormat, like a gift that had been specially delivered, waiting to be collected by its rightful owner. Indi put some tissue paper inside a Tupperware container and made a home for her broken butterfly. She carried it around lovingly and told everyone she met that it was her daddy.

That butterfly was such a thing of beauty, but it was clearly broken. It reminded me of Andy's body after he'd taken his last breath; his body was still a thing of beauty even though he was no longer here. The metaphor of the butterfly, seeing the representation of someone in the world after they have gone, is very poignant for me, and that's what the future is about now: Andy's legacy of transforming the ordinary into the extraordinary. I wanted to honour the concept of legacy – who you are, who you were and what you leave behind. And now this gorgeous little blonde curly-haired creature was holding up a very broken butterfly, but she was also adoring it because that was the legacy her father left. In that moment she could capture the essence and memory of him.

Some people fight for survival. Andy fought only to explore the purpose of his life and ultimately his death. He graciously and doggedly filmed and shared every aspect of his incredible journey to stay alive, and he invited the world into one of the loneliest and darkest times of his life. And yet in doing so, he exposed the light, the humour and the tenderness that only preparing to die will bring to you.

Andy accepted what was happening to him and he found a place where it was okay to let go, because letting go was now the bravest thing he could do. Along the way, however, he enabled us to see him in the world long after he'd gone. And he introduced me to the concept that however long or short your time is on the earth, it is how you choose to live, love and *be*, that will create your own inspiring legacy.

Andy taught us that there is a butterfly within all of us, waiting to hatch, fly, live, love and die.

Epilogue

To live, is the rarest thing in the world.
Most people exist, that is all.
— Oscar Wilde

I am filled with a tremendous sense of awe as I stand looking out at the sea of faces staring back at me. *Be Here Now* has just finished showing at Sydney's Palace Verona cinema, having already premiered around the world, and I am about to host a Q and A session with hundreds of people who are caught somewhere between being heartbroken and utterly inspired.

A bewildered woman a few rows back, whose face is vaguely familiar from somewhere around Sydney, asks, 'How do *you* go on to live life with such a positive outlook, when you've lost so much?'

As I inhale to gather my thoughts so I can intuitively respond in a way that will give her and everyone in the audience a sense of the value losing someone you love can give you, I am overwhelmed by the desire to simply answer, 'You just do your best to live, learn and let go of anything that stops you living your life to the fullest.'

But I don't say that. I stop myself momentarily. I remember that it has taken me five years of often stumbling around in the dark to live this statement with the integrity, wisdom and openness that it requires, and that, with every month and every year that has passed since Andy died, I have hurled myself into a new chapter and a new path of learning, and taken on things that many people, quite sensibly, would have turned away from.

Like the same naïve two-year-old that I once was, who in her eagerness to connect with people, dived into the middle of a swimming pool to tell the friendly strangers my name, which I could finally say, I will always, always dive in head first and learn how to swim along the way.

Standing there in the Verona, my mind turns to my blog Maybe McQueen, which over the last year or so has sat gathering dust while we worked on the birth of *Be Here Now*. Just by starting the blog, which began as a homage to Andy shortly after he died, I learned the difference I could make if I put fear and ego to the side. It became a home for my misspelled posts, chronicling every aspect of the ups and downs of learning to live without Andy, and then a guide and support structure for people wanting to be inspired to change their lives. But most of all it gave me the chance to abandon my beliefs about all the things I'd told myself I couldn't do and to start focusing on the things I could do.

The blog taught me about running before I could walk, as I bit off far more than I could chew, having forgotten that

I was now a single parent and a rather extroverted widow. It also taught me that if I was ever going to succeed as a woman running her own business, I would need all the help I could get. Most of all it taught me that I was always going to be someone who had learned from their mistakes, and that if I didn't hop right back up, dust myself off and leave my pride in the past, I would forever judge myself on my failings.

I think about the handsome, kind Italian man who'd come into my life too soon and who reminded me that I would rather be alone than be with someone with didn't make me drop to my knees with laughter. And that to be with someone for the sake of not being alone is the loneliest place that I could ever be. I also learned from new lovers, who I briefly welcomed into my life, that intimacy means nothing to me without a meeting of the minds. It doesn't matter how handsome you are or how physically appealing you might be, if you can't hold my attention, command my respect and earn a place in my heart, then we are better off apart.

I also think about my children, Jesse and Indi, who teach me every day how to be my best self, even if that means staring my worst self in the eye and accepting that she exists. In the moments where I am struggling to provide and feel a victim of the circumstances of my life, they remind me to live in the present. Teaching Indi her five times tables or watching Jesse perfect a skateboarding trick will always bring me back to the here and now, with no sadness of the past or fear of the future. They remind me that a life without purpose feels like it really has no point at all.

Epilogue

And then I think of Bondi Beach where I run daily, and the sunrise, the tide coming and going, and the different chapters of my life over the last eighteen years from when Andy and I first arrived here.

I turn back to the lady in the audience and say, 'The trick for me is choosing to view everything in life as an opportunity – the good, the bad and even the sometimes downright ugly. It's how you choose to see those things that has you either embrace life or run away from it.'

Acknowledgements

To my incredible Mum and Dad, Susi and Chris, and my sister Lowri, for teaching, challenging and loving me every step of the way. Your love and support on every level has not only allowed the last five years to be the adventure it has become, but has allowed my whole life to be the rich tapestry of crazy that most script writers would die to get their hands on. Thank you.

To Ella Doran, Louise Heywood and Ellie Hansen for being my sisters from another mother. You are some of the greatest loves of my life, my best friends and the women without whom, however far away you are, life would never ever be the same.

To my other family, the wonderful Whitfields, who I love with all my heart. Your courage, kindness and willingness to grow is more inspiring than you will ever know. Thank you for bringing Andy into this world and for holding my hand so tight as we walked him out together.

To Alex Warren and your gorgeous little family, for your kindness, curiosity and your desire to learn life's lessons through your old school friend Andy.

To Karina, Selwa, Dan, Roberta, Larissa and Sue, who not only got me started, but kept me going and stuck into me hard when I was ready to throw in the towel. Thank you for your dogged determination in turning an ordinary tale into an extraordinary love story.

To Sally, our amazing Canadian-British knock-you-off-your-feet, red-headed tornado of a guardian angel. Thank you for always being there, and for the hours and hours of time, love and commitment you have selflessly given. Thank you for being there to co-create with, to correct my insanely bad grammar and spelling, and for the never-ending supply of cinnamon chewing gum.

To Jet for listening to me go on and on and on, and for the script that we will write later this year.

And to you, beautiful Jai Courtney, for your never-waning love, support and commitment. But by the way and for the record, I can in fact sing and if you serve me a margarita without salt, I'll throw it back in your face.

To Victoria, to Jaqui, to Larraine and all of our wonderful Australian adopted family, Dini, Rich, Ben, Marisa, Con and beautiful Page who have all encouraged, supported and inspired me to keep putting myself out there.

To beautiful Kiki and Marcus Boysen for all that you were, all that you are and all that you always will be in our lives.

To Chloe Smith, Lilibet Foster and Sam Maydew, you are all responsible for playing a huge part in allowing my beautiful husband to live and die the extraordinary man who he became. Thank you for being who you are, for supporting who he was and for loving him in the way that you did. Your friendship has changed my life forever.

And to the multitude of Andy fans, *Spartacus* lovers, Maybe McQueen followers and the countless people who have reached out to me through their own personal loss, thank you for being a part of my life's journey.

To the life-changing wisdom of Byron Katie, Michael Neill, Syd Banks, Steve Griffiths, John Dashfield and Kung Fu Panda, you have all taught me that life only ever happens for you and not to you!

And lastly to my utterly beautiful son, Jesse Red, my wild and wonderful daughter, Indigo Sky, and my better half, the inspiring, funny, silly, gentle and insanely gorgeous Andy Whitfield. Thank you for choosing me to be in your life.

Nothing but love . . . to you all!